Routines-Based
Early Intervention

Routines-Based
Early Intervention
Supporting Young
Children and Their Families

by

R.A. McWilliam, Ph.D.
Siskin Children's Institute
Chattanooga, Tennessee

·P A U L·H·
BROOKES
PUBLISHING C°®

Baltimore • London • Sydney

Paul H. Brookes Publishing Co.
Post Office Box 10624
Baltimore, Maryland 21285-0624
USA

www.brookespublishing.com

Typeset by Spearhead Global, Inc., Bear, Delaware.
Manufactured in the United States of America by
Versa Press, Inc., East Peoria, Illinois.

The individuals described in this book's examples are composites or real people whose
situations are masked and are based on the author's experiences. In all instances, names
and identifying details have been changed to protect confidentiality.

Library of Congress Cataloging-in-Publication Data

McWilliam, R.A.
   Routines-based early intervention : supporting young children and their families / by
R.A. McWilliam.
     p.   cm.
   Includes bibliographical references and index.
   ISBN-13: 978-1-59857-062-5 (pbk.)
   ISBN-10: 1-59857-062-5 (pbk.)
   1. Children with disabilities—Services for—United States. 2. Parents of children with
disabilities—Services for—United States. 3. Children with disabilities—Development.
4. Developmentally disabled children—Development. I. Title.

HV890.U6M48 2010
362.4083'2—dc22
                                              2010008881

2014   2013   2012

10   9   8   7   6   5   4   3

Contents

About the Author

R.A. McWilliam, Ph.D., Director of the Siskin Center for Child and Family Research, Siskin Children's Institute, 1101 Carter Street, Chattanooga, TN 37402

Dr. McWilliam is the Siskin Endowed Chair of Research in Early Childhood Education, Development, and Intervention at Siskin Children's Institute. He is also a professor of education at the University of Tennessee at Chattanooga and an adjoint professor of special education at Vanderbilt University. He has formerly been a professor of pediatrics at Vanderbilt University Medical Center, a senior scientist at the Frank Porter Graham Child Development Institute, and a professor of education at the University of North Carolina at Chapel Hill. Dr. McWilliam's research centers on infants, toddlers, and preschoolers with and without disabilities, with a specific focus on child engagement, service delivery models, and collaboration with families. He has provided consultation, training, and technical assistance across the United States and in some countries overseas on providing early intervention in natural environments and on the Engagement Classroom Model. His Routines-Based Interview (RBI) is a widely used method of assessing families' needs and developing individualized family service plan (IFSP) outcomes and individualized education program (IEP) goals.

Prologue

This book is not intended as a survey of all the ways early intervention can be provided. It is not a balanced look at different models, strategies, and practices. Rather, it describes a framework for a coordinated, philosophically and empirically based approach to early intervention. It is a personal view of how services should be provided. This view has been shaped by my experiences providing services, supervising others who provide services, and consulting with hundreds of service providers, scores of programs, and over a dozen states. I do believe in organizing methods so people can keep the general principles in mind as they explore the complexities within those principles. From a policy development, management, and training perspective, this focus on a model prevents mushy thinking, being overwhelmed by the details, and philosophical drift. It will soon become obvious, however, that the details of each practice are clearly articulated; I have used checklists to do this.

These checklists describe steps to practices that are likely to be successful when carried out with a high level of fidelity. The practices fit within my philosophy of family centeredness and a focus on functionality. Others who share this philosophy and my interpretation of those broad constructs will find much with which they agree. They also, though, might have other ideas about how to provide services. The experts on providing support in natural environments are in general agreement about how to provide services (Workgroup on Principles and Practices in Natural Environments, 2007), even though they might use different terms, have a different model, and use different tools. Because of the similarity in our approaches, it is hard to be proprietary about the ideas or practices. I suppose how we package them in our frameworks, our terms, and our instruments is what makes us claim practices. For example, in March 2004, I sought the advice of Gerry Mahoney about a good term for what I have been calling, for years, "incidental teaching." I suggested that "responsive teaching" might be a better, less confusing term. He said, "Stay away from responsive teaching, Robin. I've co-opted that term." His tongue was in his cheek to some extent, but he also made a fair point.

As for ideas, it is hard for any of us to be too possessive. We have learned from each other and have moved with the times—often at the forefront, but nevertheless in more concert than disagreement. So the ideas presented here are not individually unique. What do set a person's work aside are the model (i.e., the combination of practices or the conceptual framework), the terms, and the tools. This book is my opportunity to put my framework, labels, and instruments in one place.

Evolution of the Model

The model described in this book comes from four principal confluences of my experience with evidence-based practices or with theory.

Family-Centered Practice

From its inception, early intervention has been interested in helping *families*, but it was only in the 1980s that serious research and theory began to attend to what this meant. One leader in this movement was Carl Dunst, who was among the first to document the importance of social support on families of young children with disabilities (Dunst, Boyd, Trivette, & Hamby, 2002; Dunst, Trivette, Boyd, & Brookfield, 1994; Dunst, Trivette, & Deal, 1994; Dunst, Trivette, & Hamby, 1996) and then what professional practices could foster families' well-being (Dunst et al., 2002; Trivette, Dunst, Boyd, & Hamby, 1996; Trivette, Dunst, Hamby, & LaPointe, 1996). I was lucky enough to work with Carl from 1983 to 1988.

My role at the Family, Infant and Preschool Program was to coordinate Project SUNRISE and eventually other classroom programs. From 1983 to 1985, Project SUNRISE was funded to operate parent-run co-ops twice a week, with children attending on both days, and parents attending on one of the days—with the other day as time without their children. Typically developing siblings also attended, making these co-ops inclusive and family like. We used this project as an opportunity to learn about families' capabilities; the value of families' having time together, particularly when there was a task for them to do; and how best to operate group settings to promote engagement. These lessons were then translated into the development of Family Place, the full-time, classroom program staffed by professionals and paraprofessionals. The impact of all these experiences can be seen in the current model.

One of the practices our team developed was a method for working with families to develop the intervention plan. This was before the passage of Education of the Handicapped Act Amendments of 1986 (PL 99-457), the law establishing federal funding for services to infants and toddlers with disabilities and their families, so there was no "individualized family service plan (IFSP)." Dunst called such a plan the Family and Child Intervention Plan (FACIP). The method we used in the classroom programs at the Family, Infant and Preschool Program was to ask the family about home routines, to talk to them about classroom routines, and to use this conversation for families to select their "goals" for the child and other family members. We developed it primarily as a tool for working collaboratively with families we only had the chance to see at arrival and departure (McWilliam, 1992). The current version of the Routines-Based Interview (RBI) is merely an elaboration of that simple but effective method.

Another luminary in the field's understanding of families has been Don Bailey, who became my next mentor. Don was involved with one of the largest studies of families (Bailey, 1987) and developed numerous measures that have advanced both research and practice (Bailey, Simeonsson, Buysse, & Smith, 1993; Bailey, et al., 2006; Bailey et al., 1998). His work has included research on personnel preparation in early intervention, on grouping (same age versus mixed age) in classroom settings, on fragile X syndrome, on longitudinal effects of early intervention, and on outcomes in early intervention. Throughout his career, he has applied his interest in families.

I worked with Don from 1988 to 2002, as a research project coordinator and eventually a senior investigator. It was while working at the Frank Porter Graham Child Development Institute at the University of North Carolina that I had the opportunity to study family issues in a serious way. Gloria Harbin invited me to work with her on evaluating North Carolina's early intervention services, where I looked at family-centered services (McWilliam, Tocci, & Harbin, 1998) while she looked at interagency collaboration. In this project, we looked at the quality of IFSPs (McWilliam, Ferguson, et al., 1998), among other things (McWilliam, Snyder, Harbin, Porter, & Munn, 2000). This was instrumental in my understanding the great need for a process to develop functional, family-centered plans. She then included me on the Early Childhood Research Institute on Service Utilization, where I conducted a case study with 72 families (McWilliam, Tocci, & Harbin, 1998). This experience was informative in honing my interview skills and led to the inclusion of some key questions in the RBI. It also helped us adopt the RBI with families served through home-based, not classroom-based, services.

Family Systems and Ecological Theories

A second influence was coming to an understanding of family systems and ecological theories. Family system theory has been described in various graphic ways. One way is to think of the family as a mobile, where movement in one part affects all the other parts. Another way is to think of the family in terms of concentric circles, with the child in the middle, those who live with the child in the next circle, people who have fairly frequent and close contact with the family in the next circle, people who have less frequent and close contact with family in the next, and distant people with whom the family has fairly circumscribed interactions in the outermost circle.

This systemic way of thinking about families matches concepts of person-centered planning and the use of the ecomap, which is described later in the book. Person-centered planning has revolutionized services for people with intellectual or developmental disabilities and is characterized by such ideas as forming a "circle of friends," planning with the person about the person's long- and short-term goals, and assessing the person's resources (Holburn, 2001; O'Brien, 2004; Orentlicher, 2008). The ecomap is a specific tool that shows people who are resources, stresses, or both in a person's life. Both person-centered planning and the ecomap involve determining the ecological factors in a person's life, including family members.

In our own family, we did not use these tools specifically, but the resources available and unavailable unquestionably shaped how we managed our family life. At times, we had friends and family to count on, but there were times and circumstances when we did not have them. We also learned that having resources available is one thing; being comfortable using them is quite another. Some people we know are not at all shy about asking favors from others. We admire these people in their audacity.

Transdisciplinary Service Delivery

Early in my career, Dunst introduced me to the concept of transdisciplinary service delivery. When I went to meetings representing Project SUNRISE, I came across Geneva Woodruff (Woodruff & Shelton, 2006) and other pioneers who articulated this approach. I realized that, before I knew the term for it, I had used transdisciplinary practices in my first home-based early intervention job. In our small team of three people working in rural Piedmont North Carolina, we had enough money only for quarterly consultation from an occupational therapist, a physical therapist, and a speech-language pathologist. That meant we had to absorb as much information as we could as we whizzed around the county with the consultant on board, going from house to house. We had to support the family in carrying out the therapists' programs. It was a marvelous way to learn about many different dimensions to early intervention.

In the co-ops, we spent so much time on functional, fun, developmentally appropriate activities that "therapy" became an afterthought. Eventually, we had therapists come into the rooms perhaps quarterly. They and we understood that their purposes were to see if the program needed to be changed (assessment) and to demonstrate interventions. They did not see the need for more frequent interventions, because they understood that the families were carrying out the interventions at home and the co-op staff were supporting the families to carry them out during co-op.

Our policy that therapists had to come into the classroom and work with us was different enough from common practice in the 1980s that I understood research was needed. Why were more people not providing integrated services? Therefore, Don Bailey and I wrote and were awarded a field-initiated grant. Our first problem on this grant was that our team of experts could not agree on the extent of pull-out services: How big an issue was this? We conducted a national survey that showed it was indeed a big problem. Incidentally, I used these data for my dissertation. Our next problem was that we discovered that it was not a simple question of in versus out of class, so we had to determine the various methods of providing services in both locations. Our third problem was that therapists would not agree to a study that involved random assignment of children to different types of therapy and they would collude with parents to refuse to participate. Our solution was to find sites and therapists who used different methods and to monitor the effects of naturally occurring therapy. These studies led to the publication of the edited book *Rethinking Pull-Out Services in Early Intervention: A Professional Resource* (McWilliam, 1996), which featured chapters by experts in six disciplines.

The integrated-services work not only taught us about classroom-based services but also taught us about how to be consultants when infants and toddlers were in child care. Early interventionists are the specialists when they visit child care centers, and we now have evidence about how to consult collaboratively.

Complexity of Home Visits

Home-based early intervention is a finely detailed masterpiece masquerading as finger painting. I know. In my early career, I was finger painting. Over time, however, I have come to understand the things we did in the early days that were indeed masterful and the things best forgotten. One study that helped me understand what worked and what did not was the large case study mentioned earlier that Gloria Harbin, Lynn Tocci, and I undertook as a part of the Early Childhood Research Institute on Service Utilization (McWilliam, Tocci, & Harbin, 1998). The case study consisted of 72 families and their 46 service providers. The families lived in nine communities—three in North Carolina, three in Pennsylvania, and three in Colorado. We interviewed the families live twice, we interviewed the service providers at least once, and we visited most settings if children were served outside the home (e.g., child care, specialized program, Head Start). The interviews in the homes and, in the case of the service providers, over the telephone gave us rich and thick descriptions of home visits. Analyzing these narratives gave us insights that advanced our thinking considerably.

As the model proposed in this book is described, its roots in family-centered practice, family systems, transdisciplinary service delivery, and home visiting will be obvious. The introduction to the model continues with a discussion of advances in early intervention that illustrate why a model was needed.

References

Bailey, D.B. (1987). Collaborative goal setting with families: Resolving differences in values and priorities for services. *Topics in Early Childhood Special Education, 7,* 59–71.

Bailey, D.B., Jr., Bruder, M.B., Hebbeler, K., Carta, J., Defosset, M., Greenwood, C., et al. (2006). Recommended outcomes for families of young children with disabilities. *Journal of Early Intervention, 28,* 227–251.

Bailey, D.B., McWilliam, R.A., Darkes, L.A., Hebbeler, K., Simeonsson, R.J., Spiker, D., et al. (1998). Family outcomes in early intervention: A framework for program evaluation and efficacy research. *Exceptional Children, 64,* 313.

Bailey, D.B., Jr. , Simeonsson, R.J., Buysse, V., & Smith, T. (1993). Reliability of an index of child characteristics. *Developmental Medicine & Child Neurology, 35,* 806–815.

Dunst, C.J., Boyd, K., Trivette, C.M., & Hamby, D.W. (2002). Family-oriented program models and professional helpgiving practices. *Family Relations: Interdisciplinary Journal of Applied Family Studies, 51,* 221–229.

Dunst, C.J., Trivette, C.M., Boyd, K., & Brookfield, J. (1994). Help-giving practices and the self-efficacy appraisals of parents. In C.J. Dunst, C.M. Trivette , & A.G. Deal (Eds.), *Supporting and strengthening families: Methods, strategies, and practices* (Vol. 1, pp. 212–220). Cambridge, MA: Brookline Books.

Dunst, C.J., Trivette, C.M., & Deal, A.G. (1994). Resource-based family-centered intervention practices. In C.J. Dunst, C.M. Trivette, & A.G. Deal (Eds.), *Supporting and strengthening families: Methods, strategies and practices* (pp. 140–151). Cambridge, MA: Brookline Books.

Dunst, C.J., Trivette, C.M., & Hamby, D.W. (1996). Measuring the helpgiving practices of human services program practitioners. *Human Relations, 49,* 815–835.

Holburn, S. (2001). Compatibility of person-centered planning and applied behavior analysis. *Behavior Analyst, 24,* 271–281.

McWilliam, R.A. (1992). *Family-centered intervention planning: A routines-based approach.* Tucson, AZ: Communication Skill Builders.

McWilliam, R.A. (Ed.). (1996). *Rethinking pull-out services in early intervention: A professional resource.* Baltimore: Paul H. Brookes Publishing Co.

McWilliam, R.A., Ferguson, A., Harbin, G.L., Porter, P., Munn, D., & Vandiviere, P. (1998). The family-centeredness of individualized family service plans. *Topics in Early Childhood Special Education, 18,* 69–82.

McWilliam, R.A., Snyder, P., Harbin, G.L., Porter, P., & Munn, D. (2000). Professionals and families' perceptions of family-centered practices in infant-toddler services. *Early Education and Development, 11,* 519–538.

McWilliam, R.A., Tocci, L., & Harbin, G.L. (1998). Family-centered services: Service providers' discourse and behavior. *Topics in Early Childhood Special Education, 18,* 206–221.

O'Brien, J. (2004). If person-centered planning did not exist, valuing people would require its invention. *Journal of Applied Research in Intellectual Disabilities, 17,* 11–15.

Orentlicher, M.L. (2008). Striving for typical: Collective experiences of person-centered planning for young adults with disabilities during transition. *Dissertation Abstracts International Section A: Humanities and Social Sciences, 69.*

Trivette, C.M., Dunst, C.J., Boyd, K., & Hamby, D.W. (1996). Family-oriented program models, helpgiving practices, and parental control appraisals. *Exceptional Children, 62,* 237–248.

Trivette, C.M., Dunst, C.J., Hamby, D.W., & LaPointe, N.J. (1996). Key elements of empowerment and their implications for early intervention. *Infant Toddler Intervention, 6,* 59–73.

Woodruff, G., & Shelton, T.L. (2006). The transdisciplinary approach to early intervention. In G.M. Foley, & J.D. Hochman (Eds.), *Mental health in early intervention: Achieving unity in principles and practice* (pp. 81–110). Baltimore: Paul H. Brookes Publishing Co.

Workgroup on Principles and Practices in Natural Environments. (2007). *Agreed-upon practices for providing early intervention services in natural environments.* Retrieved July 6, 2008, from http://www.nectac.org/~pdfs/topics/families/AgreedUponPractices_FinalDraft2_01_08.pdf

Acknowledgments

I am grateful to mentors, colleague-friends, coworkers, and my own family. Two of my most significant mentors, Carl Dunst and Don Bailey, are mentioned in the prologue. Although quite different from each other, they both have shaped my philosophy about early intervention and about how to be a successful scholar in this field. Add to them Mark Wolery, who in weekly breakfasts has tolerated my pontifications and gently told me when I was wrong. He continues to teach me about instruction and single-subject research. Over the years, Sam Odom gave me confidence, opportunities, and a model for decency. Spectacularly, my predecessors as editor of the *Journal of Early Intervention* all paved the way through friendship and example; they were, in order, Odom, Bailey, and Steve Warren.

Mary Beth Bruder has been a constant guide and example, and her influence can be seen throughout this book. Gloria Harbin made me think about leadership and policy and shared many bottles of Viognier with me. Lee Ann Jung absorbs my work and improves it with her own intelligent stamp.

Siskin Children's Institute gives me the freedom and resources to focus on scholarship, the development of new models, and experimentation in communities and our own class-rooms for young children. Jerry Jensen, the president, had the farsighted idea of creating a research center to focus on early intervention, and the Institute's board of directors backed it. Azusa Dance keeps my life organized, while managing the research center. Amy Casey, my former doctoral student, frequent study coordinator, and now colleague, represents the best of the future. Our partnership is mutually rewarding, underestimated by some people, and a rare and therefore precious gift.

Finally, my own family: These are the people who keep me honest, the people who by turns are proud of me yet who marvel that anyone cares what I think. Sonny, our younger daughter, to whom this book is dedicated, has shown us that it is possible to turn out an intelligent, hard-working, and independent young woman. Kirsten, our older daughter, is a daily lesson in rolling with the punches, working steadfastly, and laughing at the ridiculous. Finally, PJ, my wife, is a voice of reason about our field and life in general, and she has given much for me to be able to devote so many hours to work—and to Carolina and Vanderbilt basketball.

To Sonny

Introduction

T his book describes a particular approach to early intervention—one focused on the family, on functioning in everyday routines, and on a team approach to intervention. To place the approach in context, the development of early intervention is reviewed.

CHAPTER 1

Advances in
Early Intervention

The term *early intervention* is used to describe **interventions** for both at-risk children and children with developmental disabilities, and no doubt there is some overlap. But there are also fundamental differences in philosophy, approaches, and conclusions. Beginning with the possibility of overlap, however, Forrest Curt Bennett (2004), a developmental pediatrician at the University of Washington, provided an interesting overview of the evolution of early intervention. He pointed out that research in the field began by asking whether early intervention "worked"—the answer to which depended on what was meant by this term. For example, can early intervention cure potential developmental disabilities? No. Can it permanently raise IQ scores? No. Can it improve school functioning? Yes, because now the field is thinking about *function*. Can it improve adaptive behavior? Yes. It has been shown to have social and vocational benefits. Can it enhance daily care? Yes. It has been shown to enhance feeding, interacting, and behavior management. Can it help family functioning? Yes. It has been shown to improve the way families adapt to the child and pursue their interests.

According to Bennett (2004), in the medical field, there are three accepted types of early intervention:

1. Newborn screening for metabolic disorders (because there is evidence-based information)

2. Education for children with major sensory impairments (e.g., because of the success of early intervention for deaf and blind children, newborn hearing screening was developed)

3. Physical therapy for children with cerebral palsy (even though Palmer et al., 1988, showed that the commonly accepted physical therapy treatment was actually no more effective than a general early childhood education curriculum)

If these are the limits of accepted types of early intervention, Bennett leveled, questions remain about treatment for children at environmental risk for developmental disabilities (e.g., children from low-income families). In fact, Bennett said we need to look at early intervention by group (e.g., income level), biological risk (e.g., low birth weight), and established developmental disabilities, not by putting them all together. Results of the Abecedarian Project, which was the nation's first investigation of the efficacy of child care to improve the cognitive skills of children in poverty, demonstrated a 15-point IQ difference between children who received an enhanced child care intervention and the control group (Ramey & Campbell, 1984), but these differences disappeared after the end of intervention. Later, however, "sleeper" effects such as academic achievement, grade placement, and graduation emerged (Campbell, Ramey, Pungello, Sparling, & Miller-Johnson, 2002). Notably, these findings were for children from low-income families, not children with disabilities.

Similarly, the Infant Health and Development Project was most effective for children from families of low socioeconomic status, regardless of weight or health (Liaw & Brooks-Gunn, 1993). By 5 years of age (2 years after the end of intervention involving child education and family support), differences had disappeared between the intervention and follow-up groups.

For children with low birth weights, Bennett (2004) mentioned that we have moved from an infant stimulation approach to a parent-focused, infant protection approach. So now, we have individualized nursing care plans, such as "environmental neonatology" and "developmental care." Attention is being paid to brain care rather than just lung care.

Bennett said, "The most successful programs combine multiple interventions and deliver them repeatedly over time." Although important differences between early intervention for children at risk for developmental delays and early intervention for children with disabilities exist, 1) disability can be considered to exist along a continuum and 2) the system of services for children with disabilities should exist within the system of services for typically developing children.

Concepts of Family Centeredness

Since the beginning of early intervention, changes have occurred in the concept of family centeredness. In the 1970s, attention was paid to parent training and involvement (Field, Widmayer, Stringer, & Ignatoff, 1980; Forgatch & Toobert, 1979). Researchers discovered that parents could be taught to implement interventions with their children (Tudor, 1977). Later, this approach was perceived as paternalistic, especially when professionals decided what parents should be trained to do, and simplistic, when training was the extent of the involvement with the family (McWilliam, McMillen, Sloper, & McMillen, 1997). This takes us to the apparently unshakeable issue of parent involvement. Historically, professionals wanted families to become highly involved in the early intervention enterprise. The underinvolved family was blamed for underinvolvement, with scant attention paid to what the professionals had done to set the stage for family underinvolvement. In this book, I will argue that, when home visitors get it right, family involvement is a nonissue in the same way that people are "involved" when their neighbors come over. Lack of attention by a neighborhood host is a nonissue. Of course families are involved when the adults are visited. The problem is that too often the child is being visited, so the parents think their participation is optional or tangential.

Currently, we are in an era of *empowerment*—a term Carl Dunst applied to early intervention in his seminal book, *Enabling and Empowering Families* (Dunst, Trivette, & Deal, 1994). The current concept of early intervention places a high value on the family's decision-making authority; this authority is built into legislation (the Individuals with Disabilities Education Improvement Act of 2004, PL 108-446) and definitions of recommended practice (Smith et al., 2002). Perhaps owing to the tie-in with legislation, professionals can give families choices during the planning process (for which the legislation is fairly prescriptive), yet ignore concepts broader than decision making in **service** delivery (for which legislation is less prescriptive). The zeitgeist is that all professionals know that family centeredness is socially appropriate and everyone claims to use family-centered practice.

Another current principle of early intervention is one of partnership. In fact, Dunst combined (1985) the two ideas in his proactive model of empowerment through partnerships. The concept of families and professionals working as partners is an elaboration of empowerment, particularly as it is related to families having decision-making authority. It is therefore an imperfect model, because families have ultimate authority, yet professionals have more knowledge about intervention. But then, perhaps all partnerships are imbalanced in different domains.

The future of the concept might well be family quality of life, which is ironic because this was important to many of today's experts in family centeredness right from the beginning. Nevertheless, I believe that when practitioners, family advocates, administrators, and researchers consolidate the research findings and make sense of the disparate movements in the field, they will see that the concept of enhancing family quality of life will be a unifying force. Measurement systems to track this construct have been developed (Hornstein & McWilliam, 2007; Turnbull, Poston, Minnes, & Summers, 2007). One critical dimension of family quality of life is satisfaction with **routines**, which is especially salient in the context of early intervention designed to take place in **natural environments**. Put another way, routines-based early intervention will directly address families' satisfaction with their routines.

From parent training and involvement, the field of early intervention made important steps forward in conceptualizing family centeredness when empowerment and partnerships were embraced. Refinement of the concept might well come with an acceptance of the goal of improving family quality of life.

Natural Environments

The idea of providing early intervention in natural environments has probably been the hottest issue in the field since the mid-1990s. Curiously, some states and programs began the early intervention enterprise with an understanding that interventions (or at least learning opportunities) occurred throughout the child's day in places and at times that were part of the fabric of the child's and family's life. Other states and programs, however, developed their early intervention systems to be located primarily in specialized classrooms or clinics. For some people, therefore, early intervention in natural environments (EINE) is normal—familiar. For others, it is a change and a challenge.

This book is largely about EINE, so not much detail will be addressed here. But experts in this area have agreed upon the mission and principles shown in Figure 1.1. It is possible to meet the letter of the law regarding early intervention and still use a multidisciplinary model, still use a clinic-based approach on home visits, and still pull children out for treatment when they are seen in their community child care centers. This book makes the case that true EINE, however, includes transdisciplinary service delivery, support-based home visits, and integrated services in child care.

MISSION

Part C early intervention builds upon and provides supports and resources to assist family members and caregivers to enhance children's learning and development through everyday learning opportunities.

KEY PRINCIPLES

1. Infants and toddlers learn best through everyday experiences and interactions with familiar people in familiar contexts.
2. All families, with the necessary supports and resources, can enhance their children's learning and development.
3. The primary role of a service provider in early intervention is to work with and support family members and caregivers in children's lives.
4. The early intervention process, from initial contacts through transition, must be dynamic and individualized to reflect family members' learning styles and cultural beliefs and practices.
5. IFSP outcomes must be functional and based on children's and families' needs and family-identified priorities.
6. The families' priorities, needs and interests are addressed most appropriately by a primary provider who represents and receives team and community support.
7. Interventions with young children and family members must be based on explicit principles, validated practices, best available research, and relevant laws and regulations.

Figure 1.1.   Mission and key principles of early intervention. (From Workgroup on Principles and Practices in Natural Environments. [2007]. *Agreed-upon practices for providing early intervention services in natural environments.* Retrieved July 6, 2008, from http://www.nectac.org/ ~pdfs/topics/families/AgreedUponPractices_FinalDraft2_01_08.pdf; reprinted by permission.) (Key: IFSP, individualized family service plan.)

Inclusion and Embeddedness

When families want their children in group care, they mostly use inclusive, community settings such as regular child care. This is a result of EINE legislation, research findings (Odom et al., 2004), and values (Bailey, McWilliam, Buysse, & Wesley, 1998). It might be argued that we have been quite successful in increasing the extent to which inclusive placement is used, but not as successful in ensuring the quality of intervention that children receive. In addition to the general quality of the settings, we still need to pay attention to the extent to which inclusion is individualized (Purcell & Rosemary, 2008; Wolery, 1997). When it is individualized, assessment will include ecological congruence between the child's behavior and the demands of classroom routines, therapy, and early childhood special education that is integrated into classroom routines, and interventions that are embedded into regular classroom routines. Clearly, then, individualizing inclusion is consistent with EINE.

The Need for This Model

Despite these advances, a need still exists for a model that students can learn, administrators can organize, practitioners can implement, and families can advocate. First, problems still exist with early intervention as it has evolved. These problems will be elaborated upon in the following chapters, but the most common ones are a pernicious slide toward overspecialization, an absence of functional-needs assessment in the evaluation assessment process (and, therefore, nonfunctional goals), a clinic-based model applied to home visits, and pull-out services in child care.

Second, it will be useful to have an integrated system from referral through transition. Experts have developed useful practices in assessment and intervention, but have generally not provided an approach that can be used from intake through transition out of the program.

Third, there is a way to evaluate the extent to which programs are consistent with the concept of EINE and use recommended practices. A tool that allows respondents to identify their practices in various areas from not-recommended practices to highly recommended practices is useful. The Families In Natural Environments Scale of Service Evaluation (FINESSE), shown in the appendix at the end of the book and discussed further in Chapter 12, is such a measure (McWilliam, 2000a).

Fourth, despite the advances in early intervention, vast numbers of programs still are operated in an atheoretical manner with little regard to how early intervention really works. Children learn primarily through repeated interactions with the environment, with those interactions dispersed over time. They do not learn in lessons or sessions in which the "trials" are massed or the practice is concentrated, with little or no carryover to other situations. Therefore, the premise under which the common model of therapy or instruction is carried out, in which professionals work directly with children once a week or so, is questionable.

Children are better influenced by the caregivers who spend hour after hour with them during the week than they are by visitors. On the other hand, adults, because they can generalize and learn in sessions, can benefit from weekly visits from professionals. Therefore, professionals should work with adult family members, who can influence child development and skill acquisition as previously discussed. Intervention for the child therefore occurs between visits. This is when caregivers have multiple opportunities to provide learning contexts for children. In this way, early intervention really works as a process of various kinds of supports (including "training") to the caregivers who are with the child for many hours throughout the week.

Although these dimensions of early intervention have been articulated in the literature (Dunst, Bruder, Trivette, Raab, & McLean, 2001; Dunst, Herter, & Shields, 2000; Pretti-Frontczak & Bricker, 2004; Widerstrom, 2005), until now they have not been organized into a model that states, administrators, or practitioners could grasp.

CHAPTER 2

How to Use This Book

This book provides guidance about the extent to which this model should be followed and how it can be used by many configurations of programs. The relevant research is embedded within the chapters, and attempts have been made to address various people who might be able to use the information: administrators, service coordinators, service providers, and families.

Model Fidelity

The specific practices described in this book might not be the only ways to carry out those aspects of early intervention (i.e., intake, needs assessment, service decisions, home visits, classroom consultations), and the practices individually have probably been described elsewhere in one form or another. The precise techniques described here, however, are my own and have been honed over years of experience with programs around the country.

According to the model adoption literature (Hall & Loucks, 1977), when a model is *adapted* for local or individual use, it can be said that the model is well on its way to being *adopted*. On the other hand, in early intervention research, we are concerned about model fidelity. Practices are described here in detail because this is the way they have worked and this is the way they are consistent with the philosophical underpinnings.

Furthermore, communication is compromised when someone claims to employ a certain practice (e.g., "I use integrated therapy as described by McWilliam") and then does something different. The listener might actually have heard of this way of providing therapy and react accordingly (e.g., hire the person making the claim, place a child in the program of a person making the claim), unaware that the person has adapted the practice beyond recognition. Therefore, I encourage the reader to use the practices as described here with few changes. I have left enough options for specific use—what I call *local decisions*—that practitioners should not feel too constrained. The point of local decisions is that these practices should fit into different contexts.

This issue of fidelity to the model is contentious, and I have joined conversations decrying the approach of some consultants that the whole package should be taken or nothing. But a key difference here is that I have not described a whole package that must be kept intact. Each of the elements can be used separately, but I must admit that they are enhanced when other elements are used. The basic elements are

- The ecomap for understanding the family ecology (see Chapter 4)

- The **Routines-Based Interview (RBI)** for assessing needs and intervention planning (see Chapter 6)

- The **primary service provider (PSP)** model for organizing services (see Chapters 8 and 9)

- Support-based home visits (see Chapter 10)

- Integrated therapy for consultation to child care (see Chapter 11)

Each of these elements is discussed in detail in the chapters indicated. Throughout the book, tools that can be photocopied are provided to help readers implement the elements.

Implementation Across Types of Programs

Methods of providing early intervention **service** vary quite dramatically across the United States, despite one federal law, the Individuals with Disabilities Education Improvement Act (IDEA) of 2004 (PL 108-446), governing such services. Because the law does not specify the methods that must be used, but rather only the services that must be offered, methods within services are up to the state, program, or even individual practitioner. One of the most obvious variations is in the use of therapy services. Some places are focused primarily on the provision of occupational, physical, and speech therapies. Others are focused primarily on developmental or generalist services. Many combine the two, with children and families receiving both developmental-general intervention and therapy. This variation appears to be a function of history and politics. When services for infants and toddlers were first being created in states, in many cases before the passage of the Education of the Handicapped Act Amendments of 1986 (PL 99-457, the law prescribing what states participating in what was then Part H—the infant-toddler program—must do), they made decisions about service delivery models that influence today's programs. For example, some states determined that their rehabilitation hospitals were well stocked with therapists, so much of the early intervention business (a term I do not use lightly) went to them. Other states had community programs, perhaps mental health centers, so those programs were charged with organizing early intervention. Other states already had or established specialized classroom-based programs for children with disabilities and made them the nuclei of early intervention efforts.

Places with high therapy use should consider expansion of developmental-general services to ensure that developmental and family needs are being met and to help contain costs. Cost containment comes from the fact that 1) developmental generalists can address needs, at some level, in any domain; and 2) they are usually cheaper than allied health professionals. Programs that focus primarily on developmental-generalist services should ensure that enough consultation with therapists is built in so that important interventions are not missed.

Relevant Research Embedded

The research behind this model of early intervention comes from a variety of sources and is not all neatly found in convenient reviews or the same journal. Studies have documented the importance of strengthening informal supports (Barnett, Clements, Kaplan-Estrin, & Fialka, 2003; Valentine, 1993), assessing families' functioning (Bailey & Simeonsson, 1988; Dunst, Trivette, & Thompson, 1990; Higgins, Bailey, & Pearce, 2005), empowering families (Dunst, 2000; Hoagwood, 2005; Rappaport, 1981; Swick, Da Ros, & Kovach, 2001), integrating services (Bailey, 1987; Hoagwood, 2005; Jiyeon & Ann, 2003; McWilliam, 2003; Powell, Fixsen, Dunlap, Smith, & Fox, 2007), and taking a consultative approach rather than a direct, hands-on approach (Harbin, McWilliam, & Gallagher, 2000; McWilliam, 1996, 2003; McWilliam, Young, & Harville, 1996; Peck, 1993; Pohlman & McWilliam, 1999).

Unfortunately, to date, no large study has taken all the elements in the model and contrasted them with the traditional model. I'm not sure this will ever be done, because group integrity is hard to preserve in the traditional (what would be the contrast or control) group. Enough elements of the currently proposed model have seeped into the consciousness of many early interventionists that finding a "pure" control group would be very difficult. Therefore, future studies will probably address individual elements of the model, letting other elements fall where they may. Investigators will, however, need to gather descriptive data on those other elements, because they clearly all have an interrelationship. For example, if one were to study the effects of using the RBI versus a test-based approach for deciding on outcomes, the model of service delivery typically used in that program is likely to have some bearing on the group comparison result. If a primary service provider model is used, then the RBI is more likely to be beneficial than if a multidisciplinary model is used. Researchers will need to attend to these design challenges. The research I have been able to draw from is primarily in the areas of social support (Dunst et al., 1990), functional assessment (Bjorck-Akesson & Granlund, 1995; Haley et al., 2006; Wilson, Mott, & Batman, 2004), intervention planning (Jung & Baird, 2003; Jung & McWilliam, 2005; McWilliam, Ferguson, et al., 1998), service delivery models (Bruder & Dunst, 2006; Jiyeon & Ann, 2003; Powell et al., 2007), home visiting (Bronfenbrenner, 1979; Campbell & Sawyer, 2009; Peterson, Luze, Eshbaugh, Jeon, & Kantz, 2007), and integrated therapy (McWilliam et al., 1996; Palmer et al., 1988).

Cast of Characters

The references to research throughout this book will allow readers to track the empirical support for elements of this model. The application of the elements will differ depending on the role of the reader. This section describes roles used as examples in the book.

Administrator

Administrators at the state and local levels will find information in this book useful. It provides a conceptual framework for organizing services and it provides concrete practices to encourage providers to use. My work has emphasized administrative support for making changes and it has emphasized accountability. The administrative support needed is usually in the form of leadership and time to organize the implementation of the practices. Accountability in this model includes ensuring that recommended and evidence-based practices are implemented and that philosophically incompatible practices do not seep in. In each of the chapters, the checklists serve as descriptions of the model, which can be used as checks for fidelity to the model.

Service Coordinator

Throughout this book, two basic models of service coordination are described: dedicated and combined. Dedicated service coordinators are people whose jobs are solely to coordinate services, as defined in Part C. They conduct intakes, organize evaluations, and complete individualized family service plans (IFSPs), but they do not provide ongoing services beyond service coordination. They often have high caseloads because they are not involved in service provision. Combined service coordinators might do all the same service coordination activities just mentioned, but they also provide ongoing services such as special instruction, family counseling, or whatever they are qualified to provide. In the examples provided in this book, the term *service coordinators* is used when referring to people handling the official service coordination functions.

Service Provider

Service providers in early intervention include early childhood special educators (ECSEs), occupational therapists (OTs), physical therapists (PTs), and speech-language pathologists (SLPs). Others such as nurses, social workers, and psychologists also often provide ongoing services. A host of professionals are further involved in diagnosis and treatment but not in regular, frequent, and ongoing service provision in the way the "Big Four" are. Another group of service providers is generalists with child development or regular early childhood education backgrounds. One further group is paraprofessionals including certified occupational therapy assistants and physical therapy assistants. Most of this book is related to ongoing service provision by the Big Four, although the heavy weight given to needs assessment can be related to other providers. In examples, the terms *service providers* and *early interventionists* refer to providers of ongoing services, even if they also are service coordinators.

Family

The term *family* is used in the examples in this book. However, as is often the case in early intervention writing, I really mean the primary caregivers, such as parents.

Items from the FINESSE

The FINESSE (McWilliam, 2000a) was developed to measure the extent to which programs were implementing recommended practices in early intervention in natural environments. The instrument is reproduced in the appendix at the end of the book. It has been used to compare early intervention service delivery in six countries (Greece, Israel, Portugal, Spain, Turkey, and the United States) and continues to be used in international studies (McWilliam & Er, 2003). The items are derived largely from the model of service delivery described in this book. In each of the chapters in the implementation sections, relevant FINESSE items are shown and described.

Conclusion

The time has come for a model that makes sense to administrators, service coordinators and providers, and families. This does not mean that it is a package that must be swallowed hook, line, and sinker. The hook, the line, and the sinker can be swallowed separately, but they are connected.

In an endeavor as complicated and varied as early intervention, it is very difficult to examine the effectiveness of whole approaches, so the evidence behind this model is drawn from many sources. As mentioned earlier, these sources include

- Carl Dunst's work on helpgiving and empowering families (Dunst, Boyd, Trivette, & Hamby, 2002; Dunst & Bruder, 2002; Dunst, Trivette, & Deal, 1994)

- Carl Dunst's and Mary Beth Bruder's work on learning opportunities (Dunst & Bruder, 2005; Dunst, Bruder, Trivette, Raab, & McLean, 2001; Dunst, Herter, & Shields, 2000; Raab & Dunst, 2004)

- My own work on service delivery methods (Casey & McWilliam, 2005; McWilliam, 1996, 2003; Rantala, Uotinen, & McWilliam, 2009)

- Pip Campbell's work on home visiting (Campbell & Sawyer, 2009)

- Don Bailey's work on family outcomes in early intervention accountability (Bailey et al., 2006; Bailey et al., 1998)

- Tom Weisner's work on the family ecology (Weisner, Matheson, Coots, & Bernheimer, 2005)

- Mark Wolery's work on instruction in naturalistic routines (Wolery, 1997; Wolery, Anthony, Caldwell, Snyder, & Morgante, 2002; Wolery, Welts, & Holcombe, 1994)

- Sam Odom's work on inclusion (Odom et al., 1999, 2001, 2004)

- Todd Risley's work on engagement (Doke & Risley, 1972; McGee, Daly, Izeman, Mann, & Risley, 1991; Porterfield, Herbert-Jackson, & Risley, 1976; Quilitch & Risley, 1973; Twardosz, Cataldo, & Risley, 1974)

- Mike Guralnick's work on social relationships (Guralnick, 1999)

- Gloria Harbin's work on service use (Harbin, 2005; Harbin et al., 2000)

Many other researchers have contributed to the practices described here. It is almost unfair to list some without listing them all.

Unfortunately, my own colleagues and other researchers have not had the chance to investigate every strategy and technique described here. What we do have is related research and now many examples of programs and states implementing the strategies and techniques successfully. The dissemination of the approach has been enhanced by experts in early intervention who have provided their own consultation and technical assistance on this or a similar approach, most particularly by Lee Ann Jung of the University of Kentucky. Furthermore, other experts have their own approaches that are very consistent with the one described in this book. They include M'Lisa Shelden and Dathan Rush (Hanft, Rush, & Shelden, 2004; Rush, Shelden, & Hanft, 2003) and Juliann Woods (Kashinath, Woods, & Goldstein, 2006; Woods & Goldstein, 2003; Woods

& Lindeman, 2008). We know that practices in this approach are in use at one level or another in the following states: Arizona, Colorado, Connecticut, Florida, Kansas, Maryland, Michigan, Minnesota, Missouri, Nebraska, Nevada, New Jersey, New Mexico, New York, North Dakota, Ohio, Oregon, Tennessee, Texas, Utah, Vermont, Washington, Wisconsin, and Wyoming. Section II begins the description of the model.

Understanding the Family Ecology

For the purposes of the current model, *family ecology* is the social environment of the family, but one that can reach quite far. It consists of the family's informal, formal, and intermediate supports. Family ecology is important because these are the people to whom the family is already connected when we first meet them. For early intervention, one needs to determine who the existing supports are so as not to build a completely new, artificial network without exploring what the existing one can do. Social support has been found to be a good predictor of early intervention outcomes (Dunst, 2000).

Intake is a good place to begin understanding the family ecology. Many service coordinators already do this but perhaps use an unsatisfactory method. The checklist approach to finding out about families is never particularly welcome. First, families have often had to answer the same questions in the same way numerous times before. Second, unless families know why the information is important, it can seem intrusive. Third, family histories are often blended with medical histories, which families also find tedious. Service coordinators need something they can do at intake to get ecological information, to establish a positive relationship with the family, and to give the family an opportunity to speak. This section addresses methods for conducting the intake and constructing an ecomap.

Intake

The intake visit sets the stage for the rest of the early intervention experience. It must therefore be done in a family-centered (not child-centered) manner, emphasizing support (not services). So many of the family's early experiences in early intervention are related to the child, such as evaluation and development of IFSP outcomes—although family outcomes should be equally developed (Bailey et al., 1998; Turnbull et al., 2007). Furthermore, when describing the program, it can be too easy for service coordinators to list the services, as though those professional encounters were the solution. To deal with intake, I discuss first encounters, written materials, the initial referral call, intake steps, and telling the child's story. I also have created the Intake Checklist to guide the providers through the process (see Appendix 3.1).

First Encounters

The first encounters the family has with early intervention are very important for establishing expectations. Typically, these encounters occur at the intake visit, but even the telephone call to schedule the visit can be critical. Among other important considerations, these early contacts need to make clear to the family that early intervention is a support by friendly people who see that the family is like an infant's mobile. As one part of the family is moved, the other parts move accordingly. Therefore, competent early interventionists attend to the whole family, right from the beginning. In addition to the first encounters at intake, a program's written materials and the initial referral call deserve attention.

Written Materials

How does the program describe itself through its brochure and other written materials? If it describes early intervention primarily as a method for getting child-level services, such as therapies and special instruction, families can become colluders with professionals in this view. If this happens, families might get the erroneous idea that their role is to ensure that professionals work directly with children as much as possible. This has become the "more is better" phenomenon that has been documented in the field (McWilliam, Young, & Harville, 1996).

If written materials convey that early intervention is about support, however, a more accurate view can be encouraged. As described more fully in Chapter 10, the kinds of support early intervention provides are emotional, material, and informational. One of the types of information that professionals provide families is about interventions with the child. This information is what we often consider "therapy," "special instruction," or other services. With infants and toddlers and their families, therapy and special instruction consist of providing suggestions to primary caregivers for them to carry out during daily routines. Consequently, written materials should be explicit about describing *support* as the method for delivering services. If a program uses a primary service delivery model, such as that described in Chapter 9, it is helpful to mention this in written materials.

Community Impression Management

Many of the binds in which early intervention programs find themselves are attributed to referral sources. Doctors and others will tell the family to go to early intervention to get therapy, as though the direct hands-on work by the professionals is a cure-all. It is therefore necessary to educate the community, especially referral sources, about the program and how early intervention works. Programs should develop a 5-year impression management plan to include

- Visiting referral sources and explaining what early intervention is not

- Speaking at pediatric grand rounds

- Asking referral sources to make referrals to early intervention, and not for individual services

One way to help educate the community is to ensure that the written materials that community members see and distribute reflect the philosophy and knowledge desired.

Initial Referral Call

What happens when a family calls the program and says, "I was told to call early intervention. What do you do?" As with the brochure, if the person answering the telephone describes the therapy and instruction services, the family will get the wrong idea about early intervention from the very beginning. If, on the other hand, the person says the program provides support to families, the family will get the right idea. Some programs have given the receptionist a script such as the following:

> We provide support to families when there is a question about a child's development. We encourage families and other caregivers to help the child throughout the day. We make sure caregivers have the materials and information they need to do this. We pull together teams of professionals to join the family in solving problems and identifying learning opportunities. Finally, we make sure that the family is never alone in the process. We help the family

identify who they already know who can help, we make sure the family has a service coordinator, and we have a team of professionals to help.

Intake Steps

In the 1980s, studies were conducted at Western Carolina Center (now the J. Iverson Riddle Developmental Center) on the efficacy of checklist training of direct-care staff working with people with developmental disabilities. Checklists were found to be useful tools for identifying the steps in a process; for reminding practitioners what needs to be done; and for guiding supervisors, trainers, or peers when they give feedback (Lattimore, Stephens, Favell, & Risley, 1984; Realon, Lewallen, & Wheeler, 1983). A number of checklists are therefore included in this book. Checklists may be completed by individuals using the practice; as a self-check; or by a supervisor, trainer, or peer.

The Intake Checklist in Appendix 3.1 describes the steps programs should take to ensure that the first encounter, which is typically an intake visit, is positive and describes early intervention correctly. The intake visit is typically 1–2 hours in length; it is used to describe the program, tell families of their rights afforded by law, and secure their permission to evaluate the child. This checklist is designed to make the intake visit as family centered as possible, to introduce the idea that the family—not just the child—is the focus of the program, and to get important information for people potentially working with the child.

This section describes the rationale for each step in the checklist.

1. *Tell the family that the purpose for the intake is to find out their concerns and tell about the program.* Families should always be told why things are done, not just *that* they are done. Early intervention involves so much bureaucracy to which practitioners become accustomed, so families might be put through hoops without a proper rationale. An example of this first step might be the following:

    Today, I want to make sure you know what early intervention is about and what the next steps will be, if you decide this is something you want to do. In this state, early intervention is for children under the age of 36 months who have delays or certain conditions. And it's for their families. The program is voluntary. The state will provide you with three things at no charge: service coordination, an assessment of your child, and an individualized family service plan. We will discuss the costs and payment options for intervention services. On today's visit, I want to let you know about the assessment and, if you decide that's what you want to do, I need to get your permission for us to evaluate your child. I need to go over all your rights as a family receiving early intervention, and I would like to get some information about your child's vision, hearing, and possible need for assistive technology, which I will explain to you. (Such a long statement in reality would be broken up with checks with the family to ensure that they understand the process and want the conversation to continue.)

2. *Tell the family one purpose of the intake visit is also to get to know the family to better be able to serve them.* Treating families like new neighbors is a good metaphor for the first encounters, but the reason that early interventionists want to get to know families is so their intervention suggestions make sense to the family. This statement might be similar to the following:

    Early intervention is very much a family support, because your child doesn't live in a vacuum; she lives with you, so whatever is going on with you affects her—and of course, vice versa. If we know what family members and friends you have to help you, other people or agencies you can count on, as well as people or agencies who are not helpful to you, it will guide us about all the resources you have available and where we might fit in. Your life should not revolve around early intervention; rather, early intervention should reinforce the things in your life that are going well and help, if possible, with the things that aren't going well. By focusing on the whole family, it helps us focus on the whole child.

3. *Begin the intake contact by asking the family about their concerns.* Families might have existing concerns on their minds, so it is critical to ask what those are, before launching into the professional's agenda: "Before we start, tell me what's on your mind, what you hope we can help with, and what you think early intervention is all about."

4. *Tell the family that early intervention is for the whole family, not just the child* (i.e., explain family systems). Families might come to early intervention already thinking that this is like going to the doctor or going to physical therapy after an injury—something where the professional concentrates exclusively on the "patient," while giving scant attention to the context. It is vital to let the family know from the beginning that the child does not live in a vacuum, and that early interventionists need to know about the concerns, priorities, and resources of the people around the child.

5. *If appropriate, ask the family to tell the child's story, beginning at birth or before.* This is a good activity because it allows the family to describe what has happened to them, relative to their child, in their own words (see "Telling the Child's Story" later in the chapter). It also can reveal much about the family's priorities and way of life. It is inappropriate to get details about daily routines at this early stage. Furthermore, this will be explored in depth during the RBI (see Chapter 6). The interventionist may say, "Tell me Mike's story, starting from his birth or before if you like."

6. *Describe early intervention as a support program.* As mentioned earlier, this is an important alternative to describing early intervention as direct hands-on therapy or instruction:

> Early intervention is about providing you with support. Our job is to give you emotional support, to make sure you have access to any material support, such as financial programs and equipment, you might need, and informational support. We'll tell you about your child's disability [if this is an appropriate thing to say to the family], about child development, about resources including services, and about what you can do with your child to help him develop.

7. *Discuss services only in the context of supports.* Services such as the therapies and special instruction should only be discussed as a method for giving the family information (i.e., informational support), not as a method for "treating" or "teaching" the child:

> A whole team of professionals is available to help you and any other caregivers of your child. Their job is to provide you with the most relevant, up-to-date, evidence-based information to make the most of the many learning opportunities your child has throughout every day. That's what therapy and education are all about in early intervention: consultation to the people who spend time with the child.

8. *Discuss how early intervention can provide information about the child's functioning status (and disability, if appropriate).* Telling the family about the kind of information they can expect is critical:

> One of the types of information the team can help you with is about your child's diagnosis. We can talk about how this diagnosis has an impact on what she can do in her everyday life.

9. *Discuss how early intervention can provide information about child development.* Many families want to know what children of their child's age typically do and they want to know what comes next in development:

> The team will be able to tell you what children of your child's age typically do, if that's information you would like, and they can tell you what skills your child should be able to do next.

10. *Discuss how early intervention can provide information about resources, including services.* For most families, available places and activities to help with children's development and behavior might be a mystery. They are especially likely to be unaware of resources related to disabilities:

> The team will tell you about places where you can go or call to get help for your child and family. They will know people with expert knowledge. Your service coordinator will also help you figure out how these can be paid for—whether it's insurance, Medicaid, free, you yourself, and so on.

11. *Discuss how early intervention can provide suggestions about what to do with the child.* This constitutes perhaps 80% of the activity of traditional early intervention. Providing suggestions for what to do at home or in child care is the backbone of the field:

> Most of the time, the team will be helping you know what you and other caregivers can be doing in your daily activities to teach your child. That's how very young children learn—through the play and caregiving that go on in the ordinary course of a day.

12. *If necessary, screen the child for potential delays* (only necessary in programs with many inappropriate referrals). In programs where more than 10% of the referred children end up not being eligible, it might be worth screening children's development before proceeding to full-blown evaluations. The Ages & Stages Questionnaires® (ASQ) has good sensitivity and specificity, has a social and emotional questionnaire (the ASQ:SE), and has a Spanish translation (Squires & Bricker, 2009; Squires, Bricker, & Potter, 1997; Squires, Bricker, & Twombly, 2003; Squires, Bricker, & Twombly, 2004).

13. *Develop an ecomap* (see Ecomap Checklist in Appendix 4.1). The ecomap is a method for a) identifying the family's informal and formal supports and b) giving the family an opportunity to talk. It is described fully in Chapter 4.

14. *Briefly discuss families' rights, including the right to refuse services.* By law, families need to have their rights explained to them at the beginning of contact with the early intervention system. As important as this step is, it is not worth spending much time on it because families are unlikely to remember the details. Furthermore, if professionals spend too much time on this, they are spending too much time talking.

15. *Leave detailed written information about rights.* Because of the importance of families' due process rights, a clear explanation in writing should be left with the family. This should provide the information that professionals have covered, as well as details they have not covered.

16. *Ask for the family's permission to evaluate the child, if appropriate.* Two levels of evaluation are needed in early intervention: one is a multidisciplinary evaluation (MDE) that is designed to determine needs and a description of the child's current level of functioning. All children in early intervention have the right to a free MDE. The other level is testing. For children entering the system because they have a developmental delay, almost all states require that some type of testing be done to determine the extent of the delay. States have criteria for delay based on standard deviations or percentage of delay, requiring the program to assess developmental ages or quotients. It is important to note that testing is not necessary if the child enters the program because of an established condition. An MDE is necessary, but this can, in most states, consist of a description of current functioning in the five required domains: cognitive, communication, motor, social-emotional, and self-help/adaptive. Any kind of evaluation for which a report will be generated (and the "Current Level of Functioning" section of the IFSP can be considered a report) requires parental permission. Therefore, in almost all situations the family will need to give permission for the next step of the process—the MDE.

17. *Explain to the family that testing is not necessary, but some form of multidisciplinary evaluation is necessary, if the child has an established condition.* This point was explained in Step 16.

18. *Obtain financial information, if necessary.* Many programs need to determine the family's financial status early in the process because it is used to determine how much the family will pay for services. Note that by federal law, service coordination, the MDE, and the development of the IFSP must be provided to participating families at no cost to them. Because this might be a sensitive topic for some families, the reason for needing the information should be made clear.

19. *Explain fully to the family what the expected financial arrangements will be.* Finances are a primary source of worry for families, so it is vital that the family be told as soon as possible what their commitment will be. The family should be reassured that everything possible will be done not to have a negative financial impact on the family. This is a very important ethical issue in early intervention. The approach described in this book goes against the traditional pile-on of services that developmental pediatricians, rehabilitation professionals, and early interventionists have often mistakenly told families are necessary for their child to develop well. Families are quickly convinced that more is better and often pay for additional services, beyond what the Part C program is paying for. At this early stage of early intervention, at the intake visit, service coordinators should start educating parents that a high intensity and frequency of direct contact with early intervention professionals is not the answer. The issue is not just a financial one, but it does affect finances (Bairrão & de Almeida, 2003).

20. *Give the family accurate information so they do not feel they have to accept every service for which the child is eligible* (i.e., reassure them that sometimes less is more). It is a mistake to evaluate a child for services and tell the family about the child's eligibility

without discussing how early intervention works. They need to understand that piling on services and sessions will not necessarily change the amount of *intervention* the child receives. It changes only the amount of *service* the family receives. The reassurance that can be provided to the family is that a single primary service provider could work with them, perhaps visiting weekly. This service provider would have a team of other professionals who also would plan interventions, but it might not be in the family's best interest to have everyone making independent, frequent visits.

21. *Tell the family that the order is evaluation, outcome selection, service decisions.* Some families and professionals are tempted to decide on services as soon as a diagnosis is made. In fact, decisions on services need to be made after outcomes or goals are selected.

22. *If applicable, describe the benefits of the primary service provider model.*

23. *Throughout the meeting, show interest in what the family said.* Professionals should use genuine active listening.

24. *Throughout the meeting, reassure the family.* Another way of conveying emotional support is to let the family know that what they have been doing has been good for the child and that enrollment in early intervention will be worthwhile.

25. *Throughout the meeting, be positive about the child and family.* Families will be very mindful of how much they feel professionals like their child and them.

26. *Throughout the meeting, show interest in the whole family.* A sure way to encourage families to understand that early intervention is a family-oriented endeavor is to demonstrate attention to or about everyone who lives in the home.

27. *Throughout the meeting, treat the family in a friendly manner.* The nonjudgmental acceptance the professional conveys is vital for the family to feel that early intervention is supportive and something worth participating in.

28. *Cull existing family and medical history questionnaires.* Both to save time and to stop asking families unnecessary questions, existing questionnaires should be examined for any information that either is not used or is sensitive. Be careful of questions such as, "Did you smoke during your pregnancy?" Such questions serve no purpose other than to allow early interventionists to pass judgment on the mother.

Telling the Child's Story

The strategy for telling the child's story was mentioned in Step 5. This step could take a while, so intake professionals need to think carefully before making the investment. It's an optional activity, but it can provide a lot of information and convey to the family that what they have to say is important.

This step can begin as simply as, "Tell me your child's story. Why don't you start from his (or her) birth?" You can ask as many or as few follow-up questions as you think are appropriate for the situation. There's no right or wrong. You're simply trying to get the family's perspective of how things have been going. You're also giving the parents an opportunity to tell about things from their perspective.

To move the story along, you can simply ask, "And then what?" Use good conversational skills such as

- Making good eye contact
- Showing interest by nodding or saying "Mm-hmm" and "Really?"
- Avoiding passing judgment at all times

An example of a family telling the child's story might be as follows:

> When Mark was born, everything was fine. I thought I had a perfect child. Well, he was a perfect baby. Pretty. Everyone said he looked like me. Yes, that made me feel great. I was doing what I'd always wanted to do. Make a baby. Be a mother.
>
> Then around 4 months, I started to notice things that didn't seem quite right. Mark didn't react one time when my friend dropped a big old box of pans she was bringing me. We both noticed he just lay there. He didn't react like a baby should. I wondered if he was deaf. So I started making noises behind his head. He sometimes reacted, so I figured he wasn't deaf exactly, but something wasn't right. I asked the doctor about it, but she said he was too young to tell.
>
> Then I realized the nursing wasn't going well. He wouldn't stay latched on and keep sucking. So I switched him to a bottle and we still had problems. Then a couple of months later, I saw my friend with a baby born the same time as Mark. And this baby was starting to sit up by herself. And Mark couldn't do that. And this other baby responded to people in ways Mark didn't. You could make this baby laugh, play Peekaboo, and such.
>
> Yes, it made me sad. I couldn't have that kind of fun with my baby. And I was worried something was wrong....

Beyond the facts of the story (the child's delays and nonresponsiveness), the more important aspect of this mother telling the story is what this tells us about her and what we can then do to support her. When using the currently described approach, early interventionists need to remember one rule at all times: *acknowledge feelings first, deal with facts second.* To make sure we do not misinterpret indications of feelings, it is safest to ask parents how they feel, unless it is obvious. This story gives the intake coordinator an opportunity to acknowledge the feelings of sadness when the mother recounts her discovery that her child was not developing typically. The coordinator could ask her how she felt about the doctor telling her to wait. The story also gives the coordinator an opportunity to recognize what a good observer the mother was—how sensitive she was to her child's development. These family-centered behaviors are encouraging for families and they set the tone for what early intervention is supposed to be about—emotional, material, and informational support.

The previously presented steps should ensure a functional, family-centered method for conducting the intake. Chapter 4 describes the construction of the ecomap in detail.

Items from the FINESSE

The following is the Intake item from the FINESSE. It reveals a preference for ascertaining the family's desires and for connecting with the family. On the FINESSE, programs use a number ranking scale to identify which of these descriptors most closely matches what they typically do and then they identify which most closely matches what they ideally would do.

(continued)

(continued)

1. Intake consists **entirely** of a description of services, especially therapy and instruction for the child.

3. Intake consists **primarily** of a description of services, especially therapy and instruction for the child.

5. Intake consists primarily of a description of child intervention and includes **some** questions to find out what questions the family wants answered.

7. Intake consists **primarily** of questions to the family about what questions they would like answered and of questions to get to know the family.

Appendix

Appendix 3.1. Intake Checklist

APPENDIX 3.1 Intake Checklist

Intake coordinator _____ Observer _____

Use this checklist as 1) the definition of the intake visit, 2) a reminder to and self-check for the intake visitor, and 3) a guide for the feedback from an observer such as another professional, a supervisor, or a trainer. It can be used across intake visits, and therefore across families, to show progress or maintenance.

Mark as correct (+), incorrect (–), almost, (±), or not applicable or observed (NA).

Did the intake coordinator	Date	Date	Date	Date	Date
1. Tell the family the purpose for the intake was to find out their concerns and tell about the program?					
2. Tell the family one purpose was also to get to know the family to better be able to serve them?					
3. Begin the intake contact by asking the family about their concerns?					
4. Tell the family that early intervention is for the whole family, not just the child (i.e., explain family systems)?					
5. If appropriate, ask the family to tell the child's story, beginning at birth or before?					
6. Describe early intervention as a *support* program?					
7. Discuss services only in the context of supports?					
8. Discuss how early intervention can provide information about the child's functioning status (and disability, if appropriate)?					
9. Discuss how early intervention can provide information about child development?					
10. Discuss how early intervention can provide information about resources, including services?					
11. Discuss how early intervention can provide suggestions about what to do with the child?					
12. If necessary, screen the child for potential delays (only necessary in programs with many inappropriate referrals)?					
13. Develop an ecomap (see Ecomap Checklist)?					

(continued)

Did the intake coordinator	Date	Date	Date	Date	Date
14. Briefly discuss families' rights, including the right to refuse services?					
15. Leave detailed written information about rights?					
16. Ask for the family's permission to evaluate the child, if appropriate?					
17. Explain to the family that testing is not necessary, but some form of multidisciplinary evaluation is necessary if the child has an established condition?					
18. Obtain financial information, if necessary?					
19. Explain fully to the family what the expected financial arrangements will be?					
20. Give the family accurate information so they do not feel they have to accept every service for which the child is eligible (i.e., reassure them that sometimes less is more)?					
21. Tell the family that the order is evaluation, outcome selection, service decisions?					
22. If applicable, describe the benefits of the primary service provider model?					
23. Throughout the meeting, show interest in what the family said?					
24. Throughout the meeting, reassure the family?					
25. Throughout the meeting, be positive about the child and family?					
26. Throughout the meeting, show interest in the whole family?					
27. Throughout the meeting, treat the family in a friendly manner?					
28. Cull existing family and medical history questionnaires?					
Total correct					
Total possible (Items – NAs)					
Percentage correct					

Constructing Ecomaps

An **ecomap** is a graphic representation of the nuclear family surrounded by members of the family's **informal support, formal support,** and **intermediate support** and the links to those supports depict the level of support the drawer perceives. It therefore shows people and agencies, and it shows strength of support or a stressful relationship. This is a variation on ecomaps used by others (Cox, Keltner, & Hogan, 2003; Hartman, 1995; Ray & Street, 2005).

The purpose of the ecomap is shown in the following introduction script, which practitioners can use when asking families if they will participate in completing an ecomap:

> To understand who you are already dealing with, in case those people can help with our interventions, I would like to ask you about people in your life. Is that all right? Once I know this, it will make my suggestions much more relevant. If there's anything you don't want to tell me, you don't have to! You can decide when we've finished whether you want a copy in your early intervention file. Is that okay?

The unspoken purposes are also as stated earlier: to give the families an opportunity to talk during the intake meeting, which often consists of describing the program, requesting permission to evaluate, conducting screenings, and informing families of their rights.

How Do You Complete an Ecomap?

The Ecomap Checklist in Appendix 4.1 provides step-by-step instructions for completing an ecomap. The items on the checklist are reproduced next, with clarifying points where needed and figures illustrating relevant steps for a fictional family.

1. *Tell the family that the purpose of the ecomap is to get to know the family.* Then, good recommendations can be made and we will know who can help get outcomes met. Some professionals might want to write this out so they have a script when they introduce the ecomap to the family.

2. *Reassure the family that they can refuse to answer any or all questions.* This a standard reassurance for informed consent. It is also simply respectful.

3. *Ask who lives in the home with the child.*

4. *Put these people's names into a central box* (see Figure 4.1). The central "family" on the ecomap consists of the people who live in the home with the child. If the child lives in different houses, use the one belonging to the adult you are talking to. If you are talking to the mother, do not ask, "Who is the child's father?" or "Who is your husband?" Instead, simply ask who else lives in the home. If someone is named, you can ask, "How is this person related to you?" If the child is in foster care, for example, the chances are high that the ecomap would be happening with the foster parent, so the foster family is what would go in the central box. If the biological mother's name comes up, her box would be outside the central-family box. In the case of a child living with a single mother, the father's name might or might not come up (assuming the mother is participating in the ecomap construction). If it does, his box would be outside the central-family box. This is therefore not the same as a typical demographics sheet. This is about who lives in the home and then other people.

5. *Ask about the extended family not living in the household of the person giving information about the child.* Typically, we begin with the mother's parents, followed by siblings of the mother.

6. *For each person named, draw a box above the household-family box* (see Figure 4.2). Informal support sources, beginning with the child's grandparents, are, in our model of the ecomap, displayed across the top of the ecomap.

Figure 4.1.   Sample ecomap: central-family box.

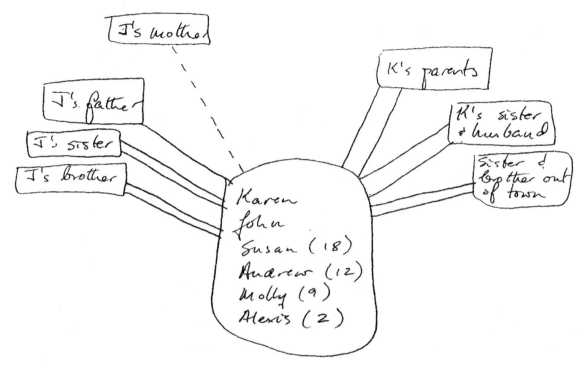

Figure 4.2. Sample ecomap: extended family of the person providing ecomap information and of any other adult in the home.

7. *Ask probe questions to determine the supportiveness or stress inducement of these people* (e.g., "How often do you talk to her?"). The person conducting the ecomap needs to ask different questions to get at this issue. When asking about nonfamily members, which comes later, families often accept simply, "How well do you get along with him [or her]?" We do not ask about relationships within the central family.

8. *Draw lines from the box back to the central box (i.e., nuclear family) reflecting supportiveness and stress,* with thick lines for much support, moderately thick lines for moderate support, thin lines for just present or somewhat supportive, and dotted lines for stress (see Figure 4.2). The person drawing the map (the professional) makes a judgment about the appropriate lines and does not seek interrater agreement from the family. We do not want to make this conversation about the thickness of the lines. Note that "thickness" of the lines, when drawn with a pen or pencil, involves the distance between parallel lines (i.e., greater distance = more support). We limit ourselves to the three thicknesses plus the dotted lines listed above. It is possible to have a continuous line of any thickness alongside a dotted line. That is, someone can be supportive but also a source of stress. For example, a grandmother of the child might a) care for the child during the day (highly supportive) but also b) make the mother feel guilty about how the mother is raising the child (stressful). We would draw a thick line next to a dotted line.

9. *Ask questions and probes and draw lines about friends of the person giving information* (boxes above the household family; see Figure 4.3). The mother's friends (BFFs) are often very important informal supports.

10. *Ask about the extended family of any other adult in the home* (boxes above the household family—e.g., the parents of the other parent). This is usually about the child's

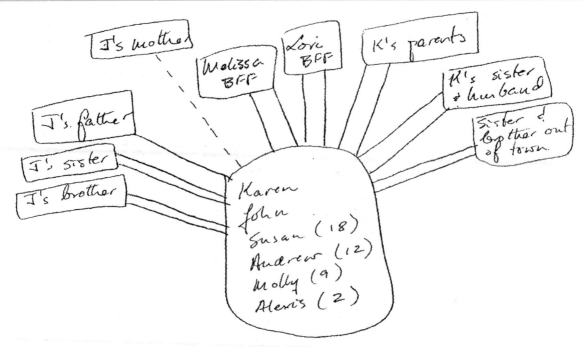

Figure 4.3. Sample ecomap: friends of the person providing ecomap information.

father's family, in traditional families. For this particular sample, both adults' extended families were added to the ecomap at the same time (refer back to Figure 4.2).

11. *Ask about friends of any other adult in the home* (boxes above the household box; see Figure 4.4). Again, this is usually about the father's friends. Sometimes, when the mother is giving the information, we draw continuous and dotted lines from these

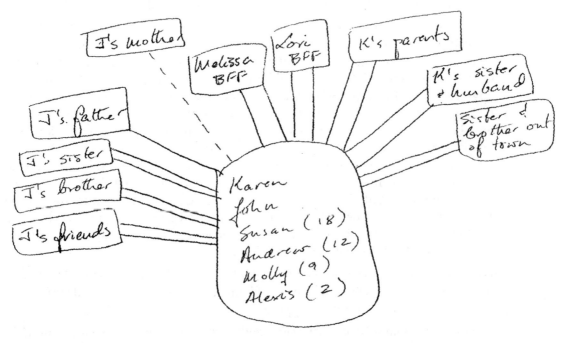

Figure 4.4. Sample ecomap: friends of any other adult in the home.

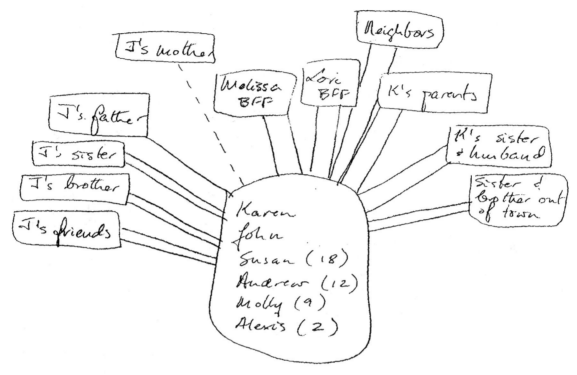

Figure 4.5.   Sample ecomap: friends and neighbors not already mentioned.

people to the central family. The continuous lines refer to the supportiveness to the father, with the dotted lines referring to the mother's view of them.

12. *Ask about family friends or neighbors not already mentioned* (boxes above the household box; see Figure 4.5).

13. *Avoid asking questions about daily routines.* A frequently asked question is whether the ecomap provides information about daily routines or the "typical day." It does not. It is limited to the issue of who is in the family's life and how supportive they are.

14. *Ask about the people at the work of the person giving information* (boxes on the sides of the household family). Many supports to families come from their acquaintances at work. We consider these neither informal nor formal supports, so we have branded them *intermediate supports* and we place them on the sides of the central box.

15. *Ask about the people at work with any other adult in the home* (boxes on the sides; see Figure 4.6).

16. *Ask about religious resources* (boxes on the sides—e.g., church, synagogue, mosque; see Figure 4.7). Some professionals are nervous about asking about this; they feel that families will consider it intrusive or that it violates the Constitution. Actually, the religious or spiritual life of families can be hugely important in early intervention (Poston & Turnbull, 2004). Most families are happy to talk about their place of worship. Occasionally, families don't like having to "admit" that they don't participate in any religious activities, so it takes a casual approach and good interviewing skills. Any time family members indicate they do not want to talk about something or are uncomfortable with a topic, the interviewer

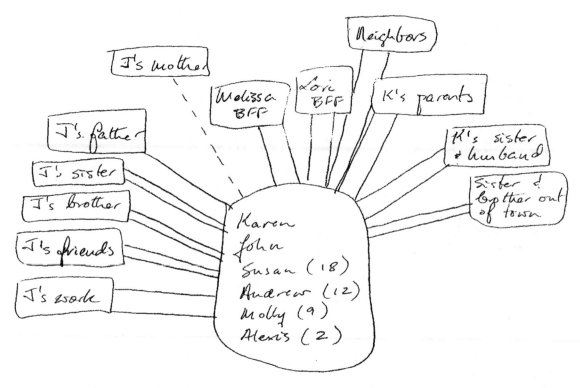

Figure 4.6. Sample ecomap: work acquaintances.

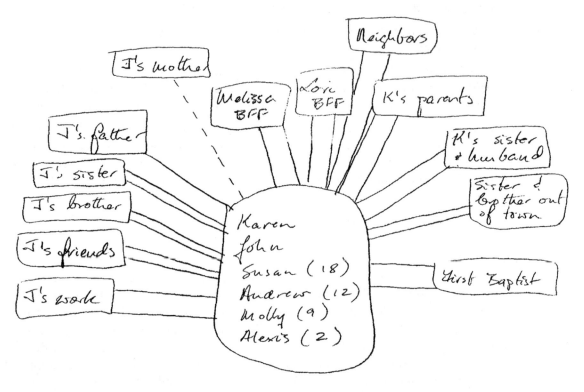

Figure 4.7. Sample ecomap: religious resources.

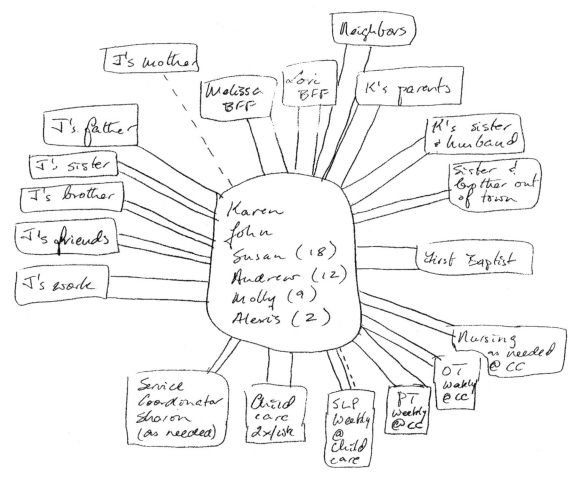

Figure 4.8. Sample ecomap: professionals involved in the child's care. (*Key:* SLP, speech-language pathologist; PT, physical therapist; OT, occupational therapist.)

should quickly affirm the parent's response and quickly move on to the next question.

17. *Ask about professionals involved in the child's care* (boxes below the household family—e.g., doctors, therapists, other early interventionists; see Figure 4.8).

18. *Ask about other services anyone in the family is receiving* (boxes below the household family; see Figure 4.9).

19. *Ask about financial resources the family is receiving* (boxes below the household family; see Figure 4.10).

20. *Ask the family if the picture looks right or if anything should be changed.* This wrap-up step is important. Most families do not add anything, but it is important to give them an opportunity to add to or even subtract from the picture. Sometimes, it is appropriate to ask the family what they think about the ecomap.

21. *Tell the family what will be done with the ecomap* (e.g., who gets copies, where it is filed). In addition to the simple respect conveyed through this step, legal considerations need to be followed.

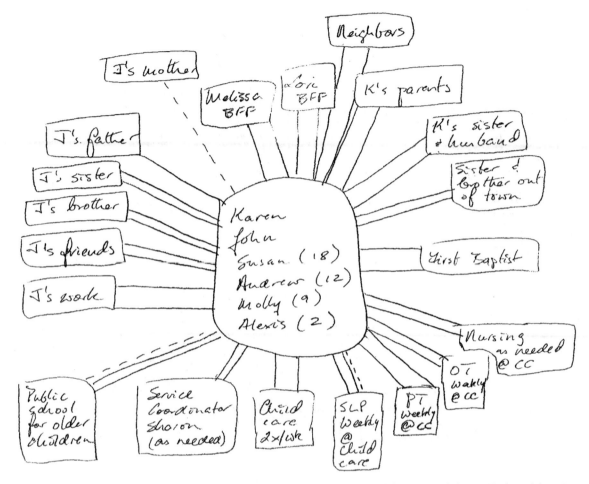

Figure 4.9. Sample ecomap: services anyone in the family is receiving. (*Key:* SLP, speech-language pathologist; PT, physical therapist; OT, occupational therapist.)

Use and Interpretation

One of the purposes of developing an ecomap is that it is a family-friendly activity that can help kick-start a positive relationship between the professional and family member. Second (the purpose stated at the beginning of the process), is that it will be used later, when intervention strategies are being developed.

When an ecomap is completed, professionals can examine it for the number of people in the informal, formal, and intermediate networks and the supportiveness of those resources. If a family has few informal supports, the professional might consider the potential for isolation. Similarly, if all the family's informal supports are at the weakest level of support, isolation might still be an issue. Professionals should be careful, however, not to psychopathologize families.

It is helpful to review ecomaps with families annually. Rather than recreating ecomaps from scratch, it is sometimes helpful to look at the previous year's ecomap. Something to be concerned about is how the support structure for a family changes over time, especially if the family's ties to the informal-support network shrink as the ties to the formal-support network expand. This might suggest that we are bombarding families with professional services to the detriment of their natural supports. The

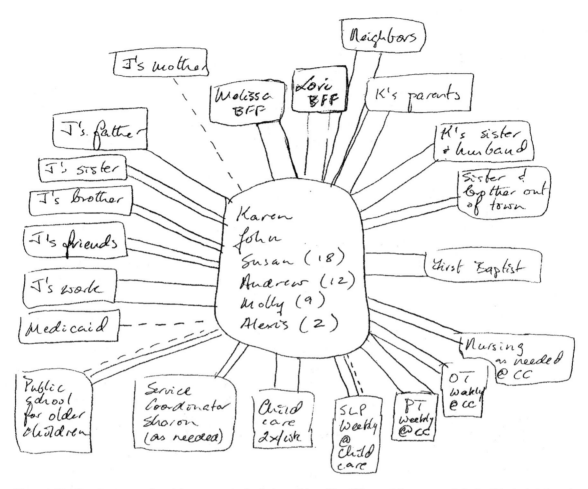

Figure 4.10. Sample ecomap: financial resources the family is receiving. (*Key:* SLP, speech-language pathologist; PT, physical therapist; OT, occupational therapist.)

shortness of the relationships with formal supports compared to the potential relationships with informal supports makes it important not to jeopardize the latter. Put simply, early intervention formal services should not supplant natural supports to the family.

Strengths and Concerns

First, developing an ecomap is a good way to get to know the family. Second, this takes only 10–15 minutes, so it does not interfere much with other intake processes. Third, it conveys, from the beginning, that early intervention is concerned with the ecology of the whole family. If we take a family-centered approach from the beginning, the family will understand why we care about all of them, not just the "target child."

Counterbalancing these three strengths is a concern of some people about intrusiveness. In my many years of experience creating hundreds of ecomaps, I have discovered that most families find the process at least painless and at most very helpful. When families are asked whether the process was intrusive, most of them say no. One parent said, "Everything in early intervention is intrusive. This is the least of it." As long as the professional doing the ecomap does it respectfully and sensitively, the family should not find it intrusive.

Review

The ecomap can be updated every 6 months or year. Service coordinators can show it to the family and ask whether anything has changed.

Ideally, service providers will examine the ecomap and do everything possible to maintain strong relationships with the informal network. This might entail asking the family from time to time about relatives and friends on the ecomap. It is also good to use informal supports instead of formal supports whenever possible and when the consumer approves. Using informal supports establishes obligations that consumers might be uncomfortable with, so professionals need to check with families before arranging any favor from an informal support member. Ideally, of course, the parents would make the calls themselves.

On the reviews, service coordinators need to make sure that informal supports are not being replaced by formal supports. One of the worst effects that early intervention can have is to weaken the informal support structure because the formal support network has become so strong and demanding. When practitioners see this happening, they need to be prepared to recommend to families that they decrease services or intensity. Most families will have nothing to do with such a change, but, if the reasons are properly given, some families will change their priorities. Other families will think that they need to sacrifice their informal support to "get therapy for my child." Our moral obligation is to encourage a family and our ethical obligation is to provide them with information. If we have encouraged them to have an easier life and informed them that the piling on of services is not likely to result in better outcomes for their child, and they still want to do that, we need to recognize that it's their life and child, not ours. That does not mean, however, that the system has to pay for more than the IFSP team, including the family, recommends.

A good example of early intervention gone awry can be seen in the real ecomap (names and identifying details changed) shown in Figure 4.11. This family had moved to their current town within the previous year, from Albuquerque. The out-of-town supports are shown in thick-lined boxes. The others are all in the current town. The child, DeeDee, had global moderate delays. The parents were both from well-educated families with a comfortable income. This is an example of a "thin" informal-support network and a "fat" formal support network. The mother said that she felt isolated, so why did she not spend more time meeting people and cultivating friends? Look at the formal supports—all those disjointed services DeeDee was getting. The saddest point of all is that, during the RBI (described in Chapter 6), the mother said the afternoons dragged on for her because she did not know what to do—how to play—with DeeDee. What were all those service providers doing? She told us they were working on cognitive, language, gross motor, fine motor, and self-help skills, but none of them addressed the mother's need to have games she could play with DeeDee. They gave her gross motor and language exercises to do with her, but DeeDee and her mother hated those. This is why it is sometimes helpful to have an ecomap.

Treatment Fidelity Issues

Some people say they do ecomaps when, in fact, they do something similar but are missing key ingredients. Developing an ecomap is a basic element of the five-component model described in this book. In other words, programs or practitioners not developing

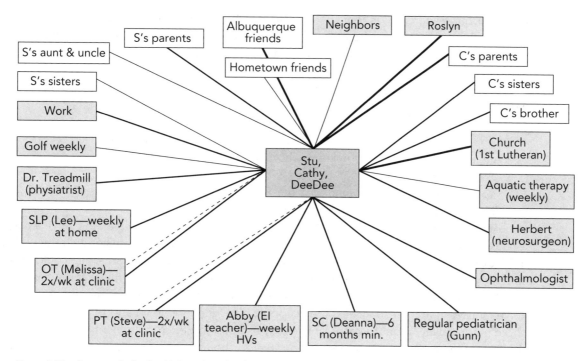

Figure 4.11. Ecomap of a family with few informal and many formal supports. (*Key:* SLP, speech-language pathologist; OT, occupational therapist; PT, physical therapist; EI, early interventionist; SC, service coordinator.)

ecomaps cannot claim to be following the model. The key ingredients of the ecomap in this model are as follows:

- The professional asks the family to participate in drawing a picture of the people and agencies in the family's life "to get a sense of who is available as resources, which will help us make our suggestions more relevant to your family."

- Only those living in the household of the child or the caregiver answering the questions are included in the central box.

- Members of the informal-support network are arrayed across the top, members of the formal-support network are arrayed across the bottom, and members of the intermediate-support network are arrayed on the sides.

- Strength of support is indicated by bands of varying thickness connecting the external supports to the family's box, with stressors indicated by a dashed line.

- Very little extraneous information is sought; definitely no information about routines is collected.

Examples

Administrator

When Annie Administrator asked Susie Service Coordinator questions about resources available to individual families, she noticed that Susie often draws blanks. Annie's reason for asking about resources was that she noticed that Susie's IFSPs were often "service heavy." Because Susie did not seem to have much information about families, Annie introduced her to the strategy of developing ecomaps with families. A few weeks later, Annie asked how the ecomaps were going.

"I did a few," said Susie, "but I felt they were too intrusive, so I've been doing them only with friendly families."

"Do you know whether Rory Rodriguez's mother is very isolated?"

"I don't think she is. There was someone at the house the other day."

Annie was hopeful. "Do you know who that was?"

"A neighbor or something."

"You haven't done an ecomap with the Rodriguez family, have you, Susie?"

"No," Susie said. "Their English isn't too good."

Annie had had enough. At a staff meeting later that week, she told all the service coordinators that ecomaps had to be completed on all new families and families with upcoming IFSP reviews. The ecomaps needed to be filed in the children's charts, so Annie could make sure they were being done. This meant that copies would need to be made for families.

Annie had become convinced that developing ecomaps with families helped both to involve families' natural resources in the "support plan" (i.e., the IFSP) and to give her service coordinators a way to get to know families. By establishing the requirement to do ecomaps, she knew the service coordinators would develop the ability to do the ecomaps. This was not rocket science, but it did demand practice. She planned to devote one staff meeting to a discussion of how it was being done. She knew she'd have to go with some of her service coordinators to give them direct feedback and maybe even to model.

Service Coordinator

Sarah Service Coordinator knew her intake visits were boring and were all about the service, not the family. She had heard about ecomaps and thought they might give some relief to her—and the families. When she first started, she was self-conscious about asking questions that weren't just about the child. She tentatively asked a few families who seemed friendly and found that the families were quite happy to tell her about who they knew and had contact with. She gained confidence. Then, she came across one mother who introduced herself as Mrs. Robinson, not by first name. Although somewhat intimidated by Mrs. Robinson's formality, Sarah plowed ahead with her newly confident approach. "Mrs. Robinson, can I ask you some questions about who you have connections with, so I can make my recommendations more meaningful?"

"What do you mean, who I have connections with?" Mrs. Robinson retorted.

"Oh, just what extended family you have, what kinds of supports you have, and so forth."

"What does this have to do with early intervention services for my child?"

"Early intervention is about the family," said Sarah, losing confidence by the mouthful. "Not just about the child."

"I think we should just concentrate on my child first, don't you?"

Sarah left the meeting feeling she'd been beaten down. She needed either to explain the process better or acknowledge that for some families the ecomap wasn't a good idea. She decided not to give up or anticipate whether families would like it. She continued to offer it, and nearly every family not only collaborated in the development of their ecomap but actually found it interesting and enlightening. Sarah realized that she would occasionally come across Mrs. Robinsons, but for most families the ecomap was successful.

Service Provider

Prunella Provider was assigned to provide ongoing home-based early intervention to the Sailor family. She had not been involved in the intake process, so she knew little about them. She did ask Sarah Service Coordinator, who worked with the Sailors, whether she had conducted an ecomap with them. Sarah said she had not; this had been during a bout of lack of self-confidence about the ecomap. Prunella was secretly delighted, even though she knew it would have been a good intake activity. Now, she got to do it with the family.

On the first home visit, Prunella told the Sailors she would like to draw a picture of the people in their lives, and the Sailors were happy to participate with her. Even though she knew the child had autism and that the family had substantial resources (from the looks of their house), Prunella discovered that there was a huge extended family living in the same town, that there were already numerous professionals involved (including some with whom the Sailors did not get along), and that church was very important to the family.

As Prunella worked with the family to develop interventions for their child, some of which involved considerable intensity of time, she talked to the Sailors about the various people in their informal support network who were willing to look after the child once a week. They discussed which family members could be trusted to carry out interventions planned with them. This information thus enlightened the team (mostly Prunella and the Sailors) about who they could count on for babysitting, giving the Sailors a rest from the intensive work with their child, and giving the child an opportunity to learn to generalize across people. Without the ecomap, it would have taken Prunella a long time to gather and use this information.

Family

The Rollos were overwhelmed at the amount of information they had received when they were referred to the early intervention program. They were sent forms and brochures in the mail, and then the nice service coordinator, Sarah, told them about services and programs and evaluations and legal rights and all sorts of other things. At one point, though, Sarah suggested they draw a picture of the people the family had connections with.

"Finally," thought Roxy Rollo. "She's going to ask questions instead of give information."

Roxy was fascinated by the picture as it evolved. She hadn't realized just how many people she and her husband had in their lives—people who were there for them as well as people who were frankly a bit of a pain. Because Sarah had described all the kinds of professionals who could be involved with them, now that they were entering early intervention, Roxy wondered where she would find time to fit them all in.

"Am I going to have a whole bunch of people down here beside the pediatrician, now that we're going into early intervention?"

"In a way, yes," said Sarah, "but you'll have one main person who you can see every week. The others will be behind the scenes, only coming out when you or your primary service provider need them."

Roxy looked at the ecomap and thought about how lucky she was and yet how busy she was. She marveled at how Sarah had obtained so much information in such a short time.

Summary

Understanding the family ecology starts with the very first encounters. This understanding is central to making early intervention family centered, which involves two concepts: how to approach families (the process) and what to talk to families about (the content). Even before families or referral sources talk to early interventionists, they might form ideas about early intervention from written products. Therefore, attention should be paid to the wording on web sites, in brochures, and in letters. Early interventionists need to emphasize support to families rather than services to children. The latter are just one form of the former.

How early interventionists handle the initial referral call and the subsequent intake steps can speak volumes about the philosophy of the program. The development of an ecomap is a strategy for getting to know the family ecology. It shows the family's informal, formal, and intermediate (work and worship) supports. It provides much information in a short time. Many people feel that they get at the same information in other ways, but the ecomap has distinct features that make it more powerful than its pretenders. In summary, so many bureaucratic activities have to happen during intake that the ecomap is a pleasant, family-centered relief.

Test on Intake

1. The intake visit should *emphasize* that early intervention is about

    a. Services

    b. Support

    c. Adaptive equipment

    d. Parent groups

2. Families should be introduced to the idea that early intervention is about families at

    a. The first visit

    b. The second visit

    c. The third visit

    d. The fourth visit

3. Because it takes a long time for referral sources to change their ideas about an agency, the early intervention program should

    a. Meet the expectations of the referral sources

    b. Accept referrals only from sources that have been trained about what early intervention is all about

    c. Develop a 5-year plan for educating the community

    d. Provide a choice between family- and child-centered services

4. The referral call should be taken by someone who

    a. Has a degree in social work or the equivalent

    b. Can handle difficult parents

    c. Can describe the services in detail

    d. Can explain early intervention in terms of support to families

5. During intake, asking the family about the child's story is

    a. A valuable way to get at the social and medical history

    b. A colossal waste of time

    c. Intrusive

    d. The best way to understand what goes on during routines

6. An ideal intake visit consists primarily of

    a. A description of child intervention and includes some questions to find out what questions the family wants answered

    b. Questions to the family about what questions they would like answered and of questions to get to know the family

    c. A description of services, especially therapy and instruction for the child

    d. Reviewing the necessary paperwork for moving into eligibility determination

7. The purpose of the ecomap is

    a. To determine the family's stress level

    b. To determine how good the family is at establishing supportive relationships

    c. To know the family, so good recommendations can be made

    d. All of the above

8. At the beginning of the ecomap process, families should be told

    a. This information is required for participation in early intervention

    b. How important it is not to leave anything out

    c. That this is just a fun, getting-to-know-you activity

    d. That they can refuse to answer any or all questions

9. Determining who the child's father is

    a. Is not necessary

    b. Is necessary

    c. Is advisable

    d. Is extremely interesting

10. The thickness of the support lines from boxes (i.e., supports) back to the central (nuclear family) box

    a. Should be verified through interrater agreement

    b. Is subject to the view of the professional, based on the family's description

    c. Is irrelevant and should be ignored

    d. All of the above

11. The informal network consists of

    a. Extended family members only

    b. Friends only

    c. Extended family members and friends

    d. People the family barely knows

12. The ecomap

    a. Covers daily routines

    b. Provides the child's story

    c. Describes the family's neighborhood

    d. None of the above

13. Asking about worship activities

    a. Recognizes that this is important to many American families

    b. Is intrusive

    c. Violates the constitutional requirement to separate Church and State

    d. Allows you to match service providers to families

14. Over time in early intervention, we need to be concerned about

    a. Having too few formal supports

    b. Depleting informal supports while expanding formal supports

    c. Depleting formal supports while expanding informal supports

    d. Formal-support providers' creeping into families' informal-support network

15. Ecomaps should be reviewed

    a. Monthly

    b. Quarterly

    c. Every 6 months

    d. Annually

16. In the five-component model of early intervention, if you're doing an ecomap, the picture (i.e., the actual ecomap) is

    a. Necessary

    b. Optional

    c. Good for some families but not for others

    d. Juvenile

17. In this model, informal-support network members are arrayed

    a. Across the bottom

    b. Across the top

    c. On the sides

    d. In the middle box

18. A dotted line between a box and the central family indicates

    a. Someone with whom the family has rare contact

    b. Someone who is just *present* in the family's life

    c. Someone who is a source of stress to the family

    d. Someone the family has heard of but has not actually met

Answers: 1) b 2) a 3) c 4) d 5) a 6) b 7) c 8) d 9) a 10) b 11) c 12) d 13) a 14) b 15) d 16) a 17) b 18) c

Appendix

Appendix 4.1. Ecomap Checklist

APPENDIX 4.1 Ecomap Checklist

Professional _____ Observer _____

Use this checklist as a self-check or for observation by a peer, supervisor, or trainer.

Mark as correct (+), incorrect (–), almost, (±), or not applicable or observed (NA).

Did the professional	Date	Date	Date	Date	Date
1. Tell the family that the purpose of the ecomap is to get to know the family so good recommendations can be made and so we know who can help get outcomes met?					
2. Reassure the family that they can refuse to answer any or all questions?					
3. Ask who lives in the home with the child?					
4. Put these people's names into a central box?					
5. Ask about the extended family, not living in the child's household, of the person giving information?					
6. For each person named, draw a box above the household-family box?					
7. Ask probe questions to determine the supportiveness or stress inducement of these people (e.g., "How often do you talk to her?")					
8. Draw lines from the box back to the central box (i.e., nuclear family) reflecting supportiveness and stress, with thick lines for much support, moderately thick lines for moderate support, thin lines for just present or somewhat supportive, and dotted lines for stress?					
9. Ask questions and probes and draw lines (boxes above the household family) about friends of the person giving information?					
10. Ask about the extended family of any other adult in the home (e.g., the parents of the other parent; box above the household family)?					
11. Ask about friends of any other adult in the home (boxes above the household box)?					
12. Ask about family friends or neighbors not already mentioned (boxes above the household box)?					
13. Avoid asking questions about daily routines?					

(continued)

APPENDIX 4.1 Ecomap Checklist (continued)

Did the professional	Date	Date	Date	Date	Date
14. Ask about the people at the work of the person giving information (boxes on the sides of the household family)?					
15. Ask about the people at work with any other adult in the home (boxes on the sides)?					
16. Ask about religious resources (e.g., church, synagogue, mosque; boxes on the sides)?					
17. Ask about professionals involved with the child (e.g., doctors, therapists, other early interventionists; boxes below the household family)?					
18. Ask about other services anyone in the family is receiving (boxes below the household family)?					
19. Ask about financial resources the family is receiving (boxes below the household family)?					
20. Ask the family if the picture looks right or if anything should be changed?					
21. Tell the family what would be done with the ecomap (e.g., who gets copies, where it is filed)?					
Total correct					
Total possible (Items – NAs)					
Percentage correct					

Needs Assessment and Intervention Planning

As the proverb says, "He who fails to plan plans to fail." The backbone of early intervention is the intervention plan. This section addresses the vital steps to developing a functional, family-centered intervention plan. These steps involve the assessment of needs, which is not commonplace in early intervention, and writing a solid plan with plenty of child and family outcomes.

Assessment

This chapter introduces material on needs assessment and intervention planning by discussing assessment in the context of early intervention in natural environments (EINE). It addresses assessment questions, assessment postulates, evaluation and assessment in Part C, assessment on the IFSP, the current level of functioning, and service coordinator roles. It concludes with the Infant/Toddler Assessment Checklist (see Appendix 5.1).

Assessment Questions

Different types of assessment are needed for infants and toddlers: assessment for diagnosis, assessment for determining eligibility, assessment for monitoring progress, and assessment for intervention planning. Each of these types might require a different way of doing it, and different types of people might be involved. A problem in early intervention is that many systems confuse the different assessment purposes or try to take short cuts by using the method for determining eligibility as the assessment of *needs*. Standardized tests might successfully sort out children who are eligible for services under the delay criterion. These tests have items that do well for the purposes intended, but those items are not necessarily meaningful for children and families in everyday life.

Assessment can be accomplished through formal testing, informal testing or clinical judgment, observation, or report. When using report, one can ask closed-ended questions (e.g., "Can she sit by herself?") and open-ended questions (e.g., "Tell me how she plays when you're hanging out in your living room."). An interview can be used to ask such questions and to elicit a report. In fact, the distinction between direct observation and interview is worth discussion. Direct observation by a professional other than a classroom teacher is based on a very small slice of life. Despite the premise behind Malcolm Gladwell's (2005) *Blink*, quick, one-time observations of children's behavior provide limited information. In a study of the amount of observation needed to produce stable engagement data, Bill Ware and I discovered that eight 15-minute observations on different days were necessary (McWilliam & Ware, 1994).

But what if you interview caregivers of children—people who have spent hours with them, day after day? What they report is their *observations* across much time, in multiple settings, with many people, and with many objects. To get a good picture of children's and families' functioning this way requires a skillful interview. Later, the RBI will be proposed as an assessment method for obtaining an observational report.

Assessment Postulates

Three challenges to assessment in early intervention are posed. First, *we overemphasize assessment, especially diagnosis, and underemphasize intervention.* For example, documentation of a child's *DSM-IV* "disorder" (*Diagnostic and Statistical Manual of Mental Disorders, Fourth Edition;* American Psychiatric Association, 1994) is often considered a major activity in a family's journey through early intervention. It is certainly expensive, costing $600 or more. In addition to the cost, many professionals actually like the professional cachet that comes with being able to administer a test—or even better, a battery of tests—and proclaim what is wrong with the child. It is rewarding to some professionals to be the people who can untangle the knotty question about what is "wrong" with a child; because this is something many families do want to know, these diagnostic assessments can be helpful. It is often said that diagnostic assessments open the gate to intervention services. Sometimes this is true, but more often testing for eligibility can be done relatively more cheaply and quickly. For professionals and parents who have a strong belief in diagnosis-specific "treatments" rather than a belief that intervention principles can cut across most learning requirements, the diagnosis is supreme.

A second proposal is that *we should provide support (i.e., intervention) and work in assessment rather than assess constantly and work in intervention.* This proposal is based on a common reason given for multiple specialists making regular home visits to a child and family: Assessment should be ongoing and only the specialist can really do the assessment. The frequency of such assessments will be challenged elsewhere in this book, but the point here is that this is another example of the overemphasis on assessment. The emphasis should be on intervention that provides ongoing information about the child's learning and progress (i.e., assessment information).

The third proposal is that *high-level expertise from multiple experts does not need to be applied to intervention for infants, toddlers, and families all the time.* As long as families have one competent professional providing ongoing support, the high-level expertise might be needed from time to time, as the child makes changes or as the family and primary service provider run into situations outside their scope of knowledge and skill. But this rarely means sending an educator, an OT, a PT, and an SLP into the home every single week.

Evaluation and Assessment in Part C

In many communities, children in Part C are being needlessly tested. Some states have even established policies requiring this needless testing. Four types of children are potentially eligible for Part C services.

1. Children with established conditions (sometimes known as *medical conditions*) are automatically eligible. States define what conditions are applicable, but often include

chromosomal abnormalities and physical impairments. These children do not need developmental testing for eligibility. All children in Part C need a multidisciplinary evaluation that must cover five domains, but this can be accomplished without formal testing. Nevertheless, some states and communities have "simplified" the process by telling professionals to test the children to get this information. Perhaps they did not realize that other forms of assessment can produce the required "current level of functioning." The case for using the RBI as the method for assessment of these children will be made later.

2. Children with developmental delays require testing to document that the delay actually exists. So, most states have established criteria about the number of months for the delay or the number of standard deviations below the mean. These children do not have known established conditions. For example, a child with Down syndrome should not need testing, but a child with delayed language and no known etiology would need testing. "Testing" usually means that a standardized instrument needs to be scored. States vary in the types of tests they allow. Some restrict testing to norm-referenced tests such as the Bayley Scales of Infant Development (1993) or the Battelle Developmental Inventory (Newborg, 2005), whereas others allow standardized but not norm-referenced tests such as the Hawaii Early Learning Profile (Parks, Furono, O'Reilly, Inatsuka, & Hosaka, 1997). It might be possible to score most of an eligibility test from the information gained in an RBI (McWilliam, Casey, & Sims, 2009), as described in Chapter 6.

3. Children with "atypical development" but no documented delay or established condition are also eligible if a qualified professional makes the determination through clinical judgment. This eligibility category is usually used for children with challenging behaviors not directly related to a disability. Although testing might not be required to establish eligibility under this category, these children are often tested to rule out a delay.

4. The final eligibility category is used only by those states that elect to serve children at risk for delays or disabilities. States decide on the risk factors that can be used for such children, who do not meet any of the other three criteria. Risk factors usually include environmental or biological conditions. Again, testing is usually used to rule out delay, so, although it is not required for eligibility, most such children in fact are tested.

Assessment on the IFSP

The IFSP requires documentation of the child's current level of performance in five domains: cognitive, communication, physical, social or emotional, and adaptive performance. The purpose is to be able to monitor that outcomes have been developed and services have been planned to match performance needs in these domains.

Usually, IFSP forms are designed with a box in which to write some information for each domain. This is good for prompting basic information, so the paperwork burden is reduced. The downside, however, is that the service coordinator might be so cryptic that the information is useless. For example, about communication, the service coordinator might write "Some receptive but needs expressive." On balance, it is better to keep this information short so the emphasis is less on assessment and more on intervention. Some states have forms or procedures where long reports on present levels of functioning are expected. The rationale for this is that an evaluation or assessment is conducted, so ethically a report should be generated. This puts a considerable burden on the service coordinator in terms of completing the IFSP process in a timely manner and sometimes in terms of having to write on the spot, in front of the family. In this model, it is recommended that the whole evaluation process be kept as streamlined as possible, which includes keeping the results short.

Unfortunately, policy organizes this by traditional domains. Understandably, the five domains were chosen because standardized instruments producing scores in these areas exist. To establish developmental delay, states can establish criteria for the amount of delay necessary to be eligible for services, so one might expect to see similar information in this section of the IFSP. The link back to standardized evaluations is logical, but the link forward to outcomes is not as logical. Better ways exist for organizing assessment of functional needs (see Chapter 6).

On some IFSPs, only positive comments are made in the boxes, presumably to emphasize the positive (Jung & McWilliam, 2005; McWilliam et al., 1998). An example is "Alison has good object permanence." But, this does not help anyone to understand why the outcomes were chosen.

On other IFSPs, only scores are placed in the boxes, sometimes because eligibility for specific services is based on domain scores. For example, a child might be able to receive speech-language services only if there is a 15-point difference between his or her language score and his or her cognitive score. This, by the way, is a flawed policy, because it can make children with cognitive impairments ineligible for services (Cole, Dale, & Mills, 1992). Another example would be in places where the discrepancy criterion is not used but the absolute or base score is. For example, a child might be eligible for speech-language services based on a delay of 25%. This implies that the age-equivalent score is accurate and that the delay has something to do with functional needs. For a host of reasons, the rules and culture around this section of the IFSP result in scores being entered into the boxes.

The notion of monitoring the match between the information in these evaluation result boxes and the outcomes has some problems. First, just because there is a delay does not mean the family has chosen to address it. The family might have more pressing needs that are even more important than the delay, such as a medical need of the child's, the family's difficulty in paying bills, or marital conflict between the parents. This is a difficult idea for professionals who are schooled in the child-centered early-intervention philosophy that we should address delays as soon as possible. Second, the method for obtaining evaluation information (e.g., a standardized test for some children) does not necessarily reveal a problem in everyday functioning. So it would be foolish to expect an outcome to match failures on those evaluations.

The policy, which is meant to ensure that systems are not denying needed supports to families, is well intended. But it does not account for the possibility that needs found in the evaluation might be met through support from a generalist. For example, a delay in adaptive performance could be addressed by the same person who is addressing delays in cognitive and communication performance. An OT and an SLP might be involved, but the rationale that the child needs separate specialists for each of these testing domains is defective (McWilliam, 2003; Rapport, McWilliam, & Smith, 2004; Woodruff & Shelton, 2006). One cannot tell from information about delay whether specialists are needed, let alone the extent to which they are needed. *This is one of the most common fundamental blunders made in the IFSP process—assigning the valuable resources of specialist time on the basis of the wrong data.*

Instead, the IFSP should consider the truly functional data, which are found in the answers to these questions:

1.   What child and family needs have been identified?

2.   If a primary service provider (PSP) model is used, who is that service provider?

3.   Given the child and family in question, what help does the PSP need to support the family in reaching the stated outcome? What intensity of support is needed?

If a multidisciplinary model is used, it is more difficult to use functional assessment data. In fact, the reason nonfunctional data (e.g., standardized-test results) are used so much is that they conform to the multidisciplinary approach: If a delay is found in a given domain, the service ostensibly related to that domain is slapped on the IFSP. For example, when a delay is found in the fine motor section of the Battelle, occupational therapy is almost automatically put on the IFSP. Nevertheless, there are ways to use functional data with multidisciplinary teams. Beginning with the top-priority outcome, the service coordinator and family decide what service might best meet that need. They need to be prepared, however, to revisit this once the whole list of outcomes has been considered.

The next question is whether the same service provider can support the family in accomplishing the second outcome. If not, they decide what service could address it. This process proceeds through the outcomes. Needless to say, the beauty of functional outcomes can become sabotaged when they are divided among different professionals who might not communicate with each other. This method also results in the family having to deal with many professionals—and often. These themes are expanded upon in Section IV, Model of Service Delivery.

Current Levels of Functioning

IDEA requires "(1) a statement of the infant's or toddler's present levels of physical development, cognitive development, communication development, social or emotional development, and adaptive development, based on objective criteria" (IDEA, § 636 (d)). This information is needed for a number of reasons. First, it is the short form of an assessment report, so monitors can determine whether the plan of action (i.e., outcomes, strategies, and services) matches the assessed needs. That is the accountability reason for an assessment report. Second, the report serves some systems as the place to document the delay that made the child eligible by virtue of his or her delay. In many systems, the age equivalence scores are entered in this part of the IFSP. Third, some people use it as the place to document progress. From year to year, they can see how the data change. In reality, the information entered in the little boxes on the form, which is the most common format, is insufficient to judge progress.

It can be assumed therefore that these reasons for documenting the present level of development will require 1) developmental scores for children being served under the "delayed" category and 2) a description of salient strengths and weaknesses. The limited space on the form is a blessing in terms of the amount of paperwork; service coordinators do not have to enter much information (see the section for child's present levels of development from the Nebraska IFSP shown in Figure 5.1). Children being served under the established condition category should not need test scores, although some systems

Nebraska Individualized Family Service Plan
(Nebraska Department of Education—Department of Health and Human Resources)

(.................... Denotes Periodic Update)   Name of Child _____   **CONFIDENTIAL**

CHILD'S PRESENT LEVELS OF DEVELOPMENT (CONT'D)

Area/Date of Evaluation   Current Abilities

Cognitive Thinking Skills
____/____/____/____yrs ____mos _____

____/____/____/____yrs ____mos _____

Communication Skills
____/____/____/____yrs ____mos _____

____/____/____/____yrs ____mos _____

Social/Behavior Skills
____/____/____/____yrs ____mos _____

____/____/____/____yrs ____mos _____

EI-1 Page 5 (57060)

(.................... Denotes Periodic Update)   Name of Child _____   **CONFIDENTIAL**

CHILD'S PRESENT LEVELS OF DEVELOPMENT (CONT'D)

Area/Date of Evaluation   Current Abilities

Self-Help/Adaptive Skills
____/____/____/____yrs ____mos _____

____/____/____/____yrs ____mos _____

Figure 5.1. Child's Present Levels of Development section of the Nebraska Individualized Family Service Plan. (From Nebraska Department of Education—Department of Health and Human Resources. [n.d.]. *Nebraska individualized family service plan.* Retrieved October 28, 2009, from http://www.nde.state.ne.us/edn/ifspform/ifsptable97.doc; reprinted by permission.) (*Key:* yrs, years; mos, months.)

Figure 5.1.   *(continued)*

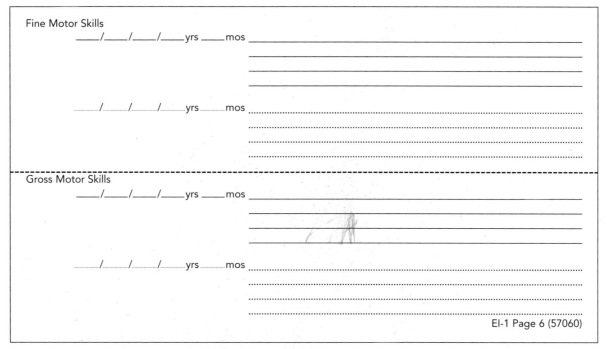

Fine Motor Skills

____/____/____/____yrs ____mos _____

____/____/____/____yrs ____mos _____

Gross Motor Skills

____/____/____/____yrs ____mos _____

____/____/____/____yrs ____mos _____

EI-1 Page 6 (57060)

require them. All children must, by law, be offered a multidisciplinary evaluation, and the results of that evaluation are usually entered in the boxes for the present level of development.

Service Coordinator Roles

In the evaluation process, service coordinators have three basic roles. First, they set up the assessment by explaining the process to families, securing their input into how the assessment should be done (this is often overlooked), and obtaining their signed consent to assess the child. In some systems, the service coordinator him- or herself might be one of the evaluators (by law, there must be two from different disciplines). In other systems, other employees of the program might do the evaluations. And in yet other systems, individuals are contracted to do evaluations. The service coordinator schedules these evaluations. For initial IFSPs, this step occurs immediately following intake. For IFSP annual reviews, they can be scheduled any time close to but preceding the IFSP.

The second role of the service coordinator is putting the information on the IFSP. This was discussed in the previous section (see "Current Levels of Functioning").

The third role of the service coordinator should be the most important: determining needs with the family. Unfortunately, this role is largely overlooked for two reasons. First, service coordinators assume the multidisciplinary evaluation discovered the child's and family's needs. Second, they focus on getting services more than on determining needs and outcomes. For reasons given earlier in this chapter, the traditional MDE is usually insufficient for determining functional needs. Therefore, the service coordinator must figure out how to determine the actual needs families with their children have. Service coordinators need to have enough training and skills to be able to assess needs. In some systems, they are unprepared for this task. In others, mercifully, they are

Items from the FINESSE

The following is the one assessment item in the FINESSE, other than those related specifically to the RBI. The FINESSE is organized with least recommended practices up to most recommended practices (see the Appendix at the end of the book for the original).

5. Identifying Family Needs

1.   Professionals do **not** ask parents about their concerns and priorities.

3.   Professionals **ask** parents about their concerns and priorities during IFSP meetings.

5.   Professionals **occasionally** (e.g., twice yearly) have conversations with families about families' aspirations.

7.   Professionals **regularly** (e.g., monthly) have conversations with families about families' aspirations.

very well prepared for this task. To assist all service coordinators, it is helpful to have a method that assesses real needs and leads to a list of functional outcomes.

The preceding FINESSE item stresses the importance of recurring discussions with families about their hopes and dreams as one dimension of assessment of their needs. As will be seen, another dimension is successful functioning in everyday routines. Many families report dealing with their situation one day at a time, but it might be important to keep alive their bigger aspirations, so they remember what they are striving for—and, more notably, so the professionals working with them can support those goals. Today, because of IDEA, it is unlikely that professionals would admit to not asking families about their concerns and priorities, but we sometimes see this in preschool programs. The law does not require assessment of concerns, priorities, and resources in Part B.

Assessment is therefore an important part of the process, but not the most important part. It needs to be kept in perspective in terms of the whole context of early intervention. Evaluation of eligibility for children coming in with delays should be conducted with alacrity and with a minimum of fuss: It is essentially answering the in-or-out question. Assessment for program planning should be conducted distinctly for that purpose; trying to use eligibility determination processes for program planning is usually a bad idea. Tests and procedures designed for one purpose are usually not much good for the other. Most important, however, in terms of this model is that the RBI exists as an ideal process for intervention planning.

Test on Assessment

1. Which of the following statements is the most accurate about sources of assessment infor-mation?

    a. Observation and parent report are mutually exclusive.

    b. Parent report is a report of multiple observations.

    c. Parent report produces an inflated view of the child's performance.

    d. Observation is the only valid source of information.

2. Assessment is

    a. Just as important as intervention

    b. More important than intervention

    c. Less important than intervention

    d. Only used for diagnosis

3. The emphasis of early intervention should be on

    a. Intervention providing ongoing information about the child's learning and progress

    b. Discovering the name of the child's condition or disability

    c. Documenting present levels of functioning

    d. Evaluating whether a child is eligible for early intervention

4. Families need

    a. Multiple professionals to see them frequently

    b. One competent professional backed up, as necessary, by other professionals

    c. Only one professional

    d. Occasional contact with a service coordinator only

5. Children with established conditions

    a. Need to be tested to determine their developmental age

    b. Need no assessment of any kind

    c. Need only a cognitive test

    d. Need to have a multidisciplinary assessment in five domains

6. Children referred to early intervention because of potential delay

    a. Need to be tested to determine their developmental age

    b. Need to have a multidisciplinary assessment in five domains

    c. Need to have parental permission to be tested

    d. All of the above

7. When a delay in a particular domain has been identified

    a. An outcome/goal must be identified to address the delay

    b. A professional from the discipline most closely related to the domain must be assigned to serve the child

    c. An outcome/goal addressing the delay might be chosen by the family

    d. A professional from a discipline different from the domain must be assigned to serve the child

8. The Individuals with Disabilities Education Improvement Act (IDEA) of 2004

    a. Requires the needs of the child and family to be assessed

    b. Requires the needs of only the child to be assessed

    c. Requires the needs of only the family to be assessed

    d. None of the above

CHAPTER 5

Appendix

Appendix 5.1. Infant/Toddler Assessment Checklist

APPENDIX 5.1 Infant/Toddler Assessment Checklist

Professional _____ Observer _____

Use this checklist as a self-check or for observation by a peer, supervisor, or trainer.

Mark as correct (+), incorrect (−), almost, (±), or not applicable or observed (NA).

Did the professional	Date	Date	Date	Date	Date
1. Include interview as part of the assessment?					
2. Include assessment or plan to include assessment as part of ongoing support?					
3. Check whether testing was required for children eligible under "medical" or "established" condition?					
4. Refrain from unnecessary formal testing?					
5. Test children for whom a documented delay was necessary?					
6. Provide a description of the current level of performance in cognitive, communication, physical, social or emotional, and adaptive performance?					
7. Indicate clearly where the child's needs are (versus glossing over them with positive language)?					
8. Refrain from using child development scores or impairment diagnoses to assign services?					
9. Set up the assessment by explaining the process to the family?					
10. Secure the family's input into how the assessment should be done?					
11. Obtain the family's signed consent to assess the child?					
12. Put assessment information (i.e., current levels of functioning) on the individualized family service plan (IFSP)?					
13. Determine the family's needs?					
14. Have or plan to have regular (e.g., monthly) conversations with families about their aspirations?					
Total Correct					
Total Possible (Items − NAs)					
Percentage Correct					

The Routines-Based Interview

The purposes of assessment were described in Chapter 5, and the case has been made for an innovative method to determine a family's functional needs. Current standardized methods do not determine these needs. First, some method is needed to identify functional goals or outcomes, otherwise known as target behaviors. Functionality of child outcomes can be thought of as addressing participation or engagement needs, addressing independence needs, and addressing social-relationship needs. Throughout this book, the importance of these three domains is stressed. Second, family priorities need to be reflected in the IFSP. Third, outcomes should be broad enough to cover a variety of ways of displaying the target behavior yet narrow enough to know what is really being addressed. Fourth, the strategies or action steps should aim directly at the function problem. Strategies such as using oral-motor exercises might be employed to address an outcome related to eating and swallowing, but a more direct approach is to teach a child to chew and swallow. The rule is *teach first*. Fifth, the process for developing IFSPs needs to foster investment by caregivers other than the family, such as child care providers, in the outcomes. The Routines-Based Interview (RBI) is a method that addresses these five needs.

Confluence of Two Models

The RBI is central to two models that have become quite widespread in the past 10 years (see Figure 6.1). It was first described in *Family-Centered Intervention Planning: A Routines-Based Approach* (McWilliam, 1992), which was written primarily for helping classroom-based staff to be family friendly. The premise was that planning with families in a way that addressed families' true concerns for their children, both at home and in the classroom, would help overcome the barrier of not seeing families for as long a time each week and on their home turf. Many of the principles from the co-ops where we tried out this and other practices have evolved into the individualizing inclusion model of classroom-based services (Wolery, 1997). That model hinges on the RBI as an assessment of the ecological congruence between a child's abilities and the classroom environment. This assessment leads directly to the development of the IFSP or individualized education program (IEP). Once a list of functional behaviors is identified, all services are provided in the classroom to ensure teamwork between classroom staff and specialists such as speech-language pathologists, itinerant special educators, occupational therapists, and physical therapists. The specialists' responsibility is to make their intervention suggestions fit into classroom routines, and teachers' responsibility is to embed those interventions into routines. The model hinges on functional outcomes or goals, which come from the RBI.

By now, it will be clear that the RBI is also central to the model of early intervention in natural environments. Again, the functionality of the child- and **family-level outcomes** in situations where the family is receiving home- and community-based services, including consultation to child care, makes the model of service delivery and the home and child care visits go more smoothly. As will be demonstrated throughout this book, the RBI is the linchpin for many of the other practices I recommend be employed in early intervention.

Research on the RBI

We recently completed the first study on the efficacy of using the RBI for IFSP development (McWilliam, Casey, & Sims, in 2009). Sixteen families were randomly assigned either to receive the RBI or to receive the business-as-usual IFSP development process. An RBI produced better outcomes than did the traditional approach to IFSP development. The families in the RBI group were more satisfied with the IFSP development process than were the families in the contrast group, and the contrast group had more variable responses. As expected, the number of outcomes was greater as a result of the RBI than as a result of the standard process. Finally, outcomes written as a result of the RBI were more functional than outcomes written as a result of the standard process.

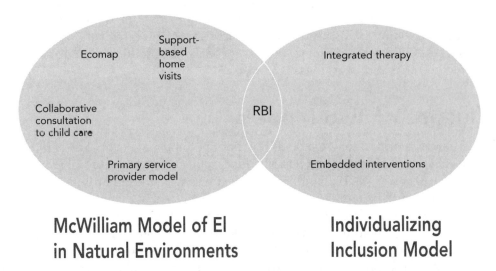

Figure 6.1. The confluence of two models. (*Key:* EI, early intervention.)

What Are Routines?

In this model, **routines** are not activities the professional impleme
stead, they are naturally occurring activities happening with some regu...
caregiving events and simply hanging-out times. As reluctant as I might be to admit ...
not everything happens in routines. Hence, at the beginning of the interview, we ask
about major concerns first. In fact, conversations about routines do lead to many concerns beyond what happens in routines. Therefore, a Routines-Based Interview is not as
circumscribed as might be thought. Another safeguard comes at the end of the interview,
when the family is asked if anything else should be discussed.

Routines-Based Interview

In the original manual (McWilliam, 1992), five stages of the RBI were described. They are
presented in the following sections.

Preparation of Families and Staff

If the child spends more than about 15 hours a week in child care, the child care provider
should be included in the interview. If this person can be present at the same meeting as
the family, the ideal situation is achieved. Often, however, caregivers and families are not
free at the same time, in which case child care providers should be interviewed before
the family. That allows the interviewer to convey what the child care provider has reported, and the family has all the information for making their decisions.

In preparing for the interview, the main point to convey to families and classroom
staff is to think about what routines (times of day, everyday events and activities) they
have and, for each one, consider the following points:

1. What the expectations are

2. What the child does

3. How well that routine is working for the family or, for classroom routines, for the
child

The Family Preparation Form (Harbin, 2005; McWilliam, 1992) is provided in Appendix 6.1 to help families get ready for the interview.

The other preparation points are logistical: where, when, who, and so forth. Families should be warned that the RBI lasts for 2 hours and that it is quite an intense conversation, so it works best if there are few distractions. This could include having
someone else watch the child, if that is convenient for the family. This request is not
made callously; the RBI is done only every 6 months and is quite different from a regular home visit. Some interviewers are self-conscious about making this request, but families appreciate being warned more than being sabotaged. Of course, some families are
not able to make arrangements, which is fine.

The Interview

The interview is a semistructured interview that must contain the following critical features for it to be considered a "Routines-Based Interview (RBI)":

1. *Main concerns.* At the beginning of the interview, the family should be asked what their main concerns are, so these can be listed and elaborated upon as the conversation moves to the day-to-day life of the family. Often families' main concerns are about walking and talking. Traditionally, that is where the outcome/goal selection ended, with a walking outcome and a talking outcome—no other child target behaviors and no family-level outcomes/goals. So, whereas the answer to the main-concerns question historically has led straight into outcome/goal development, in this approach it is merely the beginning, to determine what is on the family's mind.

2. *Go through the day.* As mentioned above, the structure of the interview is the family's progression through a typical day. To move from one time of day to another, the family is asked what happens next, rather than assuming what routines a family has and in what order they occur. During the discussion about each time of day, the interviewer attempts to find the answers to the following six questions:

   a. What everyone (both parents, siblings, other classroom children) is doing at that time

   b. What the child does

   c. The child's engagement

   d. The child's independence

   e. The child's **social relationships**

   f. The family's satisfaction with the routine

   The discussion is detailed enough for the interviewer to be able, figuratively, to paint a picture of the routine and to be able to determine what the family would like to happen differently at that time of the day. Depending on how much detail the parent gives in answer to an open-ended question such as, "What does breakfast time look like?", the interviewer might need to ask many detailed follow-up questions to be able to paint that picture. The goal is to find out what else the family would like to happen during that time of day—something that gets a star, as described next.

3. *Star concerns.* When the family mentions something a) not going well, b) they would like to be different, c) they think the child will be able to do next, or d) that raises a red flag for the interviewer, the interviewer makes a note of it and puts a star next to it. This helps with retrieval during the recap, described below. An example of something not going well might be the parent's saying, "She runs away every time I take her out of the car. That worries me to death." An example of something the parent would like to be different might be, "I'm not sure I have enough toys on the floor to entice him to crawl." An example of something the child might be able to do next might be, "She's doing really well when we go for a walk. It's a fun time. I guess the next skill will be for her to be able to step up and down at the curb with just one hand held." An example of a red flag might be, "Bedtime is no problem. I tell him he'll get a spanking if he doesn't lie there quietly." The parent might not think there is a problem, but the interviewer sees this as an opportunity to offer ideas for managing bedtime.

4. *Satisfaction ratings.* At the end of the discussion of every home routine, the interviewer asks for a judgment by the parent of how well that time of day is going—how

happy the parent is with that time of day—on a scale of 1–5. If discussing school routines with a classroom teacher or child care provider, the concluding question is how well that time of day is working for the child—a goodness-of-fit question—on a scale of 1–5.

5. *Worry and change questions.* Once the whole day is completed or time is running out (e.g., 1.5 hours have elapsed), the family is asked two questions:

   a. When you lie awake at night, worrying, what is it you worry about?

   b. If there's anything you could change in your life, what would it be?

6. *Recap.* This is the summary of the important information emanating from the interview. It will include *child-level needs,* such as for the child to sit independently at different times of the day; *child-related family needs,* such as the family's wanting to learn a way to figure out a child's preferences at meals and playtimes; or *family-level needs,* such as the parents making time for each other without the child. The interviewer quickly goes through all the starred items. Nothing is written down at this point; this is just a summing up.

7. *Family chooses outcomes.* After the recap, the family is asked to start listing the things they would like to work on, including the three types of needs mentioned above. If necessary, the interviewer shows the family the notes, particularly the starred items.

8. *Priority order.* Once the family has finished selecting outcomes and goals, as long as there is a minimum of six of them, they are asked to number them in order of importance.

The Protocol for the Routines-Based Interview (McWilliam, 2009a), available from Siskin Children's Institute (http://www.siskinresearch.org), is a tool to help guide the interviewer through the process and to document what is said. Figure 6.2 provides common questions, in order. This list can be photocopied and used as a reference during the interview.

Outcome Writing

Once outcomes have been identified, the service coordinator needs to put the **RBI outcomes** on to the IFSP. The service coordinator consults with other team members about the wording of outcomes, although the parent's words are often enough. Writing functional IFSPs and IEPs is discussed in Chapter 7.

Strategies and Review

At the same time that the service coordinator consults with other team members about the wording of outcomes or goals as necessary, he or she also consults with them about strategies. Only one or two strategies are needed for each outcome at this early stage. It is unreasonable to expect that teaching plans, for example, can be developed without knowing more about the child's functioning. Reviews occur at least every 6 months, but should occur as often as needed.

To review the structure of the RBI, families report on their routines first, and child care providers or teachers report on classroom routines second. Team members other

1. The purpose of today's meeting is to go through your day-to-day activities with your family to find out what you really want and need from early intervention. This is the best way of organizing our thoughts. Is that okay? Anything you don't want to say, don't say! You can end this at any time. Okay? At the end, we'll have a list of items that you would like the team to work on. Okay? If we don't finish today, we'll find another time, but we should try to finish today so we can get started on interventions as quickly as possible.

2. Let me begin by asking what your main concerns are.
    a. [Show interest and write these down but do not seek much elaboration.]
    b. [At any time in the interview, if the parent mentions something that is a problem, a desire, or otherwise a likely candidate for an outcome, mark it for easy retrieval. I draw a star next to it.]
    c. I will ask you more about these things as we go through the day.

3. How does your day begin?
    a. [Make sure the discussion is about how the parent's day begins, not the child's]
    b. What's everyone else doing?
    c. [If the child is awake, get a description of what the child is doing. If this early-morning routine involves interaction with the child, proceed to Question 5.]
    d. [Regardless of whether the child is awake] On a scale of 1–5, how much do you like this beginning of your day?

4. What happens next?
    a. [This is the transition question throughout the interview. It allows the parent to describe his or her day, rather than having the interviewer assume what the family does, including the order in which they do it.]
    b. Let's back up and deal just with your child's getting up.
    c. [Commonly, parents have to be slowed down, because they don't yet know the level of detail desired. These early-morning routines are the time to show the parent how much information to give in each routine.]

5. What is everyone else doing?
    a. [Try to determine normative conditions for this routine and what the family has to contend with.]

6. What is your child doing?
    a. [Allow a response to the open-ended question and then, if necessary, follow up with these next questions.]
    b. How is your child participating in this activity?
        • [Try to find out whether the child is highly engaged, just following the routine, or not participating.]
    c. How much does your child do for him- or herself?
        • [Ask developmentally appropriate questions about the child's independence. You have to know your child development!]
    d. How is your child interacting [use simpler terms if necessary] with others at this time?
        • [Ask developmentally appropriate follow-up questions about communication, self-regulation, cooperation, and social skills. Generally, ask about getting along with others during the routine.]

7. On a scale of 1–5, how well do you feel this time of day goes for you?
    a. [This is a variation on the satisfaction question.]

8. [Repeat Questions 5–7 for each routine.]
    a. [If necessary] Let's skip to dinner preparation time [or another possible later routine].
        • [With some interviews, it is necessary to move the conversation along.]

9. [After the last routine] Is there another typical event or activity we should discuss?
    a. [If time, ask about weekends.]

10. Now let me ask you a couple of general questions. When you lie awake at night, what do you worry about?
    a. [Write down the answer, marking it as a concern, if appropriate.]

11. If there's anything you'd like to change about your life, what is it?
    a. [Write down the answer, marking it as a concern, if appropriate.]

12. Now I'll go back through and remind you of the concerns you mentioned.
    a. [Review the list of marked items so the parent can see them. The parent is looking at the notes with the interviewer. This is symbolically important as well as pragmatic.]
    b. [Parents will sometimes elaborate, but this is not encouraged at this late stage.]

Figure 6.2.   Common Routines-Based Interview (RBI) questions, in order.

Figure 6.2. *(continued)*

Outcome Selection

13. [Setting the pages down] Now let me hear what you would like to be on the actual list of things to work on.
    a. [Write down what the parent chooses. If necessary, refer to the marked items.]
    b. [If the parent mentions a skill with no reference to the context or function (e.g., "I just want him to be able to talk"), ask during which times of the day it would be helpful for the child to be able to have that skill.]
    c. [If the parent mentions a service with no reference to the function (e.g., "I just want him to have physical therapy"), ask what skill that would be helpful for, and then, if necessary, during which times of the day the skill would be helpful.]
14. [Once 6–12 priorities have been listed and no more seem to be forthcoming] Now let's put this list into order of importance. Which one is the most important one to you?
    a. [Put a 1 next to that priority.] Which is next? [Continue for the whole list.]
15. This is a great list of things to work on. I'll consult with other team members and the next time we meet we'll write down their ideas and your ideas for the strategies to begin addressing these. At that time, we'll decide what services are needed to get these priorities or "outcomes" addressed.

than the interviewer who might be present can ask questions and provide information during discussions of routines, but they do not have a separate decontextualized reporting time. All professionals withhold giving advice, because as soon as they do so it changes the dynamics. The family loses confidence and seeks reassurance about what they do during their routines. If the family does specifically ask for suggestions, the interviewer says, "That's a very good question. Let me write it down, and another team member or I will be sure to answer that for you later."

Interview Strategies

Conducting a good interview requires knowing child development, knowing family functioning, and having good people skills. This leads to appropriate questions within the structure presented above. The following interview behaviors are critical for the success of an RBI.

* Be natural and as informal as is appropriate.
* Put the parent at ease with this naturalness and informality.
* Look the parent in the eye when he or she is talking.
* Avoid the use of jargon; if the parent uses jargon, ask what he or she means.
* Nod and in other ways affirm what the parent is saying.
* From time to time, express admiration for what the parent does with his or her family.
* Express understanding about how the parent might feel (e.g., "I bet you feel really good about that," or "I bet that's really frustrating"); more safely, ask the parent how he or she feels.
* Place papers flat so the parent can see what is being written—distance notwithstanding.
* Find a point of personal contact and very briefly use "self-disclosure" (any behavior or verbalization that reveals personal information to the family about the professional) (Psychopathology Committee of the Group for the Advancement of

Psychiatry, 2001) or "therapeutic use of self" (applying the accumulation of knowledge and techniques from professional education and training) (Edwards & Bess, 1998).

- If the parent cries, offer to stop the conversation.

- If the parent becomes emotional, either move on to another topic or ask if something else should be talked about.

- As much as possible, refrain from engaging in judgmental talk about the other parent, if only interviewing one parent.

- Ask about specific routines to move the interview along if it is taking a long time; the goal is to end in 90 minutes.

- Ask detailed questions at the beginning of the interview to show the parent the level of detail required.

- Keep the structure of the six questions *per routine*:

  1. What's everyone doing?

  2. What's this child doing?

  3. What's this child's engagement like?

  4. What's this child's independence like?

  5. What are this child's social relationships like?

  6. How satisfactory is this time of day (home) or how good a fit are this routine and the child (classroom)?

Missed Questions

No two interviewers will conduct an interview exactly the same way, despite the structure provided here, which is why this is called a semistructured interview. It is the follow-up questions that vary from one person to another. Inevitably, therefore, an observer might think that some questions were not asked. Correct! There is no way that all possible questions could be asked, but that is perfectly acceptable. In a way, this demonstrates the power of the process. Even with different interviewers who would ask different questions, 1) a list of functional outcomes is produced, 2) a huge amount of relevant information is discussed, and 3) a positive relationship is formed in a short time.

The Most Common Concern Among Professionals

Many professionals are concerned that families will not choose relevant things to work on or that they will have their priorities wrong. For example, when a family says that they want their child to stack eight blocks in 45 seconds, the interviewer may internally question why this is so important. First, this concern sometimes is related to a mismatch between what was found on the evaluation for eligibility and the outcomes or goals resulting from the RBI. Such a mismatch would perhaps reveal the different purposes of these assessments. The former is for determining status relative to normalcy. The latter is for determining needs for functioning in routines. Assessments conducted for different purposes can be expected to produce different ideas about what to work on. The model described here clearly puts more weight on routines-based needs than on test-based deficits.

Second, confusion between eligibility for services and necessity of services is rampant in our field. Just because a child qualifies for speech-language pathology services, for example, does not mean that he or she needs them. In fact, there is no criterion for determining "need" for services in early intervention. It is all a matter of clinical judgment. Professionals should refrain as much as possible from using the term *needing services*. The alternative is to say that services would be helpful to meet needs, goals, or outcomes. Understandably, this is not a popular notion because of the fear that payers for services will adopt the notion to say that early intervention services are unneeded and therefore should not be paid for. But the specific point being made here is that *qualification* for a service should not be translated as *necessity* for a service.

Third, just because a family does not identify a skill as a priority and an outcome, or goal, does not mean that no one will address it. Many learning opportunities are afforded to children beyond what is on their IFSPs or IEPs. For example, for a child who was determined to have delayed communication, the family may choose various eating, crawling, and toy-play outcomes and goals—but nothing about communication. Does this mean the team cannot work on language? No. As professionals work with the family about making the most of the natural learning opportunities that happen in every routine, to address their priorities, they encourage the family to talk to the child about what they are doing and to elicit communication related to eating, crawling, and toy play. So, professionals can relax when families do not select what they would have selected.

Fourth, as families obtain more information, they might add skills that, at the time of the RBI, were not important. Early interventionists who worry about "critical periods" for intervening early can relax (there is a theme here), to some extent, because the idea of critical periods has largely been replaced by the more forgiving idea of "windows of opportunity" (Bailey, 2002): There are no times after which experiences are unhelpful, nothing is predetermined by a certain age, and one cannot measure a percentage of a given domain (e.g., a child's intelligence, a child's personality) as being determined by a certain age.

Fifth, professionals do have the ethical obligation to provide families with any information they have, but when a child is first entering services they have not had a chance to convey that information. As time passes, families might learn about the importance of a skill they did not originally choose. Professionals need to be very careful about what they try to concern parents with, which leads to the sixth point: It is the parents' child, not the professional's child. Altogether, therefore, the list families produce at the end of the RBI will be a valid reflection of their functional needs.

Sample Outcome Lists

The following lists come from real interviews with families. Identifying details have been changed, but these examples show the apparent functionality of the outcomes, the level of specificity, and the extent of family outcomes. The purpose for each outcome and how it would appear on an IFSP or IEP, including criteria for measurability, are discussed in Chapter 7.

Family Outcomes for Mary (Elliott's Mother)

1. Elliott will move on stuff outside and inside (e.g., going up stairs).

2. Elliott will play and walk on different textures outside.

3. Family will find out why Elliott is eating no more than he is.

4. Elliott will eat a variety of foods.

5. Elliott will pick up foods with his fingers.

6. Mary will keep Elliott engaged during church, so it is easier for her to attend church [note that the purpose is provided already in this outcome].

7. Elliott will make choices at meals, dressing, and hanging-out times.

Priorities for Kris (Joshua's Mother)

1. Joshua will crawl, stand, and walk (moving independently).

2. Joshua will use sign language, including *yes, no, Mommy,* and *Daddy.*

3. Kris will connect with therapists.

4. Joshua will gain weight.

5. Joshua will play with toys in a coordinated way in the evening.

6. Joshua will stay in his bed through the night.

Priorities for Sandy (Bryce's Mother)

1. Bryce will communicate at mealtimes, in the morning, and in the evening, as well as communicate his needs and wants at any time.

2. When Bryce walks fast, inside, and barefoot, he will do so without falling.

3. Bryce will put on his shirt independently and pull up his pants.

4. Bryce will play and listen to stories without sucking his thumb.

5. Bryce will help with bathing.

6. Sandy will teach Calista (Bryce's sister) to communicate without screaming.

7. Sandy and Rusty (Bryce's father) will find acceptable child care for the children so they can spend time together without the children.

Priorities for Tracy (Cavanaugh's Mother)

1. Cavanaugh will keep his tongue in his mouth, including during meals, to be socially appropriate.

2. Cavanaugh will hold toys, pick up food, and hold a spoon to be engaged during play and meals.

3. Cavanaugh will sit in his highchair and his bath chair and will sit independently in his crib.

4. Cavanaugh will nurse and eat from a spoon with lip closure to get nutritional benefit and be less messy.

5. Cavanaugh will crawl to get toys to play independently.

6. Cavanaugh will babble and vocalize when playing with family members.

7. The family will finish renovations on their house to have more room for developmental equipment.

8. Cavanaugh will drink juice from a bottle from Jeff (his father) to make this time more pleasant.

Priorities for Stacey (Marcus's Mother)

1. Family will sleep throughout the night in their own beds.

2. Marcus will walk independently (outside the home, playing in the yard or on the deck, in the house).

3. Marcus will drink without using a bottle.

4. Marcus will play by himself.

5. Marcus will talk more and more clearly.

6. Marcus will feed himself with a spoon.

Priorities for Nicole (Noma's Mother)

1. Noma will pull up to stand—independent play.

2. Noma will move independently (e.g., will crawl).

3. Noma will play independently with complex toys.

4. Noma will feed herself independently with utensils.

5. Noma will say single words for what she needs.

6. Noma will use a washcloth.

7. Nicole will get more out of church experiences.

Priorities for Terry (Johnny's Mother)

1. Johnny will say words.

2. Johnny will walk in a stable way.

3. Terry will have a plan for organizing the times in the morning and after school when all the kids are at home.

4. Terry will feel emotionally supported about Johnny's development.

5. Johnny will pick up food and toys with fingers.

6. Terry will have information about schools for Johnny and Johnesia (Johnny's sister).

7. Terry will continue her studies toward a degree.

Implementation

When should the RBI be done in the intervention planning process? Options include intake, evaluation, between the evaluation and the IFSP meeting, during the IFSP meeting, or after the IFSP meeting. There are advantages and disadvantages to each, and where to fit in the RBI is a local decision; that is, it is best for programs and communities to decide this for themselves. Some discussion of the pros and cons of each option is provided next and can help this decision making.

Intake

The RBI is an effective tool for getting to know the family, which is often a goal of an intake visit. But so much official business needs to be done at intake, such as explaining rights to families, describing early intervention, and obtaining consents for evaluation, that the meeting would be awfully long. This could be especially problematic for programs with high false-positive referrals (i.e., many children—e.g., more than 10%—tested for delay being found ineligible for services). The RBI is too time-consuming to be used on an inordinate number of ineligible families. In most cases, therefore, the intake visit is not going to be an ideal option for implementation of the RBI.

Evaluation

If the evaluation for eligibility, which is only needed for children referred for delay, can be done quickly enough, it might be possible to conduct an RBI too. But it generally will make this visit too long.

Increasingly, communities are scoring instruments from the information provided during the RBI. Thus, much of the testing is obviated by the interview. A few items might need to be administered after the interview, but this is an efficient way to kill two birds with one stone. Better still, it allows the emphasis of the assessment period to be the needs-based, functional interview, rather than the decontextualized testing. This adaptation is only efficient for those children who are highly likely to be eligible. Otherwise, the interview is expensive. If a program finds that more than 10% of the children they test for eligibility are ineligible, they should either do the evaluation first or institute screening at intake. For those programs who find most children referred for delay to be eligible, scoring instruments during the RBI is increasingly popular.

Between Evaluation and IFSP

For programs that want to keep their evaluation intact, one option is to schedule another meeting between the evaluation and the IFSP meeting. Because of the 45-day limit between referral and the IFSP meeting, this can be challenging. But it is better to separate formal testing in this way than to do testing and the interview on the same day. Doing them on the same day means starting with the testing, which conveys at the beginning that professionals with their tools have valuable information about the child. It can affect the family's confidence in the value of their descriptions of the child.

A Friendly Warning

Some early interventionists have used information about routines to try to establish the times of day when outcomes that were produced from tests would be applicable. That is, they test the child, suggest outcomes, and then look for routines in which to teach the skills. This is the wrong way around. The outcomes should come from needs during the routines, not from tests. Routines are not an afterthought or just an application context. They are at the front end of identifying needs.

IFSP Meeting

Some programs do the RBI as part of the IFSP meeting, which creates the same challenge as other options that involve doing more than one thing in the meeting: It can make for an excessively long meeting. The advantage of combining these two functions is that the RBI produces the outcomes, so one might as well proceed with the IFSP. Many professionals find it helpful, however, to do some work between the outcome selection and having the IFSP meeting. They can reword the outcomes to make them more measurable and perhaps explore a strategy or two for each outcome. Of course, any of this pre-IFSP work is subject to review by the family. Professionals should not worry about doing some of this work apart from the family, because there is no question that the outcomes belong to the family. Furthermore, the RBI provides the context and functional need, so the service coordinator is likely to propose rewording and strategies consistent with the family's wishes. It is easier to do this without the pressure of having to do it live at the IFSP meeting.

After the IFSP

Occasionally, programs have opted to do the RBI after the IFSP, which is fraught with problems. The most obvious problem is that the outcomes come out of the RBI, so the team has to revise the outcomes as soon as the RBI is done. Sometimes they work with a shadow IFSP, with the outcomes developed at the IFSP meeting (which they ignore, essentially) and the outcomes developed at the RBI.

Why would early interventionists do this? If they work in a system where they have no control over the IFSP process and those who do refuse to use the RBI, they have little option. Another reason might be that the ongoing service provider is not decided upon until the IFSP meeting, and other people are involved in the evaluation, assessment, and IFSP development—and the service provider wants to hear all the information that is generated at the RBI. So, in that case, it is an issue of wanting to be the person who does the interview.

When to conduct the RBI is a local decision: The two most successful methods, by and large, are 1) fitting in an extra meeting for the RBI, between the evaluation and the IFSP meeting, and 2) combining the evaluation and the RBI, scoring the instrument during the RBI.

Numerous people can be at the RBI. The family decides who they want from the family. The child does not have to be there. When scheduling the RBI, it is suggested that professionals ask families to provide as distraction-free a setting as possible, with minimal interruptions. One would never ask this of families during regular home visits, but the RBI takes place once or twice a year. It is acceptable to ask families to reduce the likelihood of disruptions. Families should also be reassured that if they can't find someone to watch the child or handle other interruptions, it is fine.

In terms of professionals, ideally two would be present, although one is manageable. If the RBI is being used as part of the multidisciplinary evaluation (i.e., the information is going to appear in the present level of functioning section of the IFSP), two or more professionals representing different disciplines may need to be there anyway. The second person can help ask questions (although one person should take the lead), take notes, handle interruptions, and perhaps score a developmental test.

To review implementation issues for children entering the program for different reasons, first consider those with established conditions (sometimes known as "medical diagnoses"). They, like all children entering Part C, need to be offered an MDE. This is a quirk of the law because usually all that is needed for eligibility is a medical report stating the child's diagnosis related to developmental disabilities. Although children with established conditions need an MDE (an *assessment* of present level of functioning in five domains by people representing two different disciplines), they do not need to be *tested*. Scores are unnecessary for these children, so the RBI is a relevant way to get descriptions of present level of functioning.

Items from the FINESSE

The following anchors are from the item on the FINESSE related to Assessment for Intervention Planning. It addresses the problem of confusing the purposes of different assessments. Perhaps for the sake of expedience, because programs have to test many children with standardized instruments, they use those results to determine what the child needs to work on. Curriculum-based instruments tend to have somewhat more functional items than norm-referenced, diagnostic instruments, but they still do not assess what the child necessarily needs to function successfully in everyday routines. The most functional assessment for intervention planning is considered to be an RBI focusing on engagement, independence, and social relationships.

1. Only **standardized instruments** that focus on traditional developmental domains are used for intervention planning.

3. **Curriculum-based instruments** that focus on traditional developmental domains are used for intervention planning.

5. Curriculum-based instruments and Routines-Based Interviews that focus on **both** traditional developmental domains and family functioning, child engagement, social relationships, and independence are used for intervention planning.

7. **Routines-Based Interviews** that focus on family functioning, child engagement, social relationships, and independence are used for intervention planning.

Another FINESSE item related to the RBI is the one on Intervention Planning Meetings. Although the RBI could be done at a separate meeting from the IFSP meeting, this item is about the discussion related to what goes on the IFSP. Many meetings involve much talk by professionals, who discuss test results and services that match the child's diagnosis. In some meetings, families have an active role in the discussion. In the best meetings, families discuss routines and professionals seek information, priorities, and preferences.

1. During IFSP/IEP meetings, professionals **primarily** discuss test scores and services offered by the program; parents listen.

3. During IFSP/IEP meetings, professionals **occasionally** discuss test scores. The meeting focuses on child deficits and services; parents mostly listen.

(continued)

(continued)

> 5. During IFSP/IEP meetings, professionals **discuss child/family needs and functional intervention strategies;** parents are actively involved in discussion (not routines-based).
>
> 7. During IFSP/IEP meetings, parents discuss routines, priorities, and concerns; professionals **ask questions and listen.**
>
> A third item on the FINESSE related to the RBI is about Outcome/Goal Selection. Unfortunately, some outcomes are selected directly from tests. Others come from professional recommendations; the implication on the FINESSE is that those recommendations are usually not based on families' concerns, which is another response choice on this item. The most recommended practice is selecting outcomes from a Routines-Based Interview, because that would mean the outcomes were functional, necessary, and related to the family's quality of life.
>
> 1. Outcomes/goals are selected from **tests, curricula, and checklists.**
>
> 3. Outcomes/goals are selected from **professional recommendations.**
>
> 5. Outcomes/goals are selected from **family concerns** (not a Routines-Based Interview).
>
> 7. Outcomes/goals are selected from **Routines-Based Interview.**
>
> A fourth FINESSE item related to the RBI is the inclusion of Family Outcomes/Goals. In traditional practices, only child outcomes are on the plans. In at least one state, child and family outcomes are separated on the IFSP, with child outcomes on outcomes pages but family outcomes embedded within the concerns, priorities, and resources section. This suggests that the child outcomes are more important than the family outcomes, because all the outcome-specific requirements, such as criteria for attainment, are available only for child outcomes. Family outcomes related to the child's development (e.g., the mother will learn strategies to teach her child to eat independently) do not really attend to family members' needs. One could argue that the example given could have been stated as a child outcome: Eric will eat independently—and a strategy would be for the mother to learn how to teach him.
>
> Family involvement outcomes betray a notion that the role of families is to support the professionals. Compare that with the ultimate practice with family outcomes: Those outcomes unrelated to the child are included, along with child outcomes. For example, an outcome about the father getting a new job, if that would help the child's development in some indirect way, would be an appropriate family outcome.
>
> 1. Only **child** outcomes/goals are included in the IFSP/IEP.
>
> 3. Only **child-related family** outcomes/goals are included in the IFSP/IEP (along with child goals).
>
> 5. Family **involvement** outcomes/goals and child-related family goals are included in the IFSP/IEP (along with child goals).
>
> 7. Family goals **unrelated** to the child are included in the IFSP/IEP (along with child goals).

The RBI Implementation Checklist in Appendix 6.2 provides all the essential steps for doing an RBI. It also helps to separate practices that truly are consistent with the RBI from those that are "RBI-like."

Test on the RBI

1. In early intervention, RBI stands for

    a. Runs batted in

    b. Routines-based intervention

    c. Robust basting implement

    d. Routines-Based Interview

2. The RBI addresses children's functioning in

    a. Home routines

    b. Classroom (e.g., child care) routines

    c. Community (e.g., stores, playground, library) routines

    d. All of the above

3. Research on the RBI shows that

    a. Families are more satisfied with the IFSP process when an RBI is used than when it is not

    b. It leads to better child outcomes than when it is not used

    c. The IFSP process is quicker with the RBI than without it

    d. It leads to the same number of outcomes/goals as non-RBI IFSPs

4. In the context of RBI, *routines* are

    a. Procedures the early interventionist suggests the family carry out

    b. What the family naturally does in a typical day

    c. Those times of the day that are always done the same way

    d. A series of tricks on apparatus in a gym

5. To prepare families for the RBI, professionals can

    a. Bring child evaluation results

    b. Give them the Family Preparation Form

    c. Rehearse going through the day with them

    d. Give them the IFSP form

6. The RBI

    a. Is an unstructured conversation

    b. Is a questionnaire administered orally

    c. Is a semistructured interview

    d. Is a structured interview

7. To proceed through the day, using the RBI, the interviewer should

    a. Ask what happens next

    b. Have a list of routines to ask families about

    c. Let the family talk about their day in any order they want

    d. Allot 10 minutes per routine

8. During discussion of each routine, the interviewer should find out about the child's

   a. Independence

   b. Social relationships

   c. Engagement

   d. All of the above

9. Information from the interview should be captured

   a. On the daily routines form

   b. In narrative notes, with concerns starred

   c. On the IFSP, in the family assessment section

   d. On a tape recorder

10. The family's satisfaction with home routines

    a. Is not recorded; the interviewer must listen carefully

    b. Is rated by the family on a 1–10 scale

    c. Is rated by the family on a 1–5 scale

    d. Is rated by the interviewer, based on the interviewer's best guess, on a 1–5 scale

11. The worry and change questions

    a. Are too intrusive to ask most families

    b. Should not be asked by professionals who dislike dealing with families' emotions

    c. Can produce very important information related to families' desires

    d. Are an indulgence by a nosy interviewer

12. The recap

    a. Is a listing of concerns that emerged during the interview

    b. Is a reminder of what was discussed during the interview

    c. Is a review of outcomes/goals chosen during the interview

    d. Is the replacement of a top on a bottle

13. With the RBI, outcomes and goals

    a. Are chosen by the team

    b. Are chosen by the child

    c. Are selected from a bank of state-approved outcomes and goals

    d. Are chosen by the family

14. Which of the following is not true about conducting interviews?

    a. Be natural and as informal as is appropriate

    b. Use professional language to establish credibility

    c. Look the parent in the eye when he or she is talking

    d. Nod and in other ways affirm what the parent is saying

15. If the interviewer fails to ask about something

    a. The RBI needs to be redone

    b. Fewer than six outcomes are allowed

    c. It is to be expected and should not affect the outcome of the interview

    d. He or she should always go back to try to ask about it

16. If the parent does not select an outcome/goal related to a documented deficit

    a. The deficit can still be addressed while addressing other family priorities

    b. The team should propose an outcome/goal addressing that deficit

    c. The family should be referred to social services

    d. The parent should be convinced to add such an outcome/goal

17. The RBI is best implemented

    a. At intake, before evaluation

    b. After eligibility has been determined but before the completion of the IFSP

    c. Immediately after the IFSP has been developed

    d. One month into services, so rapport can be established with the family

CHAPTER 6

Appendixes

Appendix 6.1. Family Preparation Form

Appendix 6.2. RBI Implementation Checklist

APPENDIX 6.1 Family Preparation Form

Dear family:

You will soon be meeting with the rest of the team to discuss ways we can help you and your child. During the meeting, you and the other members of the team will

1. Discuss any overall questions or concerns you have.

2. Talk about what your child's day is like.

3. Choose outcomes to work on.

4. Plan who will work on these outcomes and when.

This form will help you prepare for the meeting. You may want to look over it to see the types of information that will be useful. If you think it would help to have this information written down, complete as much of the form as you have time for. If your child is in a center-based program, the center staff is preparing similar information.

The goal of the meeting is to talk about each *routine*—each different part of your child's day. The staff team members will ask questions and make suggestions as we discuss these routines. The meeting will be very flexible—its purpose is to talk about the things that are most important to *you*.

Your ideas are very important. If you have any suggestions or questions about the meeting, please share them with the rest of the team.

Please bring this form with you to the planning meeting.

Family Concerns and Routines

I.   What are your *main concerns*? Think about questions, difficulties, or needs for both your *child* and your *family* as a whole.

_____

_____

_____

_____

_____

_____

II. What are the main routines of your family's weekday?

❏ dressing   ❏ nap

❏ breakfast   ❏ watching TV

❏ leaving the house   ❏ preparing meals

❏ household chores   ❏ evening meal

❏ yard work   ❏ bath

❏ lunch   ❏ bedtime routine

❏ hanging out

❏ other routines _____

_____

_____

(continued)

APPENDIX 6.1 Family Preparation Form *(continued)*

What other events occur fairly regularly or during the weekend?

- ❑ grocery shopping
- ❑ going to the mall
- ❑ visiting relatives or friends
- ❑ going to the park
- ❑ religious services
- ❑ other routines _____

- ❑ visitors to the house
- ❑ doctor's visits
- ❑ using public transportation
- ❑ going to the library

_____
_____

Family Routines Information

For each routine you've checked, think about the following questions:

- What do you do during this routine?
- What does your child do during this routine?
- How does your child affect this routine?
- How satisfied are you with this routine?

Don't write answers to these questions if you don't want to. You might just use them to guide your thoughts about each routine. Use the space below each routine for any notes that will help you discuss the routine during the team meeting.

When you discuss center or school routines with the staff, you might ask:

- *What does my child usually do during the routine?*
- *How well does my child fit into the routine?*
- *What specific strengths or needs does my child have in this routine?*

Routine:
_____
_____
_____

Routine:
_____
_____
_____

Routine:
_____
_____
_____

(continued)

APPENDIX 6.1 Family Preparation Form (continued)

Routine:

_____

_____

_____

_____

Routine:

_____

_____

_____

_____

Routine:

_____

_____

_____

_____

Routine:

_____

_____

_____

_____

Routine:

_____

_____

_____

_____

(continued)

APPENDIX 6.1 **Family Preparation Form** (continued)

Staff Preparation Form

Child: _____

Completed by: _____ Date: _____

I. What are the main daily routines where you see the child?

  ❑ arrival   ❑ snack
  ❑ free play   ❑ lunch
  ❑ circle   ❑ music
  ❑ sand/water play   ❑ small toys
  ❑ outside   ❑ large movement
  ❑ nap   ❑ interest centers
  ❑ art   ❑ pretend play
  ❑ breakfast   ❑ story/reading
  ❑ other _____

  _____

  _____

II. What other routines occur fairly regularly?

  ❑ field trips   ❑ helping in the office
  ❑ bookmobile visits   ❑ helping in the cafeteria
  ❑ walks   ❑ visitors to the classroom
  ❑ other _____

  _____

  _____

  If you will not be attending this child's Family Centered Intervention Planning meeting, please return these forms to

  _____ (service coordinator)

  by _____ (date)

APPENDIX 6.2 RBI Implementation Checklist

Interviewer _____ Date _____

Observer _____ Score _____

	+	+/–	–	Comments
1. Did the interviewer prepare the family, at least the day before the interview, by telling them (a) that they will be asked to describe their daily routines, (b) they can choose a location, and (c) they can choose who participates (including whether it's one or both parents)?				
2. Did the interviewer greet the family, then review the purpose for the meeting (e.g., to get to know the family and to determine how best to provide support to their child and family)?				
3. Did the interviewer ask the parents if they have any major questions or concerns before starting the interview?				
4. Did the interview have a good flow (conversational, not a lot of time spent writing)?				
5. Did the interviewer maintain focus without attending too much to distractions?				
6. Did the interviewer ask follow-up questions to gain an understanding of functioning?				
7. Did the interviewer address all of the family's routines, especially by following the parent's lead?				
8. Were there follow-up questions related to engagement?				
9. Were there follow-up questions related to independence?				
10. Were there follow-up questions related to social relationships?				
11. Were follow-up questions developmentally appropriate?				
12. Were open-ended questions used initially to gain an understanding of the routine and functioning (followed by closed-ended questions if necessary)?				
13. Did the interviewer find out what people in the family other than the child are doing in each routine?				
14. Did the interviewer ask for a rating of each routine?				
15. Did the interviewer find out how satisfied the family is with each routine through both description and rating?				
16. To transition between routines, was the question "What happens next?" or something similar used?				

(continued)

From McWilliam, R.A. (Ed.). (2010b). *Working with families of young children with special needs* (pp. 44–47). New York: Guilford Press; reprinted by permission.

In *Routines-Based Early Intervention: Supporting Young Children and Their Families* by R.A. McWilliam (2010, Paul H. Brookes Publishing Co., Inc.)

APPENDIX 6.2 RBI Implementation Checklist (continued)

	+	+/–	–	Comments
17. Did the interviewer use good affect (e.g., facial expressions, tone of voice, responsiveness)?				
18. Did the interviewer use affirming behaviors (e.g., nodding, positive comments or gestures)?				
19. Did the interviewer attempt to get the parent's perspective on behaviors (why he/she thinks the child does what he/she does)?				
20. Did the interviewer use active listening techniques (e.g., rephrasing, clarifying, summarizing)?				
21. If there were no problems in the routine, did the interviewer ask what the parent would like to see next?				
22. Did the interviewer avoid giving advice?				
23. Did the interviewer avoid unnecessary questions, such as the specific time something occurs?				
24. Did the interviewer act in a nonjudgmental way?				
25. Did the interviewer use "time of day" instead of "routine"?				
26. Did the interviewer return easily to the interview after an interruption?				
27. Did the interviewer allow the family to state their own opinions, concerns, etc. (not leading the family towards what the interviewer thinks is important)?				
28. Did the interviewer get information on the parent's down time (any time for him/herself)?				
29. Did the interviewer put a star next to the notes where a family has indicated a desire for change in routine or has said something they would like for their child or family to be able to do?				
30. After the interviewer has summarized concerns, was the family asked if anything should be added?				
31. After summarizing concerns (starred items) did the interviewer take out a clean sheet of paper and ask the family what they wanted to work on? (new list)				
32. Did the interviewer ask the family to put the outcomes into a priority order for importance?				
33. Did the interviewer discuss when the services will be decided upon—this meeting or a subsequent one?				

(continued)

APPENDIX 6.2 RBI Implementation Checklist *(continued)*

	+	+/–	–	Comments
34. Did the interviewer thank everyone for their time?				
35. Did the interviewer ask the family, "When you lie awake at night worrying, what is it you worry about?"				
36. Did the interviewer ask the family, "If you could change anything about your life, what would it be?"				

Goal: 85% or better (total score of 87 or better on numbered items)
Scoring: +, 3 points; +/–, 2 points; –, 0 points.

CHAPTER 7

Writing Functional IFSPs and IEPs

Studies of IFSPs have shown the quality to be poor (Jung & Baird, 2003; McWilliam, Ferguson, et al., 1998), and many practitioners and administrators ask for help in writing **functional outcomes/goals**. The biggest problem is the outcomes: They are pathetically few (usually fewer than three), general, and unmeasurable. Functional IFSPs and IEPs can be the product of many methods of assessment and intervention planning, but they naturally follow, in this model, from the RBI. In this chapter, I discuss methods for writing goals, define functional goals, provide examples of functional goals, discuss **IFSP criteria** for attainment of goals, and present a tool for measuring the quality of goals. I use the term *goal* to refer both to IFSP outcomes (to use Part C language) and IEP goals, because *outcomes* has a double entendre. In addition to the IFSP meaning (goals), increasingly *outcome* is used to refer to programwide (sometimes even statewide or nationwide) accountability measures, such as the percentage of children in Part C who improve in meeting their own needs.

Two broad approaches to writing children's goals are the developmental and the functional approach. The former approach is based on a model of typical development, and goals are selected for those skills in a developmental hierarchy, checklist, or curriculum that the child has not mastered. It therefore consists of identifying and correcting deficits. Typically, the context of children's behavior is irrelevant. The latter approach (functional), in contrast, is based on promoting child and family success in current environments. It addresses skills needed in the home, the community, and the classroom.

In the routines-based model, outcomes/goals are derived from functional routines-based needs. They are then written to be measurable, with logical criteria, which means that they might involve generalization across routines, the duration of the desired behavior (i.e., engagement), the frequency the behavior should be displayed in 1 week, and the number of weeks in which it should be seen at that rate. There are other criteria one can use, but these are common. The most important functionality criterion is that the behaviors be *necessary,* meaning that without it the child would not be able to function in everyday routines.

Functional Outcomes/Goals

It is helpful to consider children's behavior in the three functional domains of engagement, independence, and social relationships (McWilliam, 2006a). These domains stand in contrast to traditional testing domains such as cognitive, communication, motor, adaptive, and social. Traditional domains have not even been found to be particularly useful in categorizing children's performance (Berkeley & Ludlow, 1992). The three alternative domains will help to keep outcomes/goals functional.

Some criteria for functional goals are that the goals 1) reflect the priorities of the family, 2) are useful and meaningful, 3) reflect real-life situations, 4) are free of jargon, and 5) are measurable. I discuss details of some of these criteria next. In addition to these five criteria, the following tips are worth considering:

- *Write goals that can be addressed by multiple people at multiple times of the day, during normal routines and activities.* For example, state "Auguste will participate in outside play by stepping up and down on to and off different surfaces" rather than "Auguste will step up and down on the stair equipment in the therapy room."

- *Ask yourself, "Why is the child working on this goal?"* The answer should be immediately apparent. In the above example, the first goal is clear: Auguste is working on this goal so he can participate in outside play. That is the beauty of participation-based goals, to be described later.

- *Be clear!* For example, the goal of "Folami will maintain a four-point position for 30 seconds five times a day" violates these criteria. It is not clear because most parents would not know what a four-point position is. The goal does not indicate why Folami should be working on this goal. It probably could be addressed by multiple people in normal routines, if they knew what it was.

One way to be clear is to avoid jargon. Terms such as *ambulate, mean length of utterance, pincer grasp, oral-motor skills, verbal exchanges,* and *minimal physical assistance* should be avoided in outcome/goal statements. Instead, terms such as *walk; three-word phrases; thumb and finger; bite, chew, or swallow; back and forth;* and *with a little help* are simple and understandable.

Verbs need to reflect observability and measurability and need to avoid change over time. They need to identify the end point. These are *goals*. Therefore, words such as *improve* and *increase* are not suitable. Words related to internal processes that are not observable include *understand*. Occasionally, we see goals that really indicate participation in a service, which are inappropriate. Sometimes, they even state that the goal is for the child to *tolerate* something he or she does not want to do, such as participate in a therapeutic activity. There are two problems with this type of goal. First, ethically, they are dubious, because children should be able to "deny consent with their feet," which means that by refusing they are denying consent. Second, the goal should be the skill for which the therapeutic activity is theoretically preparing the child. Good verbs are those that describe what the family wants the child to do. For example, the goal of "Muir will tolerate prone over a therapy ball" should be restated as something such as "Muir will participate in playtimes, mealtimes, and car rides by holding his head up." The good verbs in the latter example are *participate* and *holding his head up*.

Eight Steps to Writing Participation-Based Outcomes

Participation-based outcomes are applicable to almost all child outcomes (Campbell & Sawyer, 2009). They are a way of ensuring that the context in which the skill is needed comes first, so everyone working on the outcome understands that the desired behavior (i.e., the target skill) is not meaningful in and of itself but in how it helps the child participate in home, school, and community (Wilson, Mott, & Batman, 2004). This should also help to prompt adults to work on the skill at the times of day when the skill is needed.

1. *Assess functionality.* A functional outcome begins with functional assessment. It is not merely a matter of rewriting an existing outcome that might have emerged from a family's attempt to please the professional or from a failure on a standardized test. Rewriting such outcomes would merely produce well-written, nonfunctional outcomes. The RBI is an example of a functional assessment; that is, an assessment of what the child needs to be engaged, independent, and social in everyday activities.

2. *Read the informal functional outcome.* In the RBI, and other conversation-based assessments (Woods & Lindeman, 2008), fairly shorthand, informal statements will represent the family's choice of what to work on. The following are examples from an RBI; the child-level outcomes are in italics:

   a. More time as a family

   b. Boys in own bedrooms

   c. *Lance eating independently*

   d. More help for Helen (mother); Helen doing less

   e. *Lance saying words (meals, playtime, hanging out)*

   f. *Lance drinking from cup*

   g. Helen giving medicine easily

   h. Easy bedtime for Lance

3. *Determine the routines involved.* If a functional assessment was done, the routines should be obvious; they are when the RBI is used. In the above example for Lance, outcomes *c* and *f* applied primarily to breakfast, lunch, and dinner; outcome *e* has the routines specified in the informal wording.

4. *Write "[The child] will participate in [those routines].* Almost all child outcomes start this way. In the example above, therefore, the outcomes begin as follows:

   c. Lance will participate in breakfast, lunch, and dinner.

   e. Lance will participate in meals, playtime, and hanging out.

   f. Lance will participate in breakfast, lunch, and dinner.

5. *Write "...by _____ing,"* inserting the desired behavior. This step usually needs little to no change from the way the family mentioned the skill or the way it was informally recorded when the family chose outcomes. More specificity will be incorporated into the later steps. In some cases, more specificity can be built into this step. Examples of this step from above are as follows:

c. *...by feeding himself independently.* This was modified from *eating* to make sure no one would think Lance's eating (e.g., chewing, swallowing) while someone fed him would be acceptable. What Helen wanted was for Lance to feed himself by hand or with a utensil.

e. *...by saying words.*

f. *...by drinking from a cup independently.* Again, this was changed from the original, by adding *independently* so no one would think Lance's drinking (e.g., sipping, swallowing) while someone held the cup would be acceptable. Helen wanted Lance to hold the cup himself.

6. *Consider "We will know this when he or she _____" and add a measurable criterion.* Criteria, as mentioned earlier, are the measures when we can say the child has reached the goal. This does not mean we stop working on that behavior class, just on that specific skill, as specified in the criteria. The criterion helps to determine the purpose of the goal. Goals have four main purposes: to acquire a skill, to generalize a skill, to maintain a skill, and to execute a skill fluently. These purposes are not mutually exclusive. An acquisition criterion would state the extent to which the child should demonstrate the behavior or skill (e.g., 3 times per week, with 2 peers, with only a little help). Ask yourself, "What frequency, duration, or rate would be an acceptable level of the behavior?" You are basing your estimate on the information the family provided during the routines-based assessment. It is just an estimate that will be confirmed by the parents for the appropriateness of the level. Continuing the previous examples,

c. We will know he can do this when he uses his "hands" (Lance had had both his hands amputated as a result of bacterial meningitis), with or without a spoon (a spoon could be strapped to his arm), to put 10 bites into his mouth.

e. We will know he can do this when he says three different words (the rest of the criterion comes next).

f. We will know he can do this when he drinks a whole cupful, holding the sippy cup independently.

7. *Add a generalization criterion.* A generalization criterion would state the extent to which the child should demonstrate the behavior or skill across times, places, people, situations, or materials (e.g., in the classroom and on the playground; with his mother, teacher, and babysitter; when playing with three different toys). In our model, we encourage programming for generalization by writing generalization goals, which require acquisition criteria. Children can be taught a new skill in the multiple contexts they need the skill. Say to yourself, "If she did it only one time, would that be okay?" If not, ask yourself, "How often, in how many routines, with how many people, or in how many places would she have to do this to convince me that she had the skill?" In this model, because an RBI is used, we often know different routines in which the skill might be used, so they become automatic generalization criteria across routines. Using the previous examples,

c. *...at breakfast, lunch, and dinner...* (all three meals, not *or*; therefore, we mean a total of 30 bites a day)

e. *...during each of the four times of day...* (this means he can use the same three words at each routine, but he cannot use just two words in a routine, however many times he repeats them, for this criterion to be met)

f. *...at breakfast, lunch, and dinner...*

8. *Add the criterion specifying the amount of time over which the behavior needs to be displayed.* Examining the criteria we have so far for Lance related to his eating and drinking, he could meet the criterion for breakfast in March, for lunch in April, and for dinner in May, for example. Is that what was meant? No. See the following time criteria:

c. *...in 1 week*

e. *...in 2 weeks*

f. *...in 1 week*

The whole measurable outcomes for these three desires Helen had for Lance now read as follows:

c. Lance will participate in breakfast, lunch, and dinner by feeding himself independently. We will know he can do this when he uses his "hands," with or without a spoon, to put 10 bites into his mouth at breakfast, lunch, and dinner in 1 week.

e. Lance will participate in meals, playtime, and hanging out by saying words. We will know he can do this when he says three different words during *each* of the four times of day in 2 weeks.

f. Lance will participate in breakfast, lunch, and dinner by drinking from a cup independently. We will know he can do this when he drinks a whole cupful, holding the sippy cup independently at breakfast, lunch, and dinner in 1 week.

Other Criterion Types

In addition to acquisition and generalization criteria, two others might be appropriate. A *maintenance criterion* would state the extent to which the child should demonstrate the behavior or skill for a reasonable period (e.g., for 8 weeks). A *fluency criterion* would state the extent to which the child should perform the behavior or skill smoothly and rapidly (e.g., within 2 minutes, keeping up with other children).

The product of a successful needs assessment and intervention planning process therefore would be 6–10 functional outcomes. The definition of functionality in a child-level outcome is that 1) the target skill was necessary for full participation in everyday activities, 2) outcomes specify what the child or family will do, 3) the contextual need (i.e., what makes it functional) has been identified, 4) it is important to the primary caregivers, and 5) we can measure progress and achievement.

FAQs

Two questions come up often; both are presumably precipitated by professionals' wish to reduce their paperwork, which is an understandable desire.

1. *Can you combine outcomes, such as those happening in the same routine?*

It is generally preferred that outcomes not be combined. The general principle is that we want to preserve and honor the parent's desire for a specific skill, and combining skills might make it appear that we are not paying full attention to the individual skills. That does not mean we would work on them in isolation from one another. For intervention, they can be combined. Another complication is that the measurement criteria are often going to be different for the different behaviors. So the answer is no.

2. *Can you write only the top few priorities?*

Writing only the top few priorities has some merit (Hanft, Rush, & Shelden, 2004), but for two main reasons it is not advisable. First, if you have specific, uncombined outcomes, you want to ensure that interventionists (families, teachers) and their helpers (e.g., home visitors, consultants) see the panoply of skills that might be addressed in a particular routine. In our example with Lance, if only the top three outcomes were written, we might be addressing independent self-feeding and not independent drinking from a cup. That might be acceptable if the child was having a very difficult time with self-feeding, but if they could be combined for intervention they should be. Second, families often put family-level needs near the bottom of their priority list, out of a sense of self-denial. Yet, we know the importance of attending to their well-being (Barnett, Clements, Kaplan-Estrin, & Fialka, 2003; Bronfenbrenner, 1986), so to risk having lower priority, family-level needs not written on the IFSP would be a mistake.

Writing Family-Level Outcomes

Generally, family-level outcomes can be left as they are, with the addition of at least one criterion to know when the outcome has been met. Often, this can simply be a deadline by which the outcome is met. Table 7.1 lists some examples from Lance's family.

Be careful not to give the family things to do that were not meant in their interview. For example, one team saw the first outcome below and wrote, "The family will go to the mall or out to eat once a month." Those are possible strategies, but Helen did not say, at the end of the RBI, that she wanted to go to the mall or out to eat with the family.

Hiding Family Outcomes in Other Places on the IFSP

In some state or local systems, family outcomes do not appear on the same kinds of pages (paper or electronic) as child outcomes. Sometimes, they are at the bottom of the page with concerns, priorities, and resources. Sometimes, they are part of a family

Table 7.1.   Writing family-level outcomes

Original wording	Worded as IFSP outcome
More time as a family	All four family members will spend 1 hour together in a fun activity once a week for 1 month.
Boys in own bedrooms	Each boy will sleep in his own bedroom throughout the night for 7 nights in a row.
More help for Helen (mother); Helen does less	Helen will prepare dinner but not take care of the boys at that time if there is another adult in the house, 3 evenings a week for 1 month.
Helen gives medicine easily	Helen will describe giving medicine as "easy" within 6 months.
Easy bedtime for Lance	By April 30, Lance's parents will get Lance in bed for the night within 30 minutes of the beginning of the bedtime routine.

Key: IFSP, individualized family service plan.

assessment page. Sometimes, they have their own separate pages. It is best if they are on the same page(s) as child outcomes for two reasons. First, all outcomes are family outcomes, and if we go to the trouble of finding out about family-level outcomes and the priority order of importance, then that order should be preserved in the outcomes. For example, suppose a family picks the following as their first three goals:

1. More time for the parents together

2. Child will participate in dressing by pushing arms and legs through

3. Mother will get information about safe places to take the child to play outside

If the first and third outcomes were not on the regular outcomes pages, it would not be surprising if early interventionists thought first about dressing and then other child-level outcomes in that same section of the IFSP.

The second reason for putting family-level outcomes in the same place as child-level outcomes is that, historically, it seems that early interventionists have attended more to child-level outcomes than to family-level ones. By putting family-level outcomes in the same place as child-level outcomes, it might shift early interventionists' priorities.

Items from the FINESSE

The following items on the FINESSE are related to writing functional outcomes or goals. One item is about the Outcome/Goal Purpose. This item addresses the issue of whether the purpose of the outcome/goal is stated explicitly versus not being clear. The team, including the family, should have a reminder in the goal statement about why the goal is necessary. The four anchors on the FINESSE item, ranging from not recommended to recommended practices, are the following:

1. Purpose for each outcome/goal is **not clear.**

3. Purpose for each outcome/goal is simply **overall improvement** in a general developmental or skill area (e.g., talking).

5. Purpose for each outcome/goal is stated **implicitly** (i.e., we can guess why we're working on it).

7. Purpose for each outcome/goal is stated **explicitly** (i.e., we know exactly why we're working on it).

Another item is the one about the Necessity of Target Behaviors. As mentioned earlier, functional outcomes/goals are necessary for engagement, independence, and social relationships in routines. The following anchors, from not recommended to recommended practice, assess a program's practices relative to the necessity of target behaviors on the IFSP or IEP:

1. Target behaviors only **indirectly related** to functioning in current routines are recommended.

3. Target behaviors with **some developmental benefit** are recommended.

5. Target behaviors **useful** for functioning in current routines are recommended; without the behaviors, the child can just manage but not very well.

7. Target behaviors **necessary** for functioning in current routines are recommended; until the behavior is accomplished, the child cannot function well in the routine(s).

(continued)

(continued)

A third FINESSE item related to developing functional outcomes/goals is the one about the Focus of Intervention. This item assesses a program's or individual's practices relative to whether outcomes/goals are routines based versus discipline specific. Basing outcomes/goals on routines follows principles of family centeredness and functionality because routines are the natural ecocultural niches (Weisner, Matheson, Coots, & Bernheimer, 2005) of families. On the other hand, the practice of developing outcomes/goals for and by professionals from different disciplines (e.g., physical therapy goals, occupational therapy goals, speech goals) suggests that other adults cannot address them and that the goals were derived from a narrow, deficit perspective rather than from needs related to functioning across domains or disciplines. The four anchors are the following:

1. Interventions and outcomes/goals are **discipline specific.**

3. Interventions and outcomes/goals are **domain specific.**

5. Interventions and outcomes/goals are context specific but are **not** routines based.

7. Interventions and outcomes/goals are **routines based.**

Goal Functionality Scale III

In a current study (Ridgley, McWilliam, Snyder, & Davis, 2009), IFSPs are being examined to determine whether an online intervention will be associated with high-quality outcomes. This instrument is described in Chapter 12 and is provided in the appendix at the end of the book. It is also worth describing the items here.

1. *Does the goal/outcome emphasize the child's participation in a routine (i.e., activity)?* What is so important about wording outcomes/goals to emphasize the function of participation? In 1980, the World Health Organization published the *International Classification of Impairments, Disabilities, and Handicaps* as part of the World Health Organization's family of classifications. The original classification was met with criticism by advocates and self-advocates, particularly over the exclusion of the role of the environment, the settings, and situations having an impact on people's functioning. A long series of revisions was undertaken, with the involvement of representatives of people with disabilities. The revision was renamed the *International Classification of Functioning (ICF;* World Health Organization, 2007). This classification is organized into four sections: body functions, body structures, activities and participation, and environmental factors. The first two are about physiological performance and impairments, whereas the latter two provide the link from our conceptualization of functional outcomes/goals to the World Health Organization. In this classification, the most important dimension of a person's functioning, regardless of or perhaps taking into consideration his or her disability, is the person's ability to participate in activities—home, school, community, and work. In infancy and toddlerhood, this participation is **engagement**. As has already been discussed, engagement is a key foundation of this routines-based approach to early intervention. Furthermore, the fourth section of the ICF is environmental factors, which, in the context of infancy and toddlerhood, are the ways routines operate to enhance or inhibit the child's functioning. For example, a child in the car who is engaged (i.e., participating in the car-riding activity) is looking out the window, pointing, making

vocalizations, playing with toys attached to the car seat, and making eye contact in the mirror with the driver—who should be watching the road, but that's another matter altogether. The child whose functioning would be classified with lower-level codes (i.e., a child who is functioning less well) would not be engaging in all those participatory behaviors. Therefore, two children with the exact same etiology or *International Classification of Diseases* coding system could have quite different *ICF* codes. Now, one of the reasons for this difference could be the quality of the car seat for the individual child. If the car seat provided insufficient support, the child might not be able to hold his head up and might not be able to free his arms to play with the attached toys. Therefore, we would know both the participation level and the environmental factors. If for no other reason, therefore, child-level goals are written as participation goals.

2. *Does the goal/outcome state specifically (i.e., in an observable and measurable manner) what the child will do?* The specificity of the desired behavior has been identified as a key dimension of outcomes/goals and a particular weakness of IFSPs (Jung & Baird, 2003; Jung & McWilliam, 2005; McWilliam, Ferguson, et al., 1998). For example, an outcome/goal such as "Wardell will walk" is not specific enough. Instead, it could be worded as "Wardell will participate in outings to stores by walking with one hand held for 25 yards."

3. *Does the goal/outcome address a skill that is either necessary or useful for participation in home, school, or community routines?* Necessity consists of skills that the child needs in order to participate in normal activities. They exclude skills that are potentially foundational for future skills but that have no purpose in the here and now. Sometimes, goals produced by therapists are actually for strategies rather than the functional skill itself, such as crawling and kneeling. However, if the parent really wants the child to kneel for some reason, the outcome/goal should be, "Danilo will participate in toy play by kneeling while playing with toys." One might still question whether the kneeling is necessary when the child could probably play with toys by sitting or standing.

4. *Does the goal/outcome state an acquisition criterion (i.e., an indicator of when the child can do the skill)?* This first criterion is a quantifiable way of determining that the child has the skill without regard to generalization or maintenance. For example, "We will know he can do this when he plays with toys while kneeling for 3 minutes."

5. *Does the goal/outcome have a meaningful acquisition criterion (i.e., one that shows improvement in functional behavior)?* For example, "We will know he can do this when he holds a spoon for 2 minutes," not "...when he holds a spoon on 5 out of 7 trials." If kneeling while playing is the issue, the relevant acquisition criterion is probably duration. Other criteria that might make an outcome/goal meaningful are volume for an eating or drinking outcome/goal, distance for a crawling or walking outcome/goal, number of words for a language outcome/goal, and percentage of words for an articulation outcome/goal.

6. *Does the goal/outcome have a generalization criterion (i.e., using the skill across routines, people, places, materials, etc.)?* For example, "...when he holds a spoon for 2 minutes at lunch and dinner." If the child maintained kneeling for 3 minutes one time, while playing with toys, that would rarely be considered a demonstration that the skill was mastered at the level the family wanted. If, however, the child had to show this skill

3 times a day, 5 days a week, it might be considered mastered. This would be generalization across times of the day.

7. *Does the goal/outcome have a criterion for the timeframe?* For example, "…when he holds a spoon for 2 minutes at lunch and dinner on three consecutive days," or "…at lunch and dinner on 3 days in 1 week." Five days a week? If the team meant "in 1 week," that's how it should be written. If they thought 1 week was not enough to demonstrate mastery, it could be "for two consecutive weeks."

Section Summary

Traditionally, what has been missing from early intervention/early childhood special education and related services has been an assessment of the child's and family's needs. Assessment has focused on the status of the child's development and sometimes on what families want, but those are different from families' self-perceived needs. Functional assessment can take the form of an in-depth interview of natural caregivers. Many evaluations are done to determine eligibility; this is a different purpose for evaluation or assessment. Eligibility determination is based on a dichotomous outcome: in or out. Functional assessment is more complex, comprised as it is of the goodness of fit between the child or family and the demands of routines. Determining this goodness of fit should be done by those who observe the child in sufficient time and context samples, and those people are family members and child care providers.

The RBI is a helpful method for conducting such a functional assessment. It also includes a rating of the family's satisfaction with routines or the teacher's rating of the goodness of fit with classroom routines. The former might be a proxy for quality of life. The routines-based approach (e.g., McWilliam, 1992) in this model is based on a definition of routines as everyday activities and places. The RBI is a semistructured, solution-focused interview that has the same advantage as brief therapy—impact in brief encounters with adults. It produces a list of functional outcomes/goals, which then are written to satisfy requirements of the IFSP or IEP.

Functional intervention plans are founded on functional outcomes/goals, which in turn came from a functional assessment. These outcomes/goals need criteria for completion to make them measurable.

Test on Needs Assessment and Intervention Planning

1. Which of the following should be used for intervention planning?

    a.   Assessment for diagnosis

    b.   Assessment for determining eligibility

    c.   Assessment for monitoring progress

    d.   None of the above

2. Which of the following two statements are true in early intervention?

    a.   We overemphasize intervention.

    b.   We underemphasize intervention.

    c.   We overemphasize assessment for diagnosis.

    d.   We underemphasize assessment for diagnosis.

3. Which of the following types of children are automatically eligible (i.e., do not need testing to be enrolled) for Part C services under IDEA *in all states*?

    a.   Children who are biologically at risk for developmental delays

    b.   Children with suspected delays in two or more areas

    c.   Children who have established conditions

    d.   Children who are environmentally at risk for developmental delays

4. Which of the following is not true in the federal legislation about the evaluation that must be offered to families entering Part C?

    a.   Three or more qualified professionals must participate.

    b.   Functioning in five domains must be evaluated.

    c.   Narrative information is sufficient for children who are automatically eligible.

    d.   Instruments other than norm-referenced tools may be used.

5. For intervention planning, which one of the following is the most useful form of assessment of the current level of functioning?

    a.   Norm-referenced testing

    b.   Curriculum-referenced assessment

    c.   Routines-based assessment

    d.   Arena assessment

6. Which of the following is not one of the three basic roles of the service coordinator in the evaluation process?

    a.   Set up the assessment

    b.   Put the information on the IFSP

    c.   With the family, determine needs

    d.   Test the child

7. Which one of the following statements is true about the Routines-Based Interview (RBI)?

    a. It can be used for children who stay at home and for children who are in group-care or classroom settings.

    b. It can be used only for children who stay at home.

    c. It can be used only for children who are in group-care or classroom settings.

    d. It can be used only for children receiving services in clinics.

8. In the context of the RBI, *routines* are

    a. Activities the specialist conducts with the child

    b. Activities that happen with some regularity

    c. Activities that happen on schedule

    d. Activities the child knows well

9. Which of the following is not true about the RBI?

    a. The child must be present.

    b. The interview can be conducted by one or two people.

    c. The successful interview takes 1.5–2.0 hours.

    d. The successful interview results in 6–12 outcomes/goals.

10. Which of the following is a legitimate challenge to implementing the RBI?

    a. Transferring the information from the interviewer to interventionists

    b. Interviewing extremely verbose family members

    c. Interviewing family members who do not speak very much

    d. All of the above

11. Which of the following is not included in the list of functional domains in this model

    a. Social relationships

    b. Engagement

    c. Independence

    d. Motor

12. Purposes of outcomes/goals (and therefore criteria) include which of the following?

    a. Acquisition

    b. Generalization

    c. Maintenance

    d. All of the above plus fluency

13. Which of the following is not true about the definition of functionality?

    a. The outcome/goal must be able to be addressed during therapy or instruction.

    b. The outcome/goal specifies what the child or family will do.

    c. The contextual need for the outcome/goal is specified.

    d. The outcome/goal is important to the primary caregivers.

14. The purpose for each outcome/goal should be

    a. Stated implicitly

    b. Overall improvement in a general developmental or skill area

    c. Stated explicitly

    d. Recorded on a separate page of the IFSP or IEP

15. Target child behaviors on the intervention plan should be

    a. Indirectly related to functioning in current routines

    b. Have some developmental benefit, without necessarily being needed in current routines

    c. Useful for functioning in current routines, without necessarily being needed

    d. Necessary for functioning in current routines

16. Interventions and outcomes/goals should be

    a. Routines based

    b. Domain specific

    c. Discipline specific

    d. Context specific but not routines based

Answers: 1) d 2) b and c 3) c 4) a 5) c 6) d 7) a 8) b 9) a 10) d 11) d 12) d 13) a 14) c 15) d 16) a

Model of Service Delivery

Chapter 9 describes the primary service provider (PSP) approach, but that approach needs to be introduced in the next chapter, Chapter 8. Decision making, the topic of the chapter, differs between a PSP approach and a multidisciplinary or interdisciplinary approach.

- In a *multidisciplinary approach,* different professionals do their own thing and do not talk to each other. For example, a family might be visited by (or go to visit) a speech-language pathologist, an occupational therapist, a physical therapist, and an early intervention specialist. Each person typically addresses specific areas of development matching his or her training. By definition, if they are using this approach, they are working independently.

- In an *interdisciplinary approach,* different professionals do their own thing but do talk to each other.

- In a *transdisciplinary approach,* one professional (the PSP) has ongoing contact with the family, with other team members providing consultation to the family and PSP. This definition will be expanded and elaborated upon in Chapter 8.

Deciding on Services

Most service decisions are probably made on the basis of the child's diagnosis, often before outcomes have been decided. In this model, I argue for a thoughtful process of deciding on services—one that acknowledges that this decision should take multiple factors into consideration.

The Key Question

To decide on services and the intensity of those services, teams must ask the key question, *What is needed to support regular caregivers?* Support needs to 1) empower the family, 2) provide learning opportunities for the child, and also 3) be aimed at improving the overall quality of life of the family, because that quality of life has an impact on the child's development. If a PSP approach is used, the question is further refined as follows: *What services are needed to help the PSP support caregivers in carrying out interventions to meet outcomes?* This is then followed by questions about the intensity of those services. To use this approach, the outcomes must be functional. It doesn't do much good to go through this outcomes-based decision-making process with goals that are not meaningful. Decision making differs for multidisciplinary and transdisciplinary (i.e., PSP) approaches.

Multidisciplinary

Theoretically, the "team" makes decisions about services, but a defining characteristic of the multidisciplinary approach is that there really isn't a team, other than a sort of paper team—the people listed on the IFSP. Legally, the service coordinator is responsible for completion of the IFSP. This is somewhat awkward and variable across the United States: In some situations, the service coordinator is qualified to be taking the lead in this decision making, but in other situations, the service coordinator is not qualified.

Other team members might disagree with the service coordinator, especially team members who believe they should be providing more services than the service coordinator determined.

When different people are working with the family separately, the service coordinator should take the top priority and ask, "What service is needed to address this outcome?" Once the service is decided, the intensity and frequency of the service must be decided. Again, the question is, "What intensity of this service is needed to address this outcome?"

The team or service coordinator then goes to the second-priority outcome and asks two similar questions: "What *additional* services are needed to help the PSP support caregivers in carrying out interventions to meet outcomes?" and "What intensity of this service is needed to address this outcome?" This process continues through the outcomes, in priority order. By asking the question outcome by outcome, the decision making becomes *additive*. This is very important for reducing duplication of services and overburdening the family. It is additive in that we ask for the second and subsequent outcomes what additional services are needed, given that we already have decided on at least one service.

Transdisciplinary

In a transdisciplinary model, the decision making is infinitely smoother than in a multidisciplinary model and hinges on the skills, knowledge, and confidence of the PSP. This process is called the *incremental approach* to decision making, because services are added only as needed, not added to match disabilities or diagnoses. The concept map in Figure 8.1 shows this decision-making process. The branch regarding the initial IFSP, leading to the question about who the PSP should be, is addressed in the next chapter. This chapter begins at the point where the question is, "Can the PSP help the family with Outcome 1?"

The decision about who should be the PSP is addressed in Chapter 9. Once that is decided, the service coordinator, who in some places might also be the PSP (but not necessarily), asks, "Does the PSP need help supporting the family with this outcome?" If the answer is yes, the question is from whom. What individual in the agency or type of professional is needed to help the PSP with the outcome? For example, if the first outcome for a child is that the child will stand while being dressed, the service coordinator would ask the PSP whether she knew how to support the family in addressing this outcome. If the PSP says yes because she is confident about what is needed to teach the child to stand during this routine, no additional service is needed for that outcome. If the PSP, however, says that she is not confident about whether standing is viable for the child, perhaps because of the child's muscle tone or balance, she might say she needs help in supporting the family to address this outcome. In this case, she and the service coordinator (assuming, in this example, they are different people) would determine who might be needed to help with this outcome—perhaps a physical therapist.

The next question is how often the additional team member would need to help the PSP and family. In many situations, the PSP might want a consultation involving some assessment of the child from a team member. The ongoing frequency and intensity of that consulting team member would be determined after he or she had done the assessment, so the frequency on the IFSP would initially be once. At some point, either from the beginning or after assessment, the team needs to decide on the ongoing frequency and intensity. Perhaps surprisingly, this hinges more on the knowledge, skills,

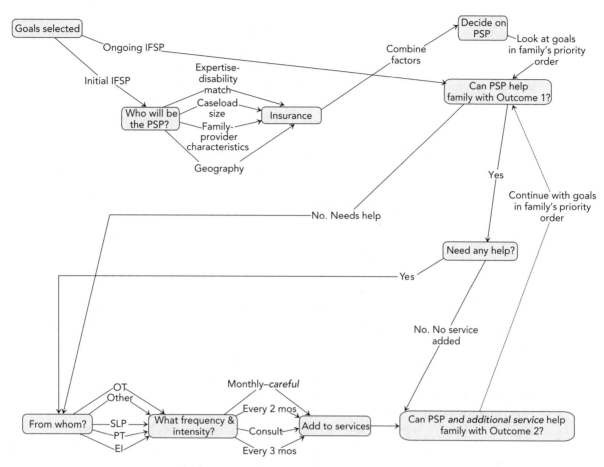

Figure 8.1.   Incremental process for deciding on services. (*Key:* PSP, primary service provider; OT, occupational therapist; PT, physical therapist; SLP, speech-language therapist; EI, early interventionist; mos, months.)

and confidence of the PSP than on the child or family. If the PSP knows the situation, has experience with the kind of outcome, and has experience with the child's special needs, less frequency is needed. If the outcome or the special needs are unfamiliar to the PSP, more frequency is needed.

Continuing the example above, in which standing while being dressed is the outcome, let us assume that the assessment revealed the child has very poor balance but normal tone. (Note that someone should refer the child to an otolaryngologist.) If the PSP has had much experience with children with balance problems and certainly with teaching children to stand, he or she probably needs consultation only every 3 months or so, from someone who can help with balance. This consultation might be with a physical or occupational therapist or another professional known to have expertise in teaching children with balance problems. If the PSP has rarely worked with children with balance problems (or is right out of school and does not even have much experience with teaching independent standing), he or she probably needs consultation every month or so. The knowledge and confidence of the PSP are the most important factors in deciding the frequency and intensity of the other services.

Because the PSP might not know how much help he or she needs, other team members might need to be consulted. This need for consultation by people who know each other is yet another reason for having existing teams, rather than ad hoc teams, in early intervention. *Existing teams* are professionals who work in the same agency or who agree to work together as a team, even if they are from different agencies or are private vendors. Ad hoc "teams" are the people who happen to be on a child's IFSP, sometimes from disparate agencies or private vendors. Existing teams can be involved in decision making during IFSP development, whereas ad hoc teams are constituted only after the IFSP is developed. The obsession with not predetermining services has been a significant challenge to good decision making in early intervention. It has prevented the involvement of providers in the IFSP development.

The service coordinator should ask other team members whether they agree with the PSP about the need for and frequency of other services. In our example, the PSP might determine that she does not need help because she has had much experience with children learning to stand independently. Another team member, perhaps a physical therapist, who has seen a report that the child does not have semicircular canals, might anticipate that this outcome is going to be especially challenging. The physical therapist therefore suggests that the PSP might need consultation regarding balance for this outcome, at least every 3 months.

The opposite opinion is also possible. That is, another team member might suggest that the PSP does not need as much consultation as the PSP might think. For example, a PSP serving a child with Down syndrome might think she should get consultation from a physical therapist monthly, while the child is an infant. The PT, however, might suggest this is too frequent. In some communities, it is almost unheard of to have a therapist suggest less frequency. In communities where the PSP model is well established, however, therapists know that if they get too committed to families when they are not absolutely necessary, they will not be available to others who might need them.

Having asked whether the PSP needs help from another team member for the first-priority outcome, the service coordinator now asks the question for the second-priority outcome. This process is continued through the remaining outcomes.

Items from the FINESSE

The following item from the FINESSE is the only one somewhat related to deciding on services. It is about the Focus of Intervention.

1. Interventions and outcomes/goals are **discipline specific**.

3. Interventions and outcomes/goals are **domain specific**.

5. Interventions and outcomes/goals are context specific but are **not** routines based.

7. Interventions and outcomes/goals are **routines based**.

A discipline-specific outcome with interventions might be "Micah will sit independently" (in itself, not a bad outcome), with the only strategy being a therapist seating him on a therapy ball, working on his trunk control. The person completing the FINESSE would have no trouble identifying domain-specific interventions and outcomes if outcomes were informally known as a "PT outcome" or a "teacher outcome."

Domain-specific outcomes, similarly, are those known as "cognitive outcomes" or "motor outcomes." Some communities even require that an outcome be determined for each of the

(continued)

(continued)

five domains required for reporting current level of functioning. Others require an outcome for each domain in which delays have been documented. For example, if a child is found to have a delay in communication, a communication outcome is expected. This requirement is understandable and even has the backing of IDEA, which stipulates that outcomes should match the findings of the multidisciplinary evaluation. Nevertheless, two other options remain for describing functional, family-centered focuses of intervention.

Context-specific but not routines-based outcomes and interventions are those that specify the place, time, or people involved when the target behavior is displayed. For example, the goal might be for the child to operate toys involving eye–hand coordination independently, and the IFSP specifies that this behavior and the interventions will occur in the small-toy area of the child care classroom. The need for this outcome might not have come from ongoing routines, and in fact adults could address it in the right place but outside ongoing routines. An adult might take the child, individually, from art and work on eye–hand coordination in the small-toy area. That would be context-specific but not routines-based intervention.

Routines-based outcomes and interventions, therefore, involve outcomes relevant to routines, rather than isolated skills that have only a presumed connection to routines. In general, if the target behavior addresses engagement in routines, which can include independence or social relationships, it is routines based. Therefore, to be routines based goes beyond the location.

Sample Outcome List

The following list of informal outcomes emerged from an RBI.

Priorities for Sandy (Bryce's Mother)

1. Bryce will communicate at mealtimes, in the morning, and in the evening, and his needs and wants at any time.

2. When Bryce walks fast, inside, and barefoot, he will do so without falling.

3. Bryce will put on his shirt independently and pull up his pants.

4. Bryce will play and listen to stories without sucking his thumb.

5. Bryce will help with bathing.

6. Sandy will teach Calista (Bryce's sister) to communicate without screaming.

7. Sandy and Rusty (Bryce's father) will find acceptable child care for the children so they can spend time together without the children

Bryce's PSP is Gloria, who is trained in early childhood special education and has worked with infants and toddlers for 6 years. The process begins by asking whether Gloria can help the family with Bryce's communication needs. She can, and she doesn't need any help because Bryce simply has delays and structural anomalies have been ruled out (i.e., nothing is wrong with his mouth, his tongue, and so forth). Gloria is experienced enough to know that if Bryce doesn't acquire some communication in the next 6 months, she will need consultation from someone, possibly a speech-language pathologist. But for now, no service in addition to special instruction, the service she provides, is necessary.

The family chose the second outcome because they think Bryce is very clumsy. Gloria is concerned that, if this is the parents' second concern, it might be more than the unstable gait of a toddler, so she wants consultation from a physical therapist. So PT is now added as a service, but only for one or a few consultations, for now. If the PT sees the need for interventions beyond what Gloria might recommend, the frequency of this additional service can be increased. But Gloria and her supervisors are careful not to set up a situation where the PT inadvertently or purposely seduces the family into thinking that frequent contact with the PT is necessary. In other words, the PT needs to support the model by empowering the PSP—to the parents' faces. Nevertheless, PT is now added, so the question about dressing, the third outcome, is whether Gloria and the PT can help the family to teach Bryce to put on his shirt independently and pull up his pants. Gloria is confident that between the two of them they can help the parents.

Can Gloria help the family with the fourth outcome—Bryce's playing and listening to stories without sucking his thumb? This is a behavior reduction outcome, with the replacement behavior being to play and listen to stories. Gloria's background makes her confident she can explain to parents how to set up a program using differential reinforcement of other behavior. Not all early childhood special education teachers have this background, incidentally, but Gloria does, so between her and the PT (we always add the already-chosen services when using the incremental approach), no additional service is added.

For the fifth outcome, Gloria feels that between the PT and herself, the family can be helped to teach Bryce to help with bathing. The family-level sixth outcome is about helping the mother, Sandy, teach Bryce's sister how to ask for things without screaming. Gloria's background (technically, with the assistance of the PT, who has already been added to the plan) makes her feel confident she can help the mother with this outcome.

Gloria needs no help with the seventh outcome—helping the family find acceptable child care. So the service list consists only of special instruction (the service provided by an early childhood special education teacher) and physical therapy. If this were a system with dedicated service coordinators, there would also be a service coordinator available to help, for example, with finding child care. If it were a system with a blended service coordinator approach, in which the PSP is also the service coordinator, both services would still be listed—as being provided by the same person. Sometimes, the blended service coordinator has to report the percentage of a visit classified as service coordination and the percentage classified as another service (e.g., special instruction), because different payment sources pertain to each service. If Medicaid is being tapped, for example, service coordination is likely to be billed for as *targeted case management*, whereas the intervention is billed under a different category.

In some unthinking, simplistic systems, the same family would be served by a speech-language pathologist (Outcome 1), a physical therapist (Outcome 2), an occupational therapist (Outcomes 3, 4, and 5), family counseling and training (Outcome 6), and service coordination (Outcome 7). Because no service is routinely available in most systems for family training and counseling, outcome 6 might not even be addressed. Often, family-level needs never even make it on to the IFSP.

The combination of the RBI and the incremental service decision approach is a powerful strategy for programming for families in early intervention. It addresses broad child and family needs through the multiple outcomes emanating from the RBI yet streamlines services to ensure that we don't rob the family of their time and role. The Service Decision Checklist in Appendix 8.1 further helps with this process.

Test on Service Decision Making

1. A transdisciplinary approach is one in which

    a. Multiple professionals each work with the child and family, separately

    b. One professional works with the child and family

    c. Multiple professionals work with the child and family but they communicate with each other

    d. Primarily one professional works with the child and family, assisted by a team of other professionals

2. Services are added to the IFSP based on

    a. The child's disability

    b. The severity of the child's delays

    c. The people needed to help the primary service provider

    d. What services are available in the community

3. Which of the following situations is problematic?

    a. A home visitor taking along another professional on every home visit

    b. A home visitor taking along another professional on every fourth home visit

    c. A home visitor's suggesting to the family that another professional provide consultation

    d. A home visitor providing the family with suggestions beyond those strictly defined by his or her training

4. An experienced home visitor

    a. Generally needs more joint home visits with other professionals than does an inexperienced home visitor

    b. Generally needs the same amount of joint home visits with other professionals as an inexperienced home visitor

    c. Generally needs fewer joint home visits with other professionals than does an inexperienced home visitor

    d. Generally needs more time to find homes when making home visits

5. The decision about whether to add a service to the primary service provider

    a. Is made by the service coordinator

    b. Is made by the service provider

    c. Is made by the administrator of the program

    d. Is made by the IFSP team

6. Child-level outcomes/goals should be

    a. Clearly identified by the developmental domain (e.g., cognitive, communication, motor) they address

    b. At least 10 words long

    c. Clearly identified by the discipline of the person who is most relevant (e.g., a physical therapy outcome, an occupational therapy outcome, a speech outcome)

    d. Usually relevant to children's engagement, independence, or social relationships

Appendix

Appendix 8.1. Service Decision Checklist

APPENDIX 8.1 Service Decision Checklist

Service coordinator _____ Observer _____

Use this checklist as a self-check or for observation by a peer, supervisor, or trainer.

Mark as correct (+), incorrect (–), almost, (±), or not applicable or observed (NA).

Did the service coordinator	Date	Date	Date	Date	Date
1. Ensure the outcomes were functional?					
2. Assess what services were needed to support the child's regular caregivers (versus simply "to maximize the child's potential")?					
3. Go through the functional outcomes in the order of importance priority identified by the family?					
4. For each outcome, ask what services the primary service provider (PSP) needed to help him or her support caregivers?					
5. For each service identified, ask what intensity of service is needed for each outcome?					
6. Base the intensity of each service on how much help the primary service provider needed?					
7. Assess both the PSP's and other team members' perspectives about how much help the PSP needed?					
Total correct					
Total possible (Items – NAs)					
Percentage correct					

Organizing Transdisciplinary Services

This chapter describes the implementation of the primary service provider (PSP) model (McWilliam, 2003), which here is considered synonymous with a transdisciplinary approach. In the PSP model, one professional provides weekly support to the family, backed up by a team of other professionals who provide services to the child and family through **joint home visits (JHVs)** with the PSP. The intensity of joint home visits depends on child, family, and PSP needs.

This model has been developed as a response to four problems with the multidisciplinary model. First, it reflects an implication that interventions for the child occur during the home visits, rather than between them. But if they have a high intensity of all services, especially if the interventionist works directly with the child, the family and others are likely to think that is where the intervention for the child is taking place.

Second, the multidisciplinary model separates child functioning into domains that do not make much sense in everyday life. When different professionals provide idiosyncratic programs for the child, the child will have a fine motor or "sensory" program, a gross motor program, a communication or feeding program, and a "cognitive" or social program. Because the actual intervention should combine these in the context of routines, this service delivery model is actually less than helpful.

Third, the multidisciplinary model requires much family time. The home visit (let alone the clinic visit, in communities that—despite policies and recommended practices—still provide such visits) requires the family to adjust their day around the business of hosting the professional. Young families are busy, and interventions occur when families are engaged in their regular activities. The home visit, as valuable as it might be, interrupts those times. Some families even believe they must be available, not to do interventions with their child necessarily, but to take the child to "therapy" or be home for the "therapist" to work with the child.

Fourth, the multidisciplinary model allocates scarce resources inappropriately. Not many people believe that early intervention services are overfunded, yet systems continue to provide services in a cost-ineffective manner. Sympathy for early intervention funding advocates will and should evaporate as long as the multidisciplinary model is used.

Principles

The principles of the transdisciplinary approach, as crafted in the model described in this book, are as follows. These reinforce what was presented in Chapter 1.

All of the Intervention Occurs Between Specialists' Visits

Infants and toddlers learn best through repeated interactions with the environment dispersed over time, not in massed trials. Therefore, it is the people who spend much time with children who have the opportunity to teach children. That is why children learn from parents and child care providers. This is a sobering fact for professionals and families who have somehow been acculturated to believe that a professional can swoop in and provide an intervention to the child, weekly. When the regular caregivers' role is framed as "following through" with some supportive activities, rather like it might be for parents of school-age children who are given homework, caregivers could be forgiven for thinking that their role is incidental rather than central to the child's learning. In fact, all the adult–child interactions that occur between specialists' visits are where learning occurs, with some learning occurring in child–object interactions—also *between* specialists' visits. Knowing where intervention actually takes place should make us rethink what the professionals' roles really are, which will lead to the realization that we do not need *multiple* professionals having regular and frequent contact with families.

Therapy and Instruction Are Not Golf Lessons

Golf is the latest sport I am slaughtering through my ineptitude. When I am having trouble with my short game (which refers to distance from the hole, not the length of my trousers), I can take a lesson from a professional. During that lesson, I will engage in massed trials: That is, I will hit many balls. This is an appropriate way for an adult to learn because adults can process information from each trial. Little children cannot process information massed together that quickly. (Note that this is different from the role of practice in motor learning, which does have a repeated- and massed-trial component. Here, we are talking about the acquisition stage of learning, before the child has the skill to practice.) Furthermore, the professional can teach me during the lessons, and I can transfer the information to nontherapy (i.e., non-golf-lesson) time. Adults can generalize like that. Little children cannot generalize as easily. The multidisciplinary approach is therefore based on a golf lesson (actually, rehabilitation) mentality that is inappropriate in work with infants and toddlers.

Regular Caregivers (i.e., Parents and Teachers) Need to Own the Goals

Rather than being the property of professionals who create them, outcomes should be the property of caregivers who decided on them. The outcomes are the backbone of the IFSP; from them, decisions about services emanate. And they are the focus of intervention, which also means they need to be appropriate and functional. The most important reason caregivers need to own the outcomes is that caregivers are the primary interventionists, so they need to see the need for the outcome and its relevance for the routines in which intervention will take place.

When we understand the concepts of intervention being what happens between visits, of children's learning through dispersed trials scattered through the day, and of caregivers owning the outcomes, the inapplicability of the multidisciplinary model becomes clear. We need instead a method that emphasizes how children really learn, that's unified around the family's functional needs, that capitalizes on families' forming close relationships with a PSP, that uses specialists as efficiently as possible, and that uses our limited resources most effectively.

Organizing the Program

Not all early intervention services are delivered through "programs," but many are—and programs have more opportunity to use a PSP model than do individual service providers. The PSP model requires a team; the section of this chapter titled "Working with Communities" addresses the formation of teams in communities. The main issues in organization of programs are 1) allocation of caseloads and time and 2) managing the big picture.

Allocation of Caseloads and Time

In a program, a beginning point can be to follow the 75/25 rule, where 75% of a generalist's time is spent visiting his or her families and 25% is spent visiting other team members' families, and 75% of a specialist's time is spent visiting other team members' families and 25% is spent visiting his or her own families. The actual percentage does not really matter, but it probably should not vary more than 10% from these to preserve the concept of transdisciplinary service delivery and to ensure that families get their needs met across disciplines.

Generalists and Specialists

It has become useful in the administration of early intervention services to divide service providers into the categories of generalists and specialists. Table 9.1 shows examples of backgrounds for the two categories. Early interventionists with one background can sometimes function in the opposite category. For example, a speech-language pathologist who spends most of his or her time in the role of a PSP, supporting the family with all kinds of needs, would be functioning as a generalist. Usually, generalists are trained to deal with a wide variety of developmental, behavioral, and family needs, whereas specialists are trained to deal with a focused scope of child functioning.

Under the 75/25 rule, a weekly schedule for a generalist might look like the one shown in Figure 9.1. Not every generalist will do four home visits a day, but the idea is

Table 9.1. Examples of backgrounds for generalists and specialists

Generalists	Specialists
Early childhood education (general or special)	Occupational therapy
Psychology	Physical therapy
Child development	Speech-language pathology
Social work	
Other disciplines aimed at the development and behavior of the whole child and family	

Monday	Tuesday	Wednesday	Thursday	Friday
Own family	Someone else's family (JHV)	In office for documentation and staffings	Own family	Own family
Own family	Someone else's family (JHV)		Own family	Own family
Own family (JHV?)	Own family		Someone else's family (JHV)	Own family (JHV?)
Own family	Own family		Someone else's family (JHV)	Own family

Figure 9.1.   Weekly schedule for generalist using the primary service provider model. Note that some visits to the PSP's own families will be with consultants. (*Key:* JHV, joint home visit.)

to show the distribution between seeing families for whom one is the primary provider and those for whom one is the secondary provider. Note that seeing someone else's family would be through a JHV made with the primary provider. Furthermore, some of the visits to one's own families would be made with another team member who was providing consultation.

Under the 25/75 rule (the numbers are deliberately reversed), a weekly schedule for a specialist might look like the one shown in Figure 9.2.

Managing the Big Picture

Program managers will need to ensure that the use of the JHV is not overdone, with the PSP taking someone with him or her on so many visits that advantages of the PSP model are lost. In such cases, it would be important to monitor why overuse is occurring. Some possible reasons include the following:

- The PSP lacks confidence.

- The PSP lacks knowledge and skills.

- The specialist is unwilling to release the role of supporting the family in carrying out the program.

Monday	Tuesday	Wednesday	Thursday	Friday
Own family	Someone else's family (JHV)	In office for documentation and staffings	Someone else's family (JHV)	Someone else's family (JHV)
Own family	Someone else's family (JHV)		Someone else's family (JHV)	Someone else's family (JHV)
Someone else's family (JHV)	Someone else's family (JHV)		Someone else's family (JHV)	Own family (JHV?)
Someone else's family (JHV)	Someone else's family (JHV)		Someone else's family (JHV)	Own family

Figure 9.2.   Weekly schedule for specialists using the primary service provider model. Note that some visits to the PSP's own families will be with consultants. (*Key:* JHV, joint home visit.)

Monday	Tuesday	Wednesday	Thursday	Friday
Own family	Someone else's family (JHV)	In office for documentation and staffings	Own family	Own family
Own family (JHV)	Someone else's family (JHV)		Own family	Own family
Own family	Own family		Someone else's family (JHV)	Own family (JHV)
Own family	Own family		Someone else's family (JHV)	Own family

Figure 9.3. Appropriate weekly schedule for generalists. (*Key:* JHV, joint home visit.)

Managers would be well advised to manage the implementation of the PSP model from three perspectives: generalist, specialist, and family. For each generalist, the majority of visits should be completed alone. An appropriate weekly schedule with joint and individual visits noted might look like that shown in Figure 9.3. The "own families" designated as a JHV change every week. For example, the second family visited on Mondays would get a JHV in the week shown in Figure 9.3, but then they might not get another JHV until 2 months from now. Next week, it might be the fourth Monday family that gets a JHV.

The generalist visiting someone else's family is there as a consultant, so the frequency is not intensive. Therefore, the four "someone else's" families that the generalist sees this week (i.e., first two visits Tuesday and last two visits Thursday) will not be the same families the generalist sees the following week. Because JHVs are challenging to plan—coordinating the family, the PSP, and the extra team member—they will not necessarily occur during the same slots every week.

Special Considerations for Consultation to Child Care

How many people should consult with a child's child care providers and how often? The principles related to consultation to family—such as the principle that one professional, with a team, provides a more unified program than do multiple professionals—still apply. On the other hand, child care providers are paid to provide a service. The rule about making joint visits, not separate visits, however, requires some latitude when the child is in child care. Because of all the activity in a classroom, the consultative ambience is quite different from a home visit. Therefore, consulting team members might make separate visits. The most important principle in this case is that children should not be pulled out of the classroom for therapy or instruction (McWilliam, 1996). Instead, therapists should use a service delivery approach called **individualized within routines** (see Figure 9.4).

One option might be to have one professional make home visits and another make visits to child care. They would be working off the same IFSP, and care would be needed to ensure that this multidisciplinary approach was integrated.

Within programs, multiple individualized IFSP teams exist, with individual professionals serving on numerous teams. On each team, one person can be the PSP. As shown in Figure 9.5, when all the teams fall under one administrative program, some amount

Individualized-Within-Routines Approach to Consultation to Child Care

1. On entering the room, observe the current activity and what the child is engaged in.
2. Join the child without interrupting his or her engagement.
3. Ensure the teaching staff can observe you.
4. Use incidental teaching
    a. To address an individualized goal
    b. To elicit more sophisticated engagement
    c. To elicit longer engagement
5. Communicate with the teaching staff about the intervention.

Figure 9.4.   Individualized-within-routines approach to consultation to child care. (*Source:* McWilliam, 1996).

of administrative control is possible, which therefore means that a team culture can be developed. Later, I will describe what happens when professionals are not joined by a common program.

Working with Communities

In some places, early intervention is provided primarily through programs, with only a little contracting to nonemployees of the program. In other places, such as Tennessee, at the time of this writing, many services are provided by independent vendors. In Ohio, many of the 88 counties have "MR-DD boards," which are teams of professionals from different disciplines and also independent vendors. The challenge to provide services with transdisciplinary teams is considerable, in the face of fragmented teams constituted family by family.

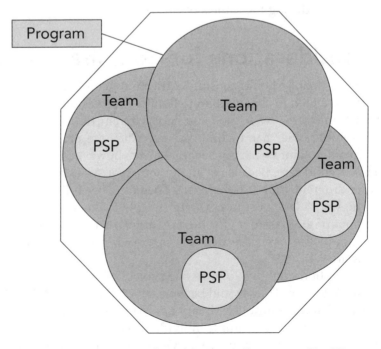

Figure 9.5.   Primary service provider model as operated by a program. (*Key:* PSP, primary service provider.)

Forming Teams

What happened to teams in early intervention (see Figure 9.6)? In communities with programs, a referral went to a service coordinator, who might be employed as a member of an early intervention program, as shown in Figure 9.6. In other communities, the service coordinator is employed by another agency, possibly dedicated to providing service coordination (Dunst & Bruder, 2006). Regardless, traditionally the service coordinator referred the child and family to the program, which then arranged for services with the coordinator. The family was a member of this team. There are, thus, two types of teams: the one that describes professionals working together in an early intervention program and the one composed for an individual child and family in the development of their IFSP. The latter type of team exists because of the law, but the former type often does not.

The features of service delivery that have killed the team concept in early intervention are the advent of the "dedicated" service coordinator (i.e., the service coordinator who is not also a service provider), the independent-vendor approach, and the fee-for-service payment method. These culprits are often interrelated.

Fortunately, there is a way out of this morass, as long as there are professionals willing to collaborate. The way out is the use of virtual teams.

The Virtual Team

In the unfortunately numerous parts of the United States where early intervention is provided in a fragmented manner by independent "vendors" (a crass term that reveals the mercantilistic mentality that service delivery has come to), the virtual team can provide a way to recover the concept of the team. It requires professionals who each have their own billing arrangements to agree to work together, still maintaining their connection to their billing agency.

As shown in Figure 9.7, the service coordinator would make the referral to this team of independent professionals, who would decide which of them would be the PSP in this situation. That person would be the family's primary partner and would use his or her regular billing mechanism to pay for those services. As the other members of the team provide their services through JHVs, they would use their own billing mechanisms. In

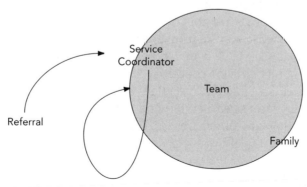

- "Dedicated" service coordinators
- Independent vendors
- Fee for service

Figure 9.6.   What happened to teams in early intervention?

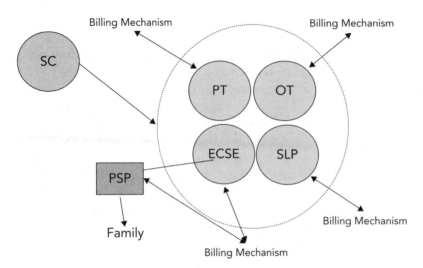

Figure 9.7. What do we do in a vendor model? (*Key:* SC, service coordinator; PT, physical therapist; OT, occupational therapist; SLP, speech-language pathologist; ECSE, early childhood special educator; PSP, primary service provider.)

the example shown, the early childhood special educator (ECSE) is the PSP, but it could as easily have been another team member. By taking turns as referrals come in, the members of the virtual team maintain their level of activity (i.e., they do not lose money), and the early intervention system can "incentivize" this process by providing more referrals to providers on teams than to totally independent providers.

It should be noted that, in vendor-driven models, providers are usually not service coordinators: That is, a dedicated-service model would be in place. The virtual team is therefore one method for simulating teamwork in a system seemingly designed to punish it.

Making the PSP Model Work: Choosing a PSP

How is the PSP chosen? Earlier, the application of the model by a virtual team was described. Such teams would presumably decide on the PSP by taking turns or some other such method to ensure fairness in the distribution of families. However, within a program in which professionals are not competing for families, the PSP might be assigned because of 1) geography (a service provider is already going to the area where the family lives), 2) caseload size, or 3) a match between the interest or expertise of a certain provider and the family's major concerns. Many providers favor the last criterion because it matches their schema that specialists are working directly with children. Care is warranted, however, because early intervention has more children enrolled with speech-language concerns than any other concern, but the number of speech-language pathologists is not great enough to allow every "speech kid" to have an SLP as the PSP.

The Joint Home Visit

As previously noted, the JHV is when the PSP and another team member go to the home. The other team member's roles are to conduct assessment through a variety of means, to provide intervention suggestions, and to model and give feedback as appropriate. The PSP's role is to ask questions, both for his or her benefit and for the benefit of the family; to ensure the family understands the information the other team member is providing; to ensure the other team member understands what the family wants and is saying; to take notes; and to handle interruptions. JHVs are therefore focused on the consultation from the specialist around needs related to functioning in routines, not around the performance of decontextualized skills. The goals of these visits are to determine problems contributing to the routines-based need, to provide information that will enhance intervention between home visits, to provide other information, and to enhance the competence and confidence of both the caregiver (e.g., parent) and the PSP.

An example of how a JHV might go is as follows. Lucia, a speech-language pathologist and the PSP for Edwin and his family, schedules a JHV with Nell, the teacher on Edwin's individualized team (i.e., on the IFSP). These JHVs occur every 3 months, according to the IFSP. Nell is on Edwin's team to provide guidance to the family about Edwin's biting others and gagging himself by squirreling food in his mouth; swallowing problems have been ruled out. Fortunately, Lucia and Nell can travel together to Edwin's house for the home visit, so they agree to catch up on the drive there. Lucia has told Edwin's mother that Nell is coming—or rather, she asked his mother if she would like Nell to come; she didn't force her on the family. When they got to the house, the early interventionists did the usual greetings with Edwin and his mother, and Nell began by asking the mother how things had been going with reducing Edwin's biting of others. The higher of the two priorities, according to Edwin's mother's prioritizing during the RBI, was addressed first. During this conversation, Lucia sat on the floor, playing with Edwin to keep him busy, while Nell and the mother talked. She was not intervening with him and she was keeping an ear on the conversation and occasionally adding to it. The biting topic lasted for about 10 minutes. There was no question of Nell's demonstrating anything because Edwin did not bite during the visit. Nell did give a few more pointers about managing the biting behavior, but the mother did not need very detailed steps; she seemed to understand how to handle the behavior.

Nell then asked about Edwin's squirreling food away. Lucia had warned her that this had not improved, which is what the mother said. Nell found out from Edwin's mother that the strategy of reinforcing every swallow wasn't working because the rate of swallowing was too low. "How do you get any nutrition in him then?" asked Nell.

"When his mouth is full and he can't fit any more in, he just refuses more food. He has nowhere to put it."

"So what do you do?"

"I make him spit it out or I stick my fingers in his mouth and pull it out. Then I give him baby food, which he eats happily. It's not solid enough to pack away."

"Are you okay with that?" asked Nell. "Or do you still want to get him eating solid food properly?"

"I still want him to eat solid food properly."

Nell discussed a shaping procedure, using the baby food as a contingency for small amounts of food, increasing the amount of food gradually. Edwin's mother wasn't sure about the timing of the baby food, so Nell offered to demonstrate. It was not exactly suppertime, but close enough, and fortunately the mother had some solid food left over. Nell showed how to show Edwin the baby food, offer him some solid food, tell him to chew it and swallow it, and then give him a jar of baby food. She drew a rough chart for increasing the amount of solids before getting the baby food but emphasized that Edwin's mother should only change the amount when Edwin had gone for three straight meals with the previous amount (i.e., a changing-criterion procedure). She thought the mother understood and she made sure Lucia understood how the procedure was to work. She made a note to herself to tell Lucia not to let Edwin's mother give up too quickly and how to handle the situation if he refused even the small amount of solids (i.e., a prompted incorrect response).

She then asked the mother and Lucia if there was anything else she could help with. There was nothing, so the early interventionists left. On the ride back to the office, Nell and Lucia went over the visit. Lucia asked a few questions about scenarios that might come up with the feeding program. Within the next couple of days, Nell sent an intervention plan (i.e., action steps or strategies) to Lucia for her own edification and to pass on to Edwin's mother.

Addressing Fears of Change

The PSP model is highly threatening to some people. Despite the fact that it is endorsed as recommended practice (McWilliam, 2000a; Rapport, McWilliam, & Smith, 2004; Workgroup on Principles and Practices in Natural Environments, 2007), the model involves a fundamental change in the traditional roles and practices of early intervention therapists. One national professional organization used to get in touch with me regularly to tell me that therapists were complaining that early intervention administrators and providers are denying therapy to families because they had moved to a PSP approach. I would often also get asked if the PSP model meant that unqualified people (usually, home-visiting teachers or early intervention specialists) were being trained to "provide therapy." What's at the root of these fears? The myths are that the PSP approach is practicing therapy without a license, it is outside the therapist's "scope of practice," it violates licensure requirements, and it diminishes the role of therapists. What do professional organizations have to say about transdisciplinary service delivery?

The American Speech-Language-Hearing Association (ASHA)'s *Emerging Consensus* states, "A natural setting must serve as the intervention context…. Services should be integrated with the natural setting such that intervention strategies can be implemented within the ongoing stream of activities typical for that setting…. The design and delivery of services should involve collaborations with families and other professional and support personnel" (Wilcox & Shannon, 1996). Although not explicitly endorsing the PSP approach, this statement conveys the same spirit.

In the recommended practices of the Division for Early Childhood (DEC) of the Council for Exceptional Children (CEC), one of the areas is "interdisciplinary models" that, despite the name, describes transdisciplinary practices (McWilliam, 2000a). In these models, teams including family members make decisions and work together; professionals cross disciplinary boundaries; intervention is focused on function, not services; and regular caregivers and regular routines provide the most appropriate opportunities for children's learning and receiving most other interventions.

Beyond professional association, Googling *transdisciplinary preschool* produced more than 44,000 results, possibly indicating this is not an uncommon approach. The following three pitfalls of the approach should be watched for.

1. *The primary service provider who lacks confidence or who tries to curry favor with therapists by requesting their assistance frequently* (e.g., "I need these people all the time"). In this case, a system could end up with every PSP visit being a JHV. This frequency of JHVs is problematic 1) because it denies families the opportunity to establish a relationship with their PSP if the visit is always focused on the other team member; and 2) it doubles the cost of early intervention, paying for two people at each home visit. We have to start regarding the economics of early intervention in terms of total costs to society, not who's paying for what. Current thinking is often that piling on of services is acceptable if other people are paying for the additional services. For example, one might find that the Part C system is paying for an early intervention generalist on a home visit, while insurance is paying for a therapist to be on that JHV. We cannot afford to say that the Part C office doesn't have to worry about the frequent JHVs just because insurance or Medicaid is covering the therapist's time. It all comes back to excessive costs borne by ordinary citizens—insurance policy holders and taxpayers.

2. *The specialist who can't release his or her role* (e.g., "No one else can support the family in carrying out these interventions but *moi*"). This person will insist on frequent visits, in truth confusing a consultative approach with a direct-service approach.

3. *The specialist who confuses intervention with service* (e.g., "This child needs therapy more than once a month"). This person does not understand that intervention is what the child receives from everyday caregivers in everyday contexts, so the frequency of services, which is what professionals provide, is unrelated to how much intervention the child receives.

By watching out for these three situations, the early intervention team or program can fend off sabotage of the PSP approach. Another source of support for this approach is from the Workgroup on Principles and Practices in Natural Environments, in which the sixth principle is "The family's priorities, needs and interests are addressed most appropriately by a primary provider who represents and receives team and community support" (2007, p. 2). This principle is one of seven agreed upon by experts in early intervention in natural environments. Attending to the natural environments principle in early intervention of course has an impact on the service page of the IFSP.

Services on the IFSP

What will happen to the service page of the IFSP when a PSP model is employed? First, we should assume that the PSP will be a weekly service, although, as discussed elsewhere in this chapter, this assumption does not always hold up. This would be the default frequency—the one recommended for most families and the one used for program budgeting. Often, the intensity of services delivered through home visiting[1] is one hour per visit. One hour a week should be adjusted as appropriate. For example, a family understanding and carrying out the intervention suggestions and not having major family issues might consider weekly visits to be too frequent. On the other hand, a family understanding interventions but having major family issues might need more frequent visits or longer visits.

---

[1]The term *the intensity of services delivered through home visiting* or *the intensity of home-based services* is technically correct, whereas *the intensity of home visits* is not because home visits are not a service; they are a setting in which services are provided.

With an initial IFSP, before the team knows the child and family well, the intensity of therapists might be more intense while they are getting to know the child and discovering why he or she had deficits revealed in the needs assessment. This helps them to recommend effective interventions. You don't need weeks to develop goals; you just need a good RBI! But developing appropriate strategies can take a number of visits. Once the short term is over, the frequency of all team members except the PSP is reduced to visits every 1–3 months. The model is supposed to be flexible within the parameters of a consultative model. This is in contrast to the prevailing method of professionals' filling up their weekly slots with the same families, week in and week out, which allows for no increase in frequency or intensity when needed. Visits might need to be more frequent if the family is in crisis or if the family is having difficulty learning an intervention through weekly visits. For most families, weekly for an hour will suffice.

Benefits of the PSP Model

The benefits of the PSP model include the following:

- The family receives strong support from one person, without having to get to know multiple people.

- The program for the child and family is coordinated, not fragmented.

- The family has to host only one visit in the home weekly, not multiple visits.

- Service providers, especially therapists, can serve more families.

- The cost to the system is reduced, which indirectly helps families.

Research is sorely needed to support *any* model of service delivery. The onus is not on the advocates for the PSP approach alone. In fact, common sense, parsimony, and theory are more on the side of the PSP approach than the multidisciplinary model, so the challenge is for advocates of the multidisciplinary model to make an argument beyond the fact that therapists and rehabilitation agencies can make more money working independently, in clinics.

Is Autism a Special Situation?

The National Research Council recommended that young children receive 25 hours a week of "educational services" (Lord & McGee, 2001). It was unfortunate that they used that term because the more cogent need is for children to receive intensive intervention, which, especially in the case of toddlers, can come from natural caregivers. It does not have to come from professionals. In fact, one might argue that it is better coming from parents or child care teachers than from professionals who are more likely to work with the child outside the context of naturally occurring stimuli (both antecedent and contingent). Intervention can be thought of as learning opportunities. For children with autism, these are opportunities to learn contingencies as well as learning to respond appropriately to discriminative stimuli. These learning opportunities can and whenever possible should be provided throughout the day in naturally occurring routines. They do not necessarily mean direct hands-on instruction from a paid professional or lessons out of context. If the regular caregivers cannot provide this intensity of instruction, the team needs to determine what *appropriate* resources are available. An excellent child care program with adequate consultation from an expert is one option. Another is a specialized program that practices inclusion and developmentally appropriate practice (Sexton, Snyder, Lobman, & Daly, 2002).

The Economics of the PSP Model

The implications for costs of implementing the PSP approach are related to who takes on the PSP role and how much business therapists lose with this model. The PSP approach can be used in a modified or pure transdisciplinary approach. In the former, most of the PSPs are generalist early interventionists, such as those trained in early childhood education or early childhood special education. Therapists are mostly reserved as the secondary team members, so they spend most of their time visiting other people's families. In a pure transdisciplinary approach, everyone has families for whom they are the PSP and then some time reserved to be the secondary for other people's families. Generally, where there is a shortage of therapists, the modified transdisciplinary approach is used and, where there are plenty of therapists, the pure transdisciplinary approach is used.

These transdisciplinary approaches have less of an impact on therapists' funding than might at first be imagined: Most third-party reimbursement systems are based on individual visits, not on caseloads. The story is different for salaried therapists not working on the fee-for-service model, such as those employed by an agency. For contract therapists or those working through a rehabilitation clinic, for example, the billable hours are especially important. In a multidisciplinary time allotment, where therapists see different families every day but carry the same schedule from week to week, assuming four families can be seen each day, we can see that 20 children can be served in 1 week (see Figure 9.8).

In a transdisciplinary time allotment, in which therapists see, say, the same five families for whom they are the PSP every week, the rest of their slots are filled up with consultations to other people's families. Because the families for which the therapist is a consultant change every week, potentially cycled back to again in 1 month, the therapist still makes 20 visits in the week. *The earnings for fee-for-service therapists are still the same.* But, in 1 month a multidisciplinary therapist can see 20 children, whereas a transdisciplinary therapist can see 5 families as the PSP and 15 different families in each of 4 weeks, which equals 60 families. The total number of families the transdisciplinary therapist can see in 1 month, therefore, is 65—compared to the 20 the multidisciplinary therapist can see. And the therapist earns the same reimbursement—for 20 visits a week (see Figure 9.9).

Monday	Tuesday	Wednesday	Thursday	Friday
X	X	X	X	X
X	X	X	X	X
X	X	X	X	X
X	X	X	X	X

Figure 9.8. Number of slots available to a therapist for seeing children.

Monday	Tuesday	Wednesday	Thursday	Friday
P	P	P	P	P
C	C	C	C	C
C	C	C	C	C
C	C	C	C	C

Figure 9.9.   Division of slots between visits in which the therapist is the primary service provider (P) and the consultant (C).

Another way to look at the economics of service delivery models is to look at a prototypical child, say a 2-year-old child with Down syndrome. In addition to the transdisciplinary versus multidisciplinary issue, the service coordination model has to be considered: Is a blended or dedicated model used? As described in Chapter 5, the blended model is one in which service coordination is added on to the role of a service provider; that is, a service provider is also the service coordinator. The dedicated model is one in which service coordinators are different people from service providers, so service coordinators do only service coordination. Our 2-year-old child with Down syndrome, receiving a multidisciplinary model with dedicated service coordination, might receive the following services:

- Occupational therapy once per week ($65)
- Physical therapy once per week ($65)
- Speech-language therapy once per week ($65)
- Special instruction once per week ($45)
- Subtotal × 50 weeks = $12,000
- Service coordination twice per year ($280 per year)
- Total = $12,280 per year

Of course, cost of services vary across the United States. These are standardized for the point of comparison of models. Realistic ones for each reader's region should be inserted, and the point will still be made.

Now, our 2-year-old child with Down syndrome, receiving a PSP model with blended service coordination, would receive the following services:

- Service coordinator/interventionist once per week ($65)
- Other specialist twice per month, which is generous ($130 per month)
- Total = $4,810

With the use of the dedicated service coordinator model, the PSP model is slightly more expensive:

- Interventionist once per week ($65)
- Other specialist twice per month ($130 per month)
- Service coordination twice per year ($280 per year)
- Total = $5,090

Obviously, the cost of serving this child in this theoretically valid way is still much lower than serving the child in a multidisciplinary way. One potential challenge, however, is that JHVs might not be reimbursed for the full time of the visit for each professional. Instead, reimbursement might be for only half of each person's visit time or for only one of the two people making the visit.

Nevertheless, some important conclusions supporting the use of the PSP approach can be drawn. With this approach, generalists spend most of their time seeing their own families, and specialists spend most of their time seeing others' families. Generalists are sometimes consultants to other PSPs, whereas specialists are sometimes PSPs. A problem with dedicated service coordination is that services are generally fragmented and generally use a multidisciplinary approach (i.e., the two usually go together), which means they are expensive. Saving money is not the main argument for the PSP model, but with the money saved, we could possibly do the following:

- Increase intensity of services for families who need more of their PSP's time.

- Hire more people to be PSPs.

- Pay providers better but then expect commensurate performance.

- Provide training to ensure the model continues to work.

- Provide educational materials for referral sources and families, so they understand the purposes and value of this approach.

Items from the FINESSE

Three items from the FINESSE pertain to organizing transdisciplinary services: Intervention Embeddedness, Focus of Intervention, and the Home-Based Service Delivery Model.

Intervention Embeddedness

The issue with intervention embeddedness is the extent to which the strategies can be incorporated into normal family routines. If strategies require *specific places*, such as a clinic setting, or *specialized equipment*, such as a commercially produced bolster, they are not "embedded." Sometimes, strategies are designed to be carried out in the home, using family materials, but the family is told to *set aside specific times*. When early interventionists recommend to families that they "work with" the child once or twice a day to "work on their goals," "do their early intervention," or "do therapy," they are not embedding interventions.

A more embedded approach, although still not totally embedded, is to recommend activities involving *significant modification of existing routines*. For example, the family may be working on the child's playing back-and-forth games with adults and decide to do this last thing at night. Therefore, the early interventionist may suggest that they have bedtime routine in the living room instead of the bedroom, use the adaptive chair instead of the rocker, and play Where's Your Nose? instead of Peekaboo. In this case, the routine has been modified significantly. A more embedded approach is to make *minor modifications of existing routines*. In the previous example, the early interventionist might have suggested they continue the bedtime routine in the bedroom; sit in the rocker with the child facing the adult; and play Peekaboo, teaching the child to take turns, imitate, and so forth. All of this intervention assumes that playing back-and-forth games is functional for the bedtime routine in this family (i.e., that the need for the target behavior came from a routines-based needs assessment).

Focus of Intervention

The critical dimension of the intervention focus is the extent to which interventions and outcomes are relevant to routines. The least routines-based interventions and outcomes are *discipline specific*. Such outcomes are described as "physical therapy outcomes" or "speech outcomes," for example. On IFSPs, they are sometimes revealed to be discipline specific because they have been written by different specialists, as can be seen by different handwritings. Some agencies or communities even have this nonrecommended practice as policy—that different outcomes have to be written by the "specialist responsible." (In case previous sections of the book dealing with this topic were overlooked, the problems with discipline-specific outcomes are that other professionals and the family do not take responsibility for those outcomes, that the outcomes tend to be separated from other outcomes, and that the outcomes are irrelevant to daily functioning.)

A similarly non–routines-based approach is interventions and outcomes that are *domain specific*. Such outcomes are described as "gross motor outcomes" or "cognitive outcomes," for example. Like discipline-specific interventions and outcomes, domain-specific ones tend not to be drawn from or relevant to everyday routines. This decreases the likelihood that they will be worked on. Even if they are, the usefulness of the skills would be questionable if the target behavior was not a skill that was needed for successful functioning in routines. Most domain-specific outcomes are taken from tests or curricula, and therefore domain-specific interventions are aimed at relatively nonfunctional behaviors.

A somewhat more functional approach is to select interventions and outcomes that are *context specific*, even if they are not routines based. This is what happens when an assessment reveals that a child has a weakness in a skill, and the early interventionist suggests working on this skill in particular contexts or routines. For example, a child might be found to have a fine pincer grasp deficieny, as was determined during an occupational therapy assessment. The OT suggests working on this skill during breakfast, picking up Cheerios. The family had not identified breakfast time as a need for intervention, because the child managed to cram Cheerios into her mouth by using a palmar grasp. Certainly, the use of a pincer grasp could make breakfast more efficient and cleaner, so the intervention context is functional. But the functionality would have been even greater if the skill and intervention were derived from a *need* that had been identified during assessment. This would make it *routines based*.

Home-Based Service Delivery Model

Home-based services can be provided in four essential ways: multidisciplinary, interdisciplinary, modified transdisciplinary, or pure transdisciplinary. The least recommended of these practices is ironically perhaps the most common—the *multidisciplinary approach*. Because of the ubiquity of some questionable practices, we must be careful not to confuse popularity of a practice with its effectiveness. In communities where the multidisciplinary approach is used, a family can receive two or more visits a week from different professionals. They often do not communicate with each other. In fact, families are often the go-betweens.

A slightly more integrated approach is where two or more professionals visit the family but they do communicate and integrate their strategies. This *interdisciplinary approach* is often claimed, but the amount of communication and integration rarely matches the claim. An integrated approach is the transdisciplinary service delivery model. In a *pure trandisciplinary model,* primary service providers come from a variety of disciplines. In a *modified transdisciplinary model,* the more available—and therefore less expensive—providers are the most common primary home visitors, with the less available—and therefore more expensive—providers mostly serving as consulting team members.

Checklists

Appendixes 9.1–9.3 provide three checklists for the organization and implementation of the transdisciplinary approach: one for the team in the organization of this approach (Transdisciplinary Service Delivery Checklist), one for the primary service provider (Primary Service Provider Checklist), and one for the consulting team member (Consulting Team Member Checklist).

Examples

Administrator

Andy Administrator runs an early intervention program that provides service coordination and direct services to families. For years, they have claimed to use an interdisciplinary approach, mostly because they conduct team assessments. Once services begin, however, different providers see families independently. Every Wednesday afternoon, they have staffings, during which three or four children are discussed fairly briefly. That's about it for interdisciplinary collaboration. Some hallway consultations occur, but they tend to be limited to discussions of crises.

Andy has slowly come to the realization that changing the model of service delivery will help professional development, provide more coordinated services to families, and make his dollars stretch further. He has not rushed headlong into this change because a number of staff members are dead against it and some families will think they are getting less intervention. He himself, however, has realized that they—and he, if truth be told—have confused amount of service with amount of intervention. The multidisciplinary approach, which is heavy on services, has resulted in too little intervention for children and families. The heavy use of services has fooled everyone into thinking that the professional time is when the children benefit, so all the time between visits (i.e., the majority of the child's life) has been more devoid of intervention than it should have been.

He discussed this irony with Priscilla PT recently. She said, "But would we be doing families a favor by turning their fun times into therapy?"

"I don't think that's what this approach should do," he replied. "If we see all kinds of routines as learning opportunities, we don't have to 'professionalize' them." He made double-quotation marks in the air.

"So each family is going to get just one service?"

"No, no. Each family will probably get a number of services; it's just that the intensity of one service will be weekly, and the others will be less often."

Priscilla looked skeptical. "What if a child needs physical therapy and the primary service provider is just a teacher?" She didn't hesitate in saying *just* a teacher.

"We'll have to rethink the concept of children 'needing' certain services" [more air quotation marks]. "Anyway, the child will still get physical therapy, but it might be, say, every 3 months."

"That's not enough."

Andy was patient. "If the therapist is a good teacher, he or she can teach the parent what to do, and the PSP will be there every week to reinforce what the PT has taught."

"Some children need a lot more than every 3 months."

"It all depends on how much support the PSP needs, actually."

"What if the child has just come out of orthopedic surgery, or some situation like that, where he or she would need direct physical therapy?" asked Priscilla.

"Then the PT can be the primary," said Andy. He thought briefly that maybe his decision had been premature. The staff was not ready, but then he remembered how long he had been contemplating the change. Priscilla would either learn this new approach or would decide not to continue working in this program. Until he made the bold administrative stand to use a transdisciplinary approach, however, making that choice was not going to happen.

Service Coordinator

Samantha Service Coordinator works as a dedicated service coordinator, meaning she does only service coordination, not service provision. She has a large caseload, which is depressing, but she is excited because she's part of a model demonstration project in her community. Small groups of providers have formed to function as permanent teams, rather than operating independently as they used to. The members of these "virtual" transdisciplinary teams all come from different agencies or are independent providers. They are SLPs, OTs, PTs, and ECSEs. When Samantha gets a referral, especially for a child that is likely to benefit from a number of services, she makes a referral to the team, not just one individual on the team.

Last week, she had a referral that exemplified how the virtual team works. The team decided which of them should be the PSP, based on a number of considerations, such as where the family lives, whose caseload can accommodate another primary family, or who has the most interest in the kind of child or family being referred. They chose Olive OT because she was already working with another child in the same neighborhood. Samantha, as service coordinator, was in charge of the IFSP, but, with the virtual team, the decision about services was easy. Once the family picked its functional outcomes, Samantha asked Olive from the virtual team whether she (Olive) could work with the family on the top-priority outcome. Olive was confident she could address the top three outcomes with the family, even though the second outcome was a language one. It was simply that the child would label various common objects found in everyday routines, on which Olive knew she could advise the family. This was not an outcome that required a speech-language pathologist. On the fourth-priority outcome, however, Olive wanted the help of someone who knew more about child strength than she did. The outcome was for the child to walk further before asking to be lifted. The behavioral aspect aside, Olive wanted to involve the PT on her virtual team to provide consultation. The PT agreed this would be a good idea, so Samantha recommended this service to the family, to be provided every other month. This decision-making process was used through the rest of the IFSP, making it easy and functional for Samantha and the family.

Service Provider

Emily Educator has landed the perfect job: a home visitor in a program that uses a transdisciplinary approach. Emily has been working in early intervention for 5 years, but has learned more in the last year than she did in all the previous time. Every time she goes on a JHV with a consulting team member, she learns more about interventions from different disciplines. She also spends about a fourth of her time as consultant to the therapists in her program. This role has given her much confidence—she feels valued. Although the opportunities to learn from colleagues are valuable, Emily also likes the fact that she and the families for whom she is the PSP are working very closely together. They see her as their major resource of professional help. She's the one who knows answers or knows people who know answers. Emily thinks she will stay in this program for a long while.

Family

Maggie Mother looks forward to Tuesdays, for that's the day Emily Educator comes to her house. She used to dread home visits when she lived in another state, where she had four different people in the house every week. Her child, Christopher, has multiple developmental problems, so an OT, an SLP, a PT, and a teacher are all involved. Where she used to live, the service coordinator also made separate visits. At first, Maggie was delighted with all the help. She quite proudly told her parents about how much help she was getting for Christopher. Everyone was delighted—until Maggie started seeing chinks in the armor. First, she was worn out with "hosting" all these visits. Second, the professionals would sometimes contradict each other. Third, each professional gave her homework, without realizing how much the others were also giving her. She was getting worn out between home visits. But then she saw these professionals "working with" Christopher on their many visits. She stopped doing the homework, partly because it was wearing her down and partly because she lost confidence. All these professionals with their years of training came in and worked directly with Christopher. She assumed his progress was because of their hands-on work. The homework was probably just something to make her feel "involved," as if she weren't fully involved with her child!

But in this new program it was different. It was scary at first, because they said she would get only one person, instead of the four people she used to get. But Emily quickly explained that Christopher would actually get more intervention with this approach. By her working with Maggie to incorporate interventions into routines, instead of Maggie's relying on the four weekly visits by different professionals, Maggie saw that all day, every day, was full of learning opportunities for Christopher. It was so much more intervention than the four therapy or instructional sessions provided.

Section Summary

Service delivery in early intervention is changing. After a rough period of unrestrained overspecialization, more and more states are seeing that less is more. That is, streamlining services can actually lead to more intervention with children. Beginning with a list of functional outcomes, services should be offered to ensure that those outcomes are met. It is important not to confuse this order (i.e., not to decide on services to match the child's diagnosis, then producing outcomes that the service providers determine are appropriate). In deciding on services, the recommended practice is to have one PSP who is backed up by a team of other professionals, as necessary. This helps to provide an integrated approach to intervention, gives the family one main person to connect with, and increases the opportunity that informal service coordination will occur as part of service delivery.

To achieve a transdisciplinary approach, either programs or communities need to be organized. In programs, policies can be set, training can be provided, and supervision can support the implementation of this approach. In communities where early intervention is not generally delivered through programs, virtual transdisciplinary teams can be established.

Test on Organizing Service Delivery

1. Service delivery involving different professionals working separately and communicating with each other, regularly, is called

    a. Multidisciplinary

    b. Modified transdisciplinary

    c. Interdisciplinary

    d. Pure transdisciplinary

2. Which of the following is *not* a purpose of supporting regular caregivers?

    a. Empowering the family

    b. Ensuring the family works with the child regularly

    c. Providing learning opportunities to the child

    d. Improving the overall quality of life of the family

3. When using a primary service provider (PSP) approach, the main consideration for deciding on what services are needed should be

    a. The diagnosis of the child

    b. The results of the multidisciplinary evaluation

    c. The outcomes chosen

    d. The needs of the PSP to support caregivers

4. Can a PSP support a family in teaching the child a skill that is outside the PSP's "scope of practice" or formal training?

    a. Yes

    b. No

    c. It depends

5. Must a child have a specialist for every area in which he or she shows deficits during the multidisciplinary evaluation?

    a. Yes

    b. No

6. The intensity of a service should be based primarily on

    a. The diagnosis of the child

    b. The results of the multidisciplinary evaluation

    c. The outcomes chosen

    d. The needs of the PSP to support caregivers

7. Ideally, who decides on intensity of any particular service?

    a. The family

    b. The team (including the family)

    c. The service provider in question

    d. The service coordinator

8. If the potential PSP is confident about supporting a family with a particular outcome, but another team member does not share that confidence (i.e., thinks that he or she should be involved), the team member should

    a. Not say anything

    b. Tell the family they are being underserved

    c. Tell the potential PSP that he or she is unqualified

    d. Offer to provide at least a consultative visit

9. Deciding on what services are needed and the intensity of those services should be done

    a. In whatever order seems natural during the meeting

    b. In the order of the busiest professional first

    c. In the order of the family's nomination of the importance of each outcome

    d. In the order of disciplines represented

10. Outcomes and interventions should be focused on

    a. Routines, to ensure they are functional for the child and family

    b. Different disciplines, to ensure that all expertise is used

    c. Different domains, to ensure that all areas of child development are covered

    d. Contexts, so appropriate routines can be chosen for working on specific interventions

Answers: 1 c 2) b 3) c 4) a 5) b 6) d 7) b 8) d 9) c 10) a

Appendixes

Appendix 9.1. Transdisciplinary Service Delivery Checklist

Appendix 9.2. Primary Service Provider Checklist

Appendix 9.3. Consulting Team Member Checklist

141

APPENDIX 9.1   Transdisciplinary Service Delivery Checklist

Professionals _____   Observer _____

Use this checklist as a self-check or for observation by a peer, supervisor, or trainer.

Mark as correct (+), incorrect (−), almost, (±), or not applicable or observed (NA).

Did the professionals	Date	Date	Date	Date	Date
1. Describe the primary service provider (PSP) model in written products about the program?					
2. Describe the PSP model during intake?					
3. Provide the rationale about how children learn and how services work?					
4. Use a routines-based, functional, family-centered, needs-based method (e.g., a routines-based interview) for selecting individualized family service plan (IFSP) outcomes?					
5. Select one professional to be the PSP?					
6. Use a variety of criteria to decide who the PSP should be (versus using only one criterion, such as matching expertise with the major disability or delay)?					
7. Arrange for the PSP to have at least weekly direct contact with the family?					
8. Agree that the PSP would provide support to the family around all the child's and family's needs (versus only around one particular developmental domain)?					
9. Ensure that professionals in addition to the PSP were available to provide services, if needed?					
10. List all the consulting services as services on the IFSP?					
11. Make decisions about services based on the PSP's need for consultation (versus on the child's diagnosis or domains of delay)?					
12. Provide administrative support for consultation to be given by non-PSP team members through joint home visits?					
13. Decide how much of each professional's time should be spent as a PSP versus as a consultant (applicable only to early intervention programs versus individual vendors)?					
Total correct					
Total possible (Items − NAs)					
Percentage correct					

APPENDIX 9.2 Primary Service Provider Checklist

Primary service provider _____ Observer _____

Use this checklist as a self-check or for observation by a peer, supervisor, or trainer. See the Support-Based Home Visiting Checklist (Appendix 10.2) as a companion checklist.

Mark as correct (+), incorrect (−), almost, (±), or not applicable or observed (NA).

Did the primary service provider	Date	Date	Date	Date	Date
1. Support the family around all the child's and family's needs (versus only around one particular developmental domain)?					
2. During the service-decision-making stage of the individualized family service plan (IFSP) development, state his or her need for consultation?					
3. Arrange for consultation from other team members to be provided through joint home visits (i.e., secured an agreement from them to consult in this manner)?					
4. During solo visits, support the family in carrying out programs developed by all members of the IFSP team?					
5. Before joint home visits, give the consultant relevant information?					
6. On joint home visits, ask questions, ensure the family understood, ensure the consultant understood, take notes, and handle interruptions?					
7. After joint home visits, debrief with the consultant?					
Total correct					
Total possible (Items − NAs)					
Percentage correct					

APPENDIX 9.3 Consulting Team Member Checklist

Consulting team member _____ Observer _____

Use this checklist as a self-check or for observation by a peer, supervisor, or trainer.

Mark as correct (+), incorrect (−), almost, (±), or not applicable or observed (NA).

Did the consulting team member	Date	Date	Date	Date	Date
1. Provide service to the child and family by making home visits jointly with the primary service provider (PSP; versus making separate visits)?					
2. Make recommendations based on his or her expertise, interest, and experience?					
3. Contribute to team decisions about the intensity of his or her service by assessing the needs of the PSP (versus simply the needs of the child and family)?					
4. Ask about the major need for each joint home visit?					
5. On joint home visits, assess child and family needs through a variety of means (e.g., hands-on, interview, observation versus just hands-on)?					
6. On joint home visits, provide intervention suggestions?					
7. On joint home visits, model and give feedback as appropriate?					
8. On joint home visits, provide information to both the family and the PSP?					
9. Before or during joint home visits, gather information from the PSP, as well as the family?					
10. During joint home visits, talk up the competence of the PSP to the family (versus usurp the PSP's role)?					
Total correct					
Total possible (Items – NAs)					
Percentage correct					

Natural Environment Locations

The number of places where children without disabilities might spend their days is considerable, so therefore the number of places that might be considered natural environments is also considerable. In early intervention, however, the most common locations are the home and the group-care setting. Home visits are discussed first, followed by consultation to child care.

Support-Based Home Visits

Home visits in Part C are different from home visits in other programs or serving other purposes. For example, nurse home-visiting programs are designed to educate mothers and monitor babies' progress. Occasional home visits by teachers or other school staff are for discussing problems or making home–school connections. Another purpose for visiting homes is to assess the home environment, as done in some social-work processes like adoption. The "rehab approach" to home visiting is to work directly with children. Nothing is quite like Part C home-based services, so the literature on efficacy from other models (Axtmann & Dettwiler, 2005; Wasik & Bryant, 2001) is only somewhat pertinent. Finally, home visits can be used to support families, which we might say is the social-support and early intervention in natural environments (EINE) approach.

Some home visits in early intervention involve professionals working directly with the child, with the parents observing, and often a toy bag is used to hold the materials the home visitor uses in his or her work with the child. Other home visits involve much talking with the family, addressing many dimensions of child and family functioning and providing informational support. These visits include the judicious use of demonstration by the home visitor, for the family, of ways of teaching the child. This chapter describes the second type of home visit, making the case for that model being more efficacious and theoretically sound than the first type of home visit.

Earlier in this book, it was established that the relationship between a primary service provider and the family is important for achieving the outcomes of early intervention (Bailey et al., 1998; Dunst, Boyd, Trivette, & Hamby, 2002; Dunst, Trivette, Boyd, & Brookfield, 1994; Rush, Shelden, & Hanft, 2003). Most families are very satisfied with their service providers, and the most family-centered practices are found in home-based services, especially by generalists (i.e., nontherapists) (McWilliam, Ferguson, et al., 1998).

The **support-based home visit** is based on four key principles that have been mentioned before, using different terms:

1. It's the family and other constant caregivers that influence the child and we can influence the family and other caregivers.

2. Children learn throughout the day, not in "lessons," "sessions," "work times," "exercise times," or "goal times" that concentrate the learning into just one time a day.

3. All the intervention for a child occurs between visits. The home visits (or clinic visits, if necessary) should be where the family gets information and encouragement so they can make the most of the learning opportunities that occur in the course of normal family life.

4. The child needs maximal intervention, not maximal services. There is little relationship between the amount and appropriateness of intervention for children and the amount of time professionals spend with the family or the number of professionals the family spends time with.

How Children Learn and How Services Work

Figure 10.1 illustrates the four principles outlined in the previous section. As shown in the figure, although professional support delivered directly to children might be assumed to have some benefit, a more realistic path to achieving child outcomes is by enhancing caregiver competence and confidence. The link between parenting and child outcomes has been well established (NICHD Early Child Care Research Network, 2002; Weisner, 2002a), and we also know that professionals can affect caregivers' competence and confidence (Barnett, Clements, Kaplan-Estrin, & Fialka, 2003; Kaiser & Hancock, 2003). Therefore, the best way to achieve child outcomes is through the parents and other caregivers. It should be noted that professionals can have a direct effect on children if they are with them for enough time in a week, as a group-care or classroom teacher would be.

Figure 10.2 shows that children learn through repeated interactions with the environment, distributed across time, better than they do in massed trials.

Figure 10.3 shows the routines-based model for children whose services are either the home or a classroom. The key to child progress through home-based services is for professional support to be aimed at family competence and confidence, as shown previously. The method of supporting families is transdisciplinary home visits. The key to child progress through classroom-based services is for professional support to be aimed at embedded interventions. The method for working with classroom staff is integrated services, which are described in Chapter 11.

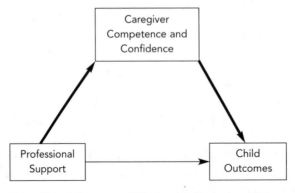

Figure 10.1.   Influences on child outcomes, showing how children learn and how services work.

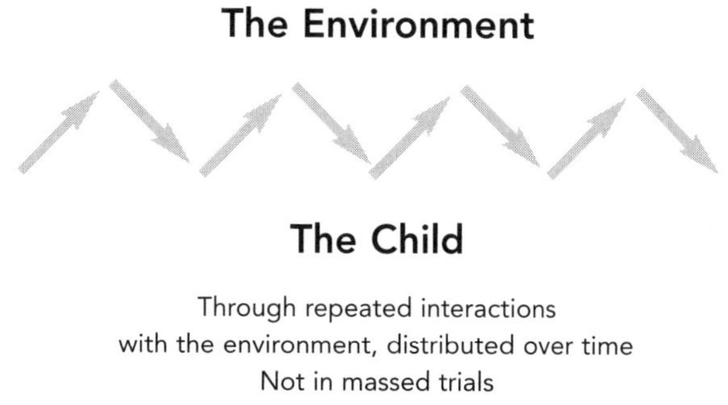

The Environment

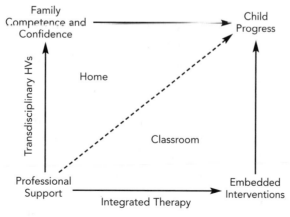

The Child

Through repeated interactions
with the environment, distributed over time
Not in massed trials

Figure 10.2. How children learn.

Figure 10.4 shows that home visits are aimed at the family. These visits might be 1 or 2 weeks apart (preferably 1 week); between them, there are family–child interactions and other learning opportunities. Those interactions and learning opportunities are what produce child learning. Therefore, the focus of the visits should be to support families in making the most of their routines.

The Need for Support-Based Home Visits

Although home visiting is one of the least studied aspects of early intervention, a number of luminaries in the field have provided guidance through their writings: Mary Beth Bruder (Bruder & Dunst, 2006), Pip Campbell (Campbell & Sawyer, 2009), Carl Dunst and Carol Trivette (Dunst et al., 2002); Rich Roberts (Roberts, Wasik, Casto, & Ramey, 1991), Jerry Mahoney and Cordelia Robinson (Mahoney, Robinson, & Powell, 1992), M'Lisa Shelden and Dathan Rush (Rush, Shelden, & Hanft, 2003), and Juliann Woods (Kashinath, Woods, & Goldstein, 2006). Their work has influenced the model described here.

What's Wrong with Dumping a Clinic-Based Model on the Living-Room Floor?

The traditional practice of working directly with children must be based on an assumption that children can learn significantly from weekly direct, hands-on intervention from

Figure 10.3. Routines-based model for children whose services are either in the home or a classroom. (Key: HVs, home visits.)

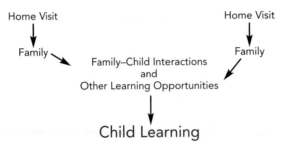

Figure 10.4.   Children learn between home visits.

a professional (Childress, 2004). Otherwise, why would those professionals ask about increasing family involvement in the home visit? What happens is that families see the professional providing therapy or instruction to the child, so some of them do other things or otherwise convey that they are leaving the professional to get on with the job. The message families are getting, therefore, is that the child is benefiting from interaction with the home visitor. This is misleading information.

What's Wrong with the Toy Bag?

The toy bag has been the icon of the early intervention home visitor. It typically contains toys considered good for children's cognitive and fine motor development. It might also contain straws, bubbles, and other materials a speech-language pathologist might believe useful. Toy bag users tend to spend most of the visit in direct interaction with the child, playing with one toy or another. Sometimes the parent is drawn into the interaction, moving it from dyadic to triadic. Typically, the toys are put back in the bag at the end of the visit and taken away. It has been useful to point to the toy bag as a symbol of what's wrong with many home visits. In actuality, the toy bag itself might not be so evil, but it stands for a misguided approach to home visiting. Here are the problems:

1. When the home visitor engages in prolonged interactions with the child and the toys, it can lead parents to believe that the direct, hands-on work is what is helping the child. Parents will tell people, "She comes and teaches [my child]." This strengthens a false belief in families—that it's the home visit that leads to improvements in child functioning, when, in fact it's what happens between visits that leads to improvements.

2. The toys are either nonfunctional or redundant. If the family does not have the exact same toys and the toys are taken away at the end of the visit, the family cannot work on the same skills, rendering the toys nonfunctional. If the family has the same toys, why bring in a parallel set?

3. Bringing in toys implies that what the family has isn't good enough. Sometimes, early interventionists who don't want to give up their toy bag will talk about families who have "literally nothing" to play with. Apart from the fact that that statement is rarely true and is usually a reflection of the early interventionist's reluctance, the solution is to leave toys, not take them into the home and then leave with them.

4. Spending so much time on toy bag activities does not match the learning opportunities children actually have during the day (Dunst et al., 2001). Put another way, children do not spend a large percentage of the time playing with toys. Many other

caregiving and play occasions happen. In the short time home visitors have with families, why would they spend such a disproportionate amount of it on toy play with the child?

Getting rid of the toy bag has turned out to be a very difficult challenge for home visitors, and many of us have likened it to an addiction, especially when trying to deal with withdrawal (see http://naturalenvironments.blogspot.com). If you take away toy bags, you have to replace them with something. Enter the **Vanderbilt Home Visit Script (VHVS).**

Vanderbilt Home Visit Script

Not just the methadone treatment for toy bag addiction, the VHVS (see Appendix 10.1) helps the home visitor stay on track. It is based, however, on an assumption that the child and family have functional outcomes/goals the family has put in priority order. As you will see, the meat of the VHVS is the discussion of how things are going with the outcomes. The VHVS is essentially seven questions, but Question 3 provides the opportunity to lead to much sophisticated partnership with the family. Here are the questions:

1. How have things been going?
2. Do you have anything new you want to ask me about?
3. How have things been going with each IFSP outcome, in priority order?
4. Is there a time of day that's not going well for you?
5. How is [family member] doing?
6. Have you had any appointments in the past week? Any coming up?
7. Do you have enough or too much to do with [your child]?

The following section describes **behavioral consultation** in home visits—what can happen as a result of the seemingly simple question, "How have things been going with [Outcome 1]?"

Behavioral Consultation

In this model of behavioral consultation (see Figure 10.5), different paths can lead from the three possible answers to the question about how things are going with a given child outcome/goal.

Not Much Improvement

If the parent says the child is still not doing the behavior on the outcome/goal, get a detailed description to find out just what the child is doing. Two options then present themselves. One is to ask for a demonstration of child functioning, if necessary—in other words, if the parent's description did not provide a clear enough report. Either listening to the description or watching the child leads to making recommendations in a method I call **ask-to-suggest**.

Ask-to-suggest involves asking the family questions about what they have tried, leading to a suggestion. It follows adult learning principles in acknowledging the

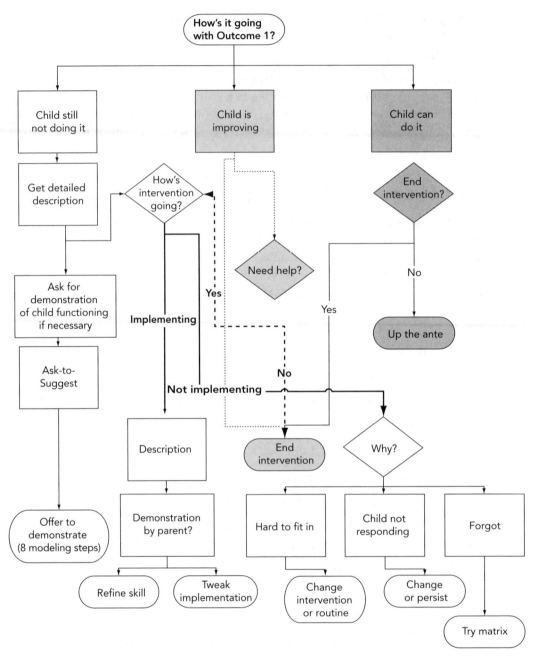

Figure 10.5. Behavioral consultation in home visits.

learner's experience before going straight into recommendations (Knowles, 1978). Once a suggestion has been made, the home visitor can offer to demonstrate how to carry out the recommendation. For example, if the mother was working on the child's moving independently from the bedroom to the kitchen, such as by crawling, and she says the child still is not moving independently, the home visitor asks for a description of what is happening. The mother says the child sits at the bedroom doorway and does not move. The home visitor says, "Can I see what you're talking about?" The mother takes the child to the bedroom doorway, puts him on the floor, and tries to coax the child to move down the hallway. The home visitor says, "Have you tried making a game out of this, like racing with him or pretending like you're animals?"

The parent says, "You mean me getting on the floor with him?"

"Well, yes. Would you like me to show you?"

"Go for it," says the parent.

The home visitor gets on hands and knees and says to the child, who she knows likes the family dog. "Look, Cherise, let's be Snoopy." And she heads off down the hallway. With any luck, the child follows. If not, the home visitor and the parent decide whether the parent will keep trying the technique through the week or they will discuss another technique. The home visitor explains that this technique is just to get the behavior started and that, as the child's rate of displaying the behavior increases, the demonstration prompt for the child will be faded to a verbal prompt.

After hearing the detailed description from the family about what the child is doing with regard to the skill, the home visitor can ask how the intervention is going—how helpful the previous techniques the family and home visitor came up with have been. If the family says they were implementing the techniques, the home visitor should ask them to describe what they were doing and how the child responded. He or she can ask the family if they would like to demonstrate what was happening. If the family does show implementation of the technique with the child, the home visitor and family can change the expectation for the skill. That is, they can aim for a different "topography" of the behavior. The home visitor can also suggest an adjustment to the technique—how the family is implementing the intervention.

For example, Rolanda is working on teaching her daughter Gigi to use her fingers to make toys work (fine motor control during small-toy play), but she says Gigi still isn't using her fingers. The home visitor asks Rolanda how the suggestion of modeling the use of the toys for Gigi was working out. Rolanda said she was showing Gigi what to do, as had been discussed at the previous home visit. The home visitor says, "Do you mind showing me how Gigi does, after you've shown her?"

Rolanda gets a couple of toys and says, "Gigi, look!" She pushes buttons on a toy cell phone and then hands it to Gigi, who puts the phone to her ear but doesn't push the buttons.

The home visitor says, "Who are you talking to, Gigi?"

Gigi doesn't respond.

"Grandma? You need to push the buttons first! Rolanda, why don't you take the phone, dial, and, while you're doing it, say, 'Mash the buttons to call Grandma'?" (We're assuming this is in rural North Carolina, where *mash the buttons* is the vernacular phrase.)

Rolanda takes the phone, does as the home visitor suggests, and hands the phone back to Gigi, saying again, "Mash the buttons to call Grandma."

Gigi pushes the buttons, while the home visitor and Rolanda clap for her and say, "Yay! You're calling Grandma. Say, 'Hi, Grandma!'" Note that they upped the ante, prompting another behavior in the play sequence. What the home visitor did was to suggest an adjustment to the technique the mother had been using.

Back to the question of how the intervention was going: If the family says they were not implementing the technique, the home visitor finds out why. Perhaps it was hard to fit in, in which case the home visitor discusses changing the intervention to something easier to fit in or changing the routine in which the intervention was to be carried out. For example, if the intervention was giving the child hand-over-hand assistance in pulling up pants at dressing time, and the parent said they were in too much of a hurry, the home visitor could discuss using the intervention after toileting.

Perhaps the family was not implementing the intervention because the child didn't respond to the intervention. The home visitor and the family then discuss whether to change the intervention or keep trying. Sometimes, especially with persistently difficult behavior—and I'm not just talking about compliance; it might be a persistent difficulty in learning a skill—the family gives up too early. The child might need to learn the consequence the family is imposing; that is, it might take many trials, distributed over time, for the child to "catch on." For example, if a family is working on teaching a child to engage in back-and-forth games during hanging-out times, they might tell the home visitor they haven't tried the pausing intervention the home visitor had suggested. This was where the parent and child would fully assist the child with no delays to roll a ball back and forth and then pause, waiting for the child to indicate he wanted the ball. The father says the child just loses interest and looks or even moves away, so he had stopped playing the game with the pause in it. The home visitor and the father talked about whether a different intervention might be better or whether the father wanted to resume trying the intervention, giving it more time. The father chose to resume it, saying he probably hadn't given it enough of a chance.

A third reason a family might not have implemented an intervention is that they forgot. One helpful way to remind the family of interventions is to develop a Routines × Outcomes matrix. In the cells, the home visitor can simply put Xs to indicate those routines that the family had picked as the ones where the behavior was needed. Or the home visitor can write a shorthand name for the intervention (e.g., "pause") in the cells (e.g., the Hanging Out × Back and Forth cell). All these options were just in response to the family's saying the child was still not doing the target behavior.

Getting Better

If the parent says the child is improving on the target behavior, the home visitor can get a detailed description, just for assessment—to know how the child is doing the skill. Another option is to ask the family if they need help with continuing to work on the skill. If the family says no, nothing else is needed during this visit on this outcome. If the family says yes, the home visitor can ask for a demonstration of the child's functioning, and the paths described above would ensue. The home visitor can also, as before, check on how the intervention has been going, with all the subsequent paths from that point.

Fine

A third response might be that the child is doing fine—can now perform the skill. The home visitor discusses with the family whether to end the intervention. If the family decides that yes, the outcome has been achieved, that's the end of it. If they say that no, they want to keep working on a more sophisticated level of the skill, the home visitor discusses with them what that upped ante might be. Technically, the outcome as originally written is achieved, and the family chose to have a new outcome: It's the same behavior but with different criteria. For accountability, it is better to document the first one as achieved rather than keep the outcome and just change the criteria.

Clearly, the question of how Outcome 1 is going is not a question with a simple consequence. Many opportunities to provide the family with information, which is a form of coaching, with demonstration with the child as necessary, occur. On some visits only one outcome can be dealt with, so the home visitor has to respect the family's original

---

Items from the FINESSE

The following items address the Home-Based Service Delivery Model:

1. **Multidisciplinary** home visits by two or more professionals: Professionals provide regular home visits and do not communicate with each other.

3. **Interdisciplinary** home visits by multiple professionals: Professionals provide regular home visits and exchange information occasionally.

5. **Modified transdisciplinary** home visits: A teacher or other "generalist" provides regular home visits and receives consultation from specialists.

7. **Pure transdisciplinary** home visits: Any professional team member provides regular home visits and receives consultation from other professionals.

The distinctions among these approaches are described in Section IV.

The following items address the Home Visitor's Primary Role:

1. To provide direct, hands-on instruction to the child, while the parent **might be doing other things.**

3. To provide direct, hands-on instruction to the child with the parent **present and attending.**

5. To **listen** to parent concerns and **model** for and **instruct** the parent.

7. To provide material, informational, and emotional **support** by talking with families.

This item is related to what has been described as a support-based approach to early intervention (McWilliam & Scott, 2001a).

---

priority order but needs to check with the family about what outcome or outcomes to work on in each home visit.

Support-Based Early Intervention

Home visits should be a vehicle for providing three kinds of support: emotional, material, and informational. These supports are similar to Guralnick's (1998) notion of how to provide early intervention from a developmental perspective.

Emotional Support

In a qualitative study of very supportive early intervention service providers, five key characteristics were identified (McWilliam, Tocci, & Harbin, 1998):

1. *Positiveness:* This is being positive about the child and the family. Early interventionists are generally overtly complimentary of children for their accomplishments, their sociability, or even their appearance. But they might be more reticent about complimenting adult members of the family.

2. *Responsiveness:* When families express needs, home visitors should be prepared to address those needs in some manner. Emotionally supportive early interventionists return calls and e-mails quickly.

3. *Orientation to the whole family:* It means a lot to families to have their home visitor acknowledge that the parents have a number of people in the family to deal with. When early interventionists show interest in other family members, parents sense they are not treating the home visits as just a job. Increasingly, it is becoming apparent that paying attention to the emotional well-being of the primary caregiver, who is often the mother, is a hallmark of emotional support (Barnett et al., 2003).

4. *Friendliness:* Treating families, interpersonally, the way one might treat a neighbor characterized emotionally supportive home visitors (McWilliam, Tocci, et al., 1998). This is contrasted with treating families strictly as clients. However kind and well-meaning professionals are, families can spot someone who is being professionally friendly and therefore only superficially caring.

5. *Sensitivity:* Home visitors need to put themselves in families' shoes. This is especially important in the kinds of suggestions given. If given a chance to talk about their routines, families often express frustration with certain times of the day, and the problem is that the child cannot occupy him- or herself while the parent attends to something. The home visitor who suggests the parent teach the child at that time would not be sensitive to what the parent is saying.

These five characteristics are not the only ways of being emotionally supportive, but they do provide a reasonable framework for how home visitors should approach families. It is equally important, however, to meet families' family-level needs. It is not enough to be nice and friendly to them or to attend only to child-level needs.

Material Support

Home visitors are in a unique position to observe and respond to families' needs for the material things that allow them to function.

1. *Basic necessities:* If families do not have enough food, if their housing is unsafe, or if they cannot afford any more diapers, they are hardly going to be in a position to engage in developmentally enhancing activities with their children (Maslow, 1948, 1958). Home visitors need to be prepared to handle emergency situations when they come across needs such as these. They need to be prepared to spend the home visit seeking solutions to the problem with the family. This might necessitate calling the service coordinator, calling informal supports of the family's, or calling agencies that help families in dire straits.

2. *Financial resources:* Families in early intervention sometimes have access to financial support by virtue of the child's disability (e.g., supplemental security income) or their income level (e.g., temporary assistance to needy families). The home visitor should ensure that the service coordinator, if that is a different person, has explored all these resources.

3. *Equipment:* To function well, a family might need specialized equipment for the child, such as a communication device, splints, supported seating, and so forth. The home visitor should ensure the family has any needed equipment. At the same time, he or she should not obtain equipment willy-nilly. This model follows the principle that there's nothing a bolster can do that a good pair of sturdy thighs can't do just as well!

Informational

When families are asked what more they want from their early intervention programs, they almost always say "information" (Bailey & Simeonsson, 1988). The four topics they most commonly want information about are the following:

1. The child's disability

2. Resources, including services

3. Child development, such as what's typical for their child's age and what can be expected next

4. What to do with the child

Assuming that what home visitors from any discipline do is largely give families information about what to do with their child, one hopes along with all the other support indicators mentioned here, it might be argued that therapy and special instruction in early intervention are the provision of support. *In fact, it is more accurate to describe early intervention as support to families than services to families.* Support, as described here, is more than just delivering a service—and delivering a service in the absence of a supportive approach would only be doing part of the job. Refer to the Support-Based Home Visiting Checklist in Appendix 10.2 for a guide to ensuring that principles of social support are used during a home visit.

Summary

Home visits in early intervention are for the purpose of providing multiple kinds of supports for families: emotional, material, and informational. They are not supposed to be just another location for a professional to work with the child. By giving families and other caregivers, such as teachers, information on what they can do with the child, home visitors acknowledge that those who spend hours with the child during the week are in the best position to provide interventions. The limited amount of time for home visits is best spent following adult-learning principles, being a consultant, coach, or guide. Problems with the toy-bag approach to home visits have been articulated. To provide home visitors with some structure, the VHVS is suggested. This script leads to opportunities for the home visitor to use behavioral consultation with child-level outcomes/goals, with three paths depending on whether the child is making progress, is not performing the skill at all, or has accomplished it.

Test on Home Visits

1. The purpose of visiting homes in early intervention is

    a. To educate mothers and monitor babies' progress

    b. To discuss problems or make home–school connections

    c. To assess the home environment

    d. To work directly with the children

    e. To support families

2. Very young children learn best through

    a. Concentrated lessons where the rate of interaction is high

    b. Repeated interactions distributed throughout the day

    c. Drill work with flash cards

    d. Listening to Mozart

3. Which of the following is true?

    a. Maximum service is most likely to produce child outcomes.

    b. Maximum intervention is most likely to produce child outcomes.

4. Which of the following is *not* true?

    a. Toy bags establish the agenda for the home visit.

    b. Toy bags can make families feel their toys and materials are inadequate.

    c. Toy bags suggest the way the child learns is by interactions with a professional.

    d. Toy bags are never made of canvas.

5. The Vanderbilt Home Visit Script (VHVS)

    a. Provides a general guide to home visits

    b. Is a home visit curriculum

    c. Provides all the questions and statements professionals should make, like standardized test items

    d. Describes a font for completing progress reports

6. When two professionals work with the same child, seeing the child on separate visits, they are practicing

    a. Multidisciplinary service delivery

    b. Interdisciplinary service delivery

    c. Modified transdisciplinary service delivery

    d. Pure transdisciplinary service delivery

7. The home visitor's primary role is

    a. To weigh the child and measure the child's head circumference

    b. To provide support to the family

    c. To work directly with the child

    d. To train the parent to be a good parent

8. When evaluating the child's and family's progress in meeting a given outcome/goal, which of the following is true?

    a. If the child has accomplished the outcome/goal, the outcome/goal is worked on no longer.

    b. If the child has made some progress, all the home visitor has to do is congratulate and encourage the family.

    c. If the child has made no progress, first the home visitor finds out why not.

    d. If the child has made no progress, the home visitor reminds the mother that it's her job to work with the child.

Appendixes

Appendix 10.1.   Vanderbilt Home Visit Script (VHVS)

Appendix 10.2.   Support-Based Home Visiting Checklist

APPENDIX 10.1 Vanderbilt Home Visit Script (VHVS)

Directions

The purpose of the Home Visit Script (VHVS) is to give home visitors in early intervention a structure for providing support-based home visits, attending to functional needs of families and the children in those families. It supports professionals in using an alternative to a hands-on, activity-based approach (i.e., "the toy bag approach") that implies that the visitor is directly helping the child's development. The script instead gives the home visitor a guide for talking to the family about the many dimensions of child and family life that are part of early intervention in natural environments.

The process is applicable for all disciplines—for professionals from all backgrounds who are providing comprehensive home visits. Such home visits are generally conducted by professionals serving in a primary service provider, primary coach, or transdisciplinary role. Professionals who make discipline-specific home visits (e.g., a physical therapist providing physical therapy only during home visits) might need to adapt the script. The script is very applicable for service coordinators.

Throughout the home visit, the home visitor should provide the following evidence-based emotional support (McWilliam, Tocci, & Harbin, 1998):

- *Positiveness:* Be positive about the child and other family members.
- *Responsiveness:* Respond to the family's overt or covert requests.
- *Orientation to the whole family:* Show interest in other family members, especially the well-being of the primary caregiver.
- *Friendliness:* Treat the family as you would treat neighbors.
- *Sensitivity:* Walk in the family's shoes.

At any time in the home visit, it is likely to be appropriate to stop and provide information about how to do something with the child (in the context of discussing regular routines, of course), as prompted in the script.

Script Overview

1. How have things been going?
2. Do you have anything new you want to ask me about?
3. How have things been going with each IFSP outcome, in priority order?
4. Is there a time of day that's not going well for you?
5. How is [family member] doing?
6. Have you had any appointments in the past week? Any coming up?
7. Do you have enough or too much to do with [your child]?

General Well-Being

How Have Things Been Going?

The opening question is open ended to give the family an opportunity to set the agenda for the visit.

Follow-Up Prompts

1. The 4 *E*s: Ears (listen), Elicit (ask), Empathize, Encourage
2. Do you need any information to help with this?
3. Should we try to solve this?
4. Would you like me to show you?

Notes

(continued)

page 2 of 5

APPENDIX 10.1 **Vanderbilt Home Visit Script (VHVS)** *(continued)*

New Questions or Concerns

Do You Have Anything New You Want to Ask Me About?

This question is a little more specific, giving the family an opportunity to think about new issues, skills, problems, and so on.

Follow-Up Prompts

1. The 4 *Es*: Ears (listen), Elicit (ask), Empathize, Encourage

2. Do you need any information to help with this?

3. Should we try to solve this?

4. Would you like me to show you?

Notes

Outcomes in Priority Order

The outcomes should be functional needs the family has identified. This is best accomplished through some form of routines-based assessment, such as the Routines-Based Interview (McWilliam, 1992), instead of or in addition to developmental assessment. This type of assessment tends to result in 6–12 quite specific, functional child and family outcomes. It is helpful to have families put their outcomes in priority order. Child outcomes are always discussed in the context of routines.

How Have Things Been Going with [Priority No. 1]?

Discuss this in the context of routines.

Follow-Up Prompts

1. The 4 *Es*: Ears (listen), Elicit (ask), Empathize, Encourage

2. Do you need any information to help with this?

3. Should we try to solve this?

4. Would you like me to show you?

Notes

How Have Things Been Going with [Priority No. 2]?

Discuss this in the context of routines.

Follow-Up Prompts

1. The 4 *Es*: Ears (listen), Elicit (ask), Empathize, Encourage

2. Do you need any information to help with this?

3. Should we try to solve this?

4. Would you like me to show you?

Notes

(continued)

APPENDIX 10.1 Vanderbilt Home Visit Script (VHVS) *(continued)*

How Have Things Been Going with [Priority No. 3]?

Discuss this in the context of routines.

Follow-Up Prompts

1. The 4 *E*s: Ears (listen), Elicit (ask), Empathize, Encourage

2. Do you need any information to help with this?

3. Should we try to solve this?

4. Would you like me to show you?

Notes

How Have Things Been Going with [Priority No. 4]?

Discuss this in the context of routines.

Follow-Up Prompts

1. The 4 *E*s: Ears (listen), Elicit (ask), Empathize, Encourage

2. Do you need any information to help with this?

3. Should we try to solve this?

4. Would you like me to show you?

Notes

How Have Things Been Going with [Priority No. 5]?

Discuss this in the context of routines.

Follow-Up Prompts

1. The 4 *E*s: Ears (listen), Elicit (ask), Empathize, Encourage

2. Do you need any information to help with this?

3. Should we try to solve this?

4. Would you like me to show you?

Notes

How Have Things Been Going with [Priority No. 6]?

Discuss this in the context of routines.

Follow-Up Prompts

1. The 4 *E*s: Ears (listen), Elicit (ask), Empathize, Encourage

2. Do you need any information to help with this?

3. Should we try to solve this?

4. Would you like me to show you?

Notes

(continued)

APPENDIX 10.1 Vanderbilt Home Visit Script (VHVS) *(continued)*

How Have Things Been Going with [Priority No. 7]?

Discuss this in the context of routines.

Follow-Up Prompts

1. The 4 *Es*: Ears (listen), Elicit (ask), Empathize, Encourage

2. Do you need any information to help with this?

3. Should we try to solve this?

4. Would you like me to show you?

> Notes

How Have Things Been Going with [Priority No. 8]?

Discuss this in the context of routines.

Follow-Up Prompts

1. The 4 *Es*: Ears (listen), Elicit (ask), Empathize, Encourage

2. Do you need any information to help with this?

3. Should we try to solve this?

4. Would you like me to show you?

> Notes

Problematic Routines

Is There a Time of Day that's Not Going Well for You?

This question provides the family an opportunity to discuss a routine that continues to be or has become unsatisfactory.

Follow-Up Prompts

1. The 4 *Es*: Ears (listen), Elicit (ask), Empathize, Encourage

2. Do you need any information to help with this?

3. Should we try to solve this?

4. Would you like me to show you?

> Notes

Other Family Members

How Is [Family Member] Doing?

This question reinforces to the family that you understand that the child lives in the context of a whole family.

Follow-Up Prompts

1. The 4 *Es*: Ears (listen), Elicit (ask), Empathize, Encourage

2. Do you need any information to help with this?

3. Should we try to solve this?

4. Would you like me to show you?

> Notes

(continued)

APPENDIX 10.1 Vanderbilt Home Visit Script (VHVS) *(continued)*

Appointments

Have You Had Any Appointments in the Past Week? Any Coming Up?

These questions help the family organize the information they receive from other professionals and questions they might want to ask other professionals.

Follow-Up Prompts

1. The 4 *Es*: Ears (listen), Elicit (ask), Empathize, Encourage

2. Do you need any information to help with this?

3. Should we try to solve this?

4. Would you like me to show you?

Notes

Work Load Related to Intervention

Do You Have Enough or Too Much to Do with [Your Child]?

This question demonstrates your sensitivity and responsiveness.

Follow-Up Prompts

1. The 4 *Es*: Ears (listen), Elicit (ask), Empathize, Encourage

2. Do you need any information to help with this?

3. Should we try to solve this?

4. Would you like me to show you?

Notes

APPENDIX 10.2 Support-Based Home Visiting Checklist

Home visitor _____ Date _____

Observer _____

Use this checklist as a self-check or for observation by a peer, supervisor, or trainer.

Mark as correct (+), incorrect (–), almost, (±), or not applicable or observed (NA).

Did the home visitor	+ – ±	Notes
Emotional support		
1. Make positive statements about the child?		
2. Make positive statements about the adult family members?		
3. Respond to the family's overt or covert requests?		
4. Show concern for family members other than the target child (see also 21)?		
5. Treat the family in a friendly manner, as one would treat a neighbor?		
6. Demonstrate sensitivity to the family's situation?		
The visit		
7. When appropriate, provide information about how to do something with the child?		
8. Provide information about what to do with the child in the context of discussing regular routines?		
9. Consistently listen to the family?		
10. Consistently ask questions (rather than just provide information)?		
11. Consistently empathize?		
12. Consistently encourage the family?		
13. Appropriately offer information to help with a concern?		
14. Appropriately ask whether the concern needed solving (e.g., "Should we try to solve this?")?		
15. Appropriately offer to show the family a technique (instead of not showing or showing without asking)?		

(continued)

APPENDIX 10.2 Support-Based Home Visiting Checklist (continued)

Did the home visitor	+ − ±	Notes
The script		
16. Ask an open-ended opening question to give the family an opportunity to set the agenda for the visit (e.g., "How have things been going?")?		
17. Ask the family whether they have anything new they want to discuss?		
18. Ask the family how things have been going with each of the outcomes or goals on the individualized plan?		
19. Ask the family about outcomes or goals in the family's priority order of importance?		
20. If time, ask the family if there is a time of day that's not going well for them?		
21. If time, ask about family members other than the child (see also 4)?		
22. If time, ask about any appointments since the previous visit or before the next visit?		
23. If time, ask whether the family has enough or too much to do with the child?		
Behavioral consultation		
24. If the child is still not doing the target skill, get a detailed description of what he or she is doing?		
25. Ask how the intervention is going?		
26. Ask for a demonstration of child functioning, if necessary?		
27. Use the ask-to-suggest procedure?		
28. If the family reported implementing the intervention but the child is still not doing the target task, ask for a description of what they have been doing?		
29. Ask the family if they would like to show what they have been doing with the child?		
30. Refine the skill or tweak implementation?		

(continued)

From McWilliam, R.A. (2010a). Support-based home visiting. In R.A. McWilliam (Ed.), *Working with families of young children with special needs* (pp. 27–59). New York: Guilford Press; adapted by permission.

In *Routines-Based Early Intervention: Supporting Young Children and Their Families* by R.A. McWilliam (2010, Paul H. Brookes Publishing Co., Inc.)

APPENDIX 10.2 **Support-Based Home Visiting Checklist** *(continued)*

Did the home visitor	+ − ±	Notes
31. If the family reported not implementing the intervention, ask why, politely?		
32. If the intervention was hard to fit in, change the intervention or the routine?		
33. If the family was not implementing the intervention because the child was not responding, ask the family if they wanted to change the intervention or persist?		
34. If the family forgot to implement the intervention, try an Outcome/Goal X Routine matrix?		
35. If the child is improving in doing the target skill, ask whether the family needs help?		
36. If the child is improving and the family does not need help, end the intervention?		
37. If the child can do the target skill, ask the family if they want to end the intervention?		
38. If the family does not want to end the intervention, up the ante for the child?		

Collaborative Consultation to Child Care

In March 2004, the Administration on Developmental Disabilities and the Administration on Children, Youth, and Families convened a forum on inclusion. Veterans from the disability side were startled that some of the participants treated the information as new. There was much discussion about the need to train child care workers so inclusion could work, but it's also important to ensure that the specialists going into those child care programs are trained to provide good consultation. When they are trained, they in turn can provide training to early childhood educators in the course of delivering itinerant special education or related services. Then, *therapy = training*. As federal officials worry about how to fund training, they should not forget that an infrastructure exists within Part C and Section 619 services.

Some participants, however, pointed out that in some places specialists were still not going to child care programs, but families were taking their children to clinic-based therapies. This is a systemic issue that I hope eventually gets remedied. The federal policy is there, with respect to natural environments and least restrictive environment, but enforcement and resources are lagging. This chapter explains how early intervention provided to children in community child care or in specialized classroom settings needs to be consistent with the consultative approach described in this book for home visits.

Settings

Home visitors often go to children's care settings. This chapter does not deal with family child care homes, such as informal arrangements or licensed family child care facilities. It deals with settings where larger groups are cared for: community child care, other community settings, and specialized programs.

Community Child Care

Community child care settings can include private child care or public child care. The staffing of these facilities is usually by people who have a high school diploma and some further training—sometimes an associate's degree, such as a child development associate credential. The class sizes range from as few as 4 infants to a room of up to more than 20. These settings either depend on a threshold number of children paying fees or exist to serve the most children on a limited public budget. Therefore, the quality of the programs varies, posing substantial challenges to the early interventionist who must consult in sometimes poor conditions.

Other Community Settings

Other community group settings the early interventionist might go to on a "home visit" are a mother's day-out program, a toddler book group, a moms-and-tots class, and so forth. Unfortunately, not enough home visitors manage to visit children's worship-location care programs (e.g., church nurseries, Sunday school). This chapter will concentrate on visiting programs that the child attends 15 hours a week or more—enough time to make a difference in the child's learning new skills.

Specialized Programs

Some children in early intervention attend programs specifically established to serve children with special needs, such as Early Head Start (for children living in poverty or with disabilities) and specialized centers, some of which are inclusive and some not. The practices described in this chapter pertain to any group setting that an early interventionist visits. In a specialized program where the child's teacher is a special educator, one would not ordinarily expect the child to receive special instruction aside from what that person provides. So, it might be argued that special instruction is already integrated into the ongoing routines. On the other hand, if the IFSP calls for the early interventionist to consult with the teacher, if the early interventionist is a "special instructor," such as an early childhood special educator, he or she does become a consultant from the outside—and the principles and practices described in this chapter become relevant. Furthermore, therapists visit children in classrooms in specialized programs, whether the teacher is a special education teacher or not. Therefore, integrated therapy is an issue in specialized programs as much as it is in community programs.

Consultation

Peter Drucker, the business guru, is reputed to have said, "My greatest strength as a consultant is to be ignorant and ask a few questions" (n.d.). This might summarize the point of collaborative consultation. An early interventionist is an expert in young children with disabilities. This expertise is augmented by training in a specific discipline, such as early childhood special education, occupational therapy, physical therapy, or speech-language pathology. There is no question of such a professional's expertise. One might think, therefore, that an expert-consultation approach would be appropriate (Graham, 1998). In such an approach, the consultant 1) decides what the problem is, 2) suggests what to do about the problem, and 3) evaluates whether the solution has worked. This kind of consultation is rampant in the medical field, where the tacit agreement by both professional and patient is that these responsibilities lie with the expert. When, however, the topic is not a consultee's health but another human being (a child) and the expertise is not as decontextualized as a medical condition (i.e., the environment is not the issue; the illness resides in the patient, regardless of environment), the expert model of consultation is not appropriate (Erchul, 1999; Pryzwansky & White, 1983; Reinking, Livesay, & Kohl, 1978; Tanner Jones, 1997).

Collaborative consultation, in contrast, involves joint decision making between the consultant and consultee on the problem, the solution, and the evaluation of the solution (Horne & Mathews, 2004; Rush, Shelden, & Hanft, 2003). In this model, early interventionists come with their expertise, but they have Drucker's philosophy. They are there to find out what's going on and to ask questions. In the course of that conversation, they will make suggestions, but always in the spirit of brainstorming with the teacher.

Collaborative consultation follows the principles of adult learning or *andragogy* (Knowles, 1978). These principles include the following (Brookfield, 1986; Knowles, 1977; Merriam, Caffarella, & Baumgartner, 2007).

- Adults are lifelong learners.

- Adults differ widely in their interests, abilities, and experiences.

- Adults' experiences are a resource in training.

- Adults move from dependence to independence as they become more competent and self-confident.

- Adults relate what they are learning to their life situations.

- Adults are motivated to learn by a variety of factors.

- Adults learn best by actively participating in the learning.

- Adults learn best in comfortable, supportive environments.

If early intervention consultation follows andragogical principles, the odds of caregivers' implementing the strategies are increased. Part of a consultant's task is to gain trust and credibility, and the social-task orientation of both the consultee and the consultant needs to be considered (see Figure 11.1).

Some teachers want to know about the consultant as a person, such as where he or she goes to church, where he or she grew up, and whether he or she has children, before they will listen to what the consultant has to say. If the early interventionist is similarly socially oriented, this match works well. Other teachers first want to know what the consultant knows and how useful he or she will be. If the early interventionist is similarly

Figure 11.1. Two characteristics of consultees and the approaches to take with them.

task oriented, the match is likely to work. If, however, the early interventionist is socially oriented and the teacher is task oriented, the early interventionist has to adjust.

Rules of Consultation

The following rules of consultation have been derived from research, experience, and adult learning theory.

Work in the Classroom (Don't Pull the Child Out)

To ensure the child has the opportunity for "wrap-around" learning, the teachers need to get suggestions from consultants, and consultants need to see what functional needs exist for the child and for the teaching staff. The best way for these needs to be met is for consultants to work in the classroom, rather than pulling children out to a therapy room.

Establish Ground Rules with the Teachers

To maximize the likelihood that everyone will be able to work collaboratively, teachers and consultants should talk about how they picture the therapist's time in the classroom. The consultant might negotiate with the teacher on the following points, for example:

1. The teaching staff should pay attention to what the consultant is doing.
2. The teaching staff should stay in the classroom. This is not a time to take a break just because there's an extra pair of hands to keep the child–adult ratios legal.
3. Teachers should be prepared to change the specific activity if the therapist can't find a way to fit into the existing routine.
4. Teachers should be able to report on progress with each outcome (see Chapter 10).

    For their part, teachers might negotiate with the therapist on the following points:

1. If something is working with the child, make sure someone on the teaching staff is shown how to do it.
2. Work only on skills that are actually needed in everyday routines.
3. Allow other children to participate in the interactions the therapist has with the child.
4. Leave every session with concrete ideas or feedback for the teaching staff.

Respect Whose Turf You're On

The classroom belongs to the teacher, so the consultant should not interfere with the running of activities, unless this has been worked out with the teacher.

Aim to Make Routines More Successful for Teachers and the Child

To combat some teachers' fear that enrolling children with significant disabilities will overburden the teacher, consultants should have suggestions that result in more successful routines for the child and for the teacher. If it's successful for the child, by definition the child is engaged, independent, and interacting with others. If it's successful for the teacher, he or she will appreciate that the consultant's suggestions are not making extra work (i.e., are feasible) and are helpful.

Communicate During the Activity

The purpose of the consultant's being in the classroom is to model and provide suggestions to the teaching staff. Therefore, the consultant needs to state this as an expectation. The communication should be both about assessment (what is needed) and intervention (what is being done to address the need).

Position Yourself to Model and to Observe

The consultant should be constantly aware of the potential to be observed. Good modeling also means talking about the specifics of the intervention, so the teaching staff does not miss salient features of the intervention. Similarly, the consultant should be in a position to observe the teachers' interactions with children, to learn from them, and to give them feedback and suggestions.

Model Incidental Teaching

In the classroom, consultants can model incidental teaching. Because good incidental teaching looks playful, they might need to describe what they are doing: establishing something for the child to be interested in, following the child's interest, eliciting more sophisticated behavior, and ensuring there is a consequence for that behavior.

(Some readers might need a reminder that a *behavior* is any action by the child; it is not necessarily a "problem behavior." Similarly, a *consequence* can be a reinforcer—natural or artificial. A *reinforcer* is a contingent stimulus that results in an increase in the frequency, duration, rate, or intensity of the behavior. A consequence can also be corrective feedback and other things. The point is not to confuse neutral behavioral terms, as used here, with erroneous terminology.)

Aim for Child Engagement, Independence, and Social Relationships

Rather than aiming just for the little skills the consultant might have noticed are missing from the child's repertoire, the consultant should keep a focus on the bigger picture of the foundations of learning: engagement, independence, and social relationships (McWilliam, 2006). Whenever possible, when giving suggestions to teachers, consultants should specifically state how they will help engagement, independence, and social relationships.

Debrief Before Leaving

In the same way that a visitor should not leave someone's house without saying good-bye, consultants should have some contact with some member of the classroom staff before leaving. At whatever detail level is appropriate for the situation, they should review what was done that day, remind the staff what to do, and tell them what steps the consultant is going to take next (e.g., send information, look up information, make materials).

Make Friends with the Teachers

I found that classroom staff–consultant dyads that had stronger relationships carried out interventions suggested by the consultants more than did dyads that had weaker relationships (McWilliam, 1996). The value of establishing a personal relationship cannot be overstated.

Rapport Building

Consultants have all sorts of tricks for building rapport with teaching staff. The following are a few of the more successful tricks.

- *Sniff out poopy diapers.* If working in a classroom where children are in diapers, the wise consultant will eventually detect a diaper that needs changing. Offering to change the diaper and actually following through will earn a huge number of brownie points. Consultants who use this trick are to be treasured.

- *Clean up after an activity.* This is a fairly simple task a visitor to the classroom can offer to do. With any of these tricks, the consultant keeps in mind that these are not precedents being set; they are steps toward a goal of securing the teaching staff's alliance.

- *Distract a disruptive child.* As a temporary help to the staff, distracting a disruptive child is a good idea. But, ultimately, the consultant should help the staff figure out how to deal with the situation on their own.

- *Bring in something of personal interest to the teacher.* At workshops, I often ask consultants to think about teachers they work with and then to list one or two topics of personal interest to those teachers. Such topics might be a college team they support, grandchildren, a course they're taking, a hobby, something they collect, and so forth. It's amazing how often I come across a consultant who has no idea what the teacher he or she has chosen is interested in. That's the first step. The trick, then, is to bring in something free or cheap related to that interest, whether it be a clipping from the newspaper, a coupon, or a book to lend.

- *If meeting at lunch, bring lunch.* Consultants sometimes use teachers' lunchtimes to talk to them. If they make the suggestion, they should be prepared to take lunch for the teachers. Lunchtime is supposed to be their break.

Integrated Therapy and Special Education

A definition for *integrated specialized services* is when therapy and specialized instruction occur in the classroom with other children usually present, and in the context of ongoing routines and activities. The definition addresses the disciplines involved, the location, the presence of peers, and the classroom context. The context is especially important.

Serving children in group care settings can occur in six ways, although not all are effective (McWilliam, 1996):

1. *Individual pull-out:* The consultant takes the child from the classroom, works with him or her, returns the child to the classroom, and leaves. Sometimes, there is some communication, perhaps with the consultant trying to tell the teacher what went on in the isolated, artificial setting where the consultant worked with the child. The consultant has maximal control over the session in this model.

2. *Small-group pull-out:* Similar to the previous model, the consultant takes two or more children from the classroom to work with them. Small-group pull-out is sometimes used for efficiency's sake and sometime to provide the children with a peer during the session.

3. *One-on-one in classroom:* The consultant stays in the classroom, taking the child to the side to work on skills not necessarily having anything to do with the current activity. If they did, it would be the model called individualized within routines. One-on-one in classroom is sometimes known as pull-aside or push-aside therapy. Consultants using this approach have their own agenda; they are not concerned with what the teacher is doing at that time. Teaching staff are not expected to pay any attention to what the consultant is doing, because the purpose of this session is for the consultant to work with the child, not to have the consultant model for the teaching staff.

4. *Group activity:* The consultant interacts with the whole class or a group of the children, for the benefit of the child he or she came to see. What the consultant does might have been planned with the teacher or might be spontaneous, but it is consistent with what is going on in the classroom at that time. The teaching staff can see the techniques the consultant uses, because they are involved also. Examples are a physical therapist having all the children go through an obstacle course in the classroom or a speech-language pathologist interactively reading a book to a group of children. In both cases, the activity was designed to benefit a particular child, but the intervention is carried out in a group setting.

5. *Individualized within routines:* This model involves the consultant's joining the child in whatever the child is engaged in and weaving intervention into the child's activity. It does not interrupt the activity, and the teaching staff can see what the consultant is doing.

6. *Consultation only:* Sometimes, consultants merely observe, without interacting with the child, and give feedback to the teaching staff. To count as a therapy session, according to some systems, consultants have to have direct contact with the child, so consultation only might not be reimbursable.

The six models can be considered along a continuum from most segregated to most integrated. The most effective is individualized within routines, because the teaching staff can see how they can intervene in the context of their own activities. Furthermore, the consultant can see the demands of the routine and can help figure out how to make intervention work in that context.

The second most effective model is **group activity,** again because the teaching staff can see how they can help the child in the context of a regular activity. The difference between these two models is that in individualized within routines, the regular teaching staff are running the activity. In group activity, the consultant is running the activity.

There are almost no legitimate reasons to remove a child from a classroom. Those few reasons are not given here, however. Experience has taught me that if you give a pulling-out consultant some reasons for pull-out, he or she will find many ways to argue that those reasons apply to many children. Consultants who tend to use one model with some children tend to use it with all the children they serve. What can interfere with that pattern is the expectations or rules of a given site (McWilliam, 1996).

Research Findings

Some of the research findings reported in *Rethinking Pull-Out Services: A Professional Resource* (McWilliam, 1996) are summarized here.

- Individualized within routines was the most effective model, followed by group activity.

- Four times as much communication occurred in in-class methods versus out-of-class methods.

- It's not just a location issue. When children were taught similar tasks by the same person in the classroom and in a separate, pull-out room, no difference in the children's behavior was observed. The interventionist was a researcher, not a teacher of the child.

- In a study in which teachers had experience with both integrated and pull-out specialized services, they were more satisfied with integrated services. This was especially true when they liked the therapist.

- Parents were asked their preference for specialized services for their child—in class or pull-out. After 1 year of random assignment to one or the other, parents who were assigned to the condition they did not prefer had not changed their preference. After 2 or more years of integrated therapy, however, parents switched what they preferred from out of class to in class. It therefore can take parents over a year to acknowledge the benefits if they are predisposed to segregated models.

- Early childhood special education is the most integrated, followed by occupational therapy. In a national survey of ECSEs, OTs, PTs, and SLPs working with children younger than the age of 6 in classroom programs, the discipline of the respondent was the strongest predictor of their choice of models. ECSEs reported choosing in-class practices the most, followed by OTs. SLPs and PTs were the least likely.

- Most practitioners say that their choice of method depends on the child. In fact, after controlling for discipline, goals worked on, the family's choice of in versus out of class, and teacher characteristics, child characteristics accounted for only 10% of the variance in their decision making about which model to implement.

"Direct" versus "Consultative"

The integrated-services model is consultative, but in some systems, *consultative* means infrequent—sometimes ad hoc. In contrast, *direct* means frequent and scheduled. Because an integrated-services model is frequent and scheduled, it should be documented as direct. There will be some hands-on for demonstration and, anyway, it is the most effective method—so why should a consultant get reimbursed at a lower rate? The definitions of *direct* and *consultative* are problematic because they have been applied to intensity rather than model of service delivery.

Challenges

Although there is no question that individualized within routines is the most effective model, that does not mean it is always easy.

1. Developmentally inappropriate classrooms are challenging for implementing integrated services. Those that are too academic tend to be rigidly run with not enough play. Therefore, the activities are under the tight control of the teacher, and it is awk-

ward at best for a consultant to join the child. Those classrooms that are too "special ed" tend to have a high ratio of adults to children (meaning few children per adult), so yet another adult in the classroom can seem too many. Furthermore, in those classrooms children are often engaged in one-on-one or two-on-one highly structured activities or "work stations," so again the interactions are not fluid enough for a consultant to join the child.

2. Some parents do not trust the integrated-services model. Even when the math is explained to them, showing that children receive more intervention throughout the day, they have become such fanatics of one-on-one direct hands-on instruction or therapy that they do not want to give it up.

3. Some teachers do not, in fact, embed goals and strategies into their everyday teaching, which contributes to parents' mistrust of the model.

4. Some classroom teachers do not want consultants involved. They may react by saying, "Don't come at all" or "If you come, take the child out." In this situation, we can go in to the classroom but only to take out the "problem" child. Or perhaps those teachers' message is, "Go do your thing elsewhere." A third reaction might be, "Don't talk to me about classroom management." This is a killer because often reluctant teachers have bigger (i.e., classroom) problems that need to be solved before specific interventions with the child are likely to be tried.

5. Poor communication between consultants and teacher can occur for at least three reasons: a) the classroom activities when the consultant is in the classroom are not amenable to the consultant's help; b) classroom teachers won't talk during activities; or c) no planning time, when teachers and the consultant can sit down and talk, is available.

There are no quick fixes to these situations, but developing a good relationship with the teaching staff should be a very high priority. Some suggestions are listed above. For some teachers, the task-oriented ones, the consultant's credibility might be as important as his or her people skills. Therefore, consultants need to size up the teacher and, if necessary, have concrete, feasible suggestions to contribute to the joint planning. See the Consultation Checklist in Appendix 11.1 for more information.

Items from the FINESSE

The FINESSE has one relevant item: Group Care Consultation.

1. When consulting in classrooms, we use individual or small-group **pull-out**.

3. When consulting in classrooms, we use **1:1 in classroom**.

5. When consulting in classrooms, we use **group activities**.

7. When consulting in classrooms, we use **individualized activities within routines**.

Test on Collaborative Consultation

1. Natural environments typically include

    a. Rehabilitation hospital clinics

    b. Self-contained preschool classrooms in elementary schools

    c. Child care programs

    d. Ponds and streams

2. In this model, consultation means

    a. Checking in with children intermittently

    b. Giving advice, without seeing the child

    c. Pulling the child out of the classroom

    d. Increasing the knowledge and skills of adults

3. Which one of the following practices is not part of collaborative consultation

    a. Dictating what the teaching staff should do with the child

    b. Deciding with the teaching staff why the child needs help

    c. Deciding with the teaching staff what interventions to try

    d. Deciding with the teaching staff whether interventions have worked

4. Which one of the following is not a principle of adult learning?

    a. Adults relate what they are learning to their life situations.

    b. Adults are motivated to learn by money alone.

    c. Adults learn best by actively participating in the learning.

    d. Adults learn best in comfortable, supportive environments

5. If a classroom teacher is very sociable, consultants should

    a. Keep the teacher on task

    b. Put up barriers to let the teacher understand that therapy or instruction is serious business

    c. Get to know the teacher as a person before being too task oriented

    d. Report the teacher to the director

6. The most effective location for providing services to children in child care is

    a. A distraction-free room

    b. The hallway

    c. Wherever class activities take place

    d. A clinic in a hospital

7. While the consultant is in the room

   a. The teacher should do what the consultant wants

   b. The consultant should do what the teacher wants

   c. Neither the teacher nor the consultant should do anything

   d. The teacher and the consultant should establish ground rules for each other and them-selves

8. If collaborative consultation succeeds

   a. Routines (activities) should run more smoothly

   b. Routines will be harder to run

   c. Routines will cease to exist

   d. Routines will run more smoothly for the target child but not for anyone else

9. While the consultant is in the room, which of the following is not true?

   a. Teachers and the consultant should communicate with each other.

   b. The consultant should position him- or herself to observe and to demonstrate.

   c. The consultant should model discrete trials of decontextualized behaviors.

   d. The consultant should aim for engagement, independence, and social relationships.

10. Which of the following is not a trick for building rapport?

   a. Sniff out poopy diapers

   b. Clean up after an activity

   c. Make a disruptive child stay at the activity

   d. Bring in something of personal interest to the teacher

11. Joining a child in what he or she is already engaged in and weaving intervention into that engagement is called

   a. Pure consultation

   b. Group activity

   c. One-on-one in classroom

   d. Individualized within routines

12. Which of the following disciplines has the professionals reporting the most integrated serv-ices?

   a. Occupational therapy

   b. Physical therapy

   c. Early childhood special education

   d. Speech-language pathology

13. Time spent talking to a teacher, with the child present, should count as

    a.   Direct service

    b.   Indirect service

    c.   Consultative service

    d.   Administrative time

Appendix

Appendix 11.1. Consultation Checklist

APPENDIX 11.1 Consultation Checklist

Consultant _____ Observer _____

Use this checklist as a self-check or for observation by a peer, supervisor, or trainer.

Mark as correct (+), incorrect (–), almost, (±), or not applicable or observed (NA).

Did the consultant	Date	Date	Date	Date	Date
1. Establish ground rules with the teachers?					
2. Consult with the teacher about what is needed to address the child's individualized family service plan (IFSP) outcomes/goals (i.e., what the problems are)?					
3. Consult with the teacher about what intervention the teacher will implement?					
4. Consult with the teacher about how things were going with each outcome being addressed in the classroom?					
5. Use behavioral consultation by following procedures, differentially, for answers of *child still not doing it*, *child is improving*, or *child can now do it*?					
6. Use ask-to-suggest if the child is still not doing it?					
7. Offer to demonstrate, using the eight modeling steps, if necessary?					
8. Refine the skill or tweak the intervention if the teacher is implementing the intervention but the child still cannot perform the behavior satisfactorily?					
9. Change the intervention or the routine if the teacher found it hard to fit in an intervention?					
10. Discuss making changes to the program versus persisting with the intervention if the teacher was not implementing the intervention because of the child's lack of responsiveness to the program?					
11. Make a Goal X Routine classroom matrix if the teacher forgot to carry out the intervention?					
12. Treat the teacher like an adult learner (ask about his or her experiences, encourage the teacher to relate the suggestions to his or her life situation)?					
13. Match the teacher's social to task orientation?					
14. Work in the classroom?					
15. Demonstrate respect for the teacher's turf?					

(continued)

Did the consultant	Date	Date	Date	Date	Date
16. Make suggestions that should make routines more successful?					
17. Communicate during the activity?					
18. Position him- or herself to model and to observe?					
19. Model incidental teaching?					
20. Mention child engagement, independence, or social relationships?					
21. Give specific feedback to teachers?					
22. Debrief before leaving?					
Total Correct					
Total Possible (Items – NAs)					
Percentage Correct					

Effecting Change

The closing section describes implementation issues related to the model presented throughout this book. In the following chapter, I discuss systems, service coordination, personnel preparation, and evaluation. Effecting change in these areas and providing adequate means of measurement will yield successful outcomes for children and families participating in routines-based intervention.

CHAPTER 12

Implementing the Model

Systems, Service Coordination,
Personnel Preparation, and Evaluation

To make the transition to the approach described in this book, various systems have to be addressed. A *system* is defined, for this purpose, as an organized entity that has formal or informal impact on—in this case—early intervention service delivery. The four systems dealt with here are programs, communities, states, and professional associations.

Programs

Individual programs providing early intervention are sometimes point-of-entry offices (addressed as a community system in the next section), sometimes comprehensive early intervention programs, sometimes therapy or "rehab" agencies, and so forth. State programs are described in the States section. At the program level, this model of routines-based early intervention can be supported or undermined through policies, management, and in-service training.

On the premise that you can't expect someone to do something if he or she hasn't been told to, program-level policies can be put into place to support this approach. Examples include the following:

1. Do not use toy bags on home visits; instead, use the Vanderbilt Home Visit Script (VHVS) and behavioral consultation.

2. RBIs must be completed when developing IFSPs.

3. Only the PSP can make a home visit alone; otherwise, it must be a joint home visit.

4. Ecomaps must be developed before every initial IFSP and must be reviewed at every annual IFSP.

5. IFSPs must have 6–12 functional, family-centered, measurable outcomes/goals; any exceptions have to be discussed with the supervisor.

6. Data must be collected on child and family progress.

7. Do not use a pull-out approach when seeing a child in child care; instead, the individualized-within-routines approach must be used.

8. Hold no "staffings" without inviting the family; call them "team meetings."

9. Use evidence-based practices.

10. Write child-level outcomes/goals as participation-based goals.

The keys to successful management supporting this model are 1) systematic feedback; 2) strong team leadership skills; and 3) knowledge of early intervention, child development, and family functioning. Systematic feedback can be achieved with the use of the various checklists provided in this book (Realon, Lewallen, & Wheeler, 1983). The need for strong team leadership skills comes from the problem of different professionals on an individual IFSP team having different viewpoints, especially different philosophies about serving children. For example, if an early interventionist is trying to use a PSP approach and another person serving the child and family insists on seeing the family separately and at a high frequency, the service coordinator has to resolve this dispute when completing the frequency and intensity section of the service page. This is where a program manager might be needed to settle the conflict. Knowledge of early intervention is not only highly desirable in early intervention managers but also necessary. In particular, program administrators need to understand how children learn and how services work, so they don't simply assume that early intervention is about either the piling on of services or the denial of services. A well-informed, knowledgeable (and these are different characteristics) manager would support an incremental decision-making process that looked at the ecology of the whole team.

Professionals can receive training in their programs. Traditional in-service workshops with no follow-up are ineffective (Sexton, Snyder, Wolfe, & Lobman, 1996). Unfortunately, too few programs plan in-service as an ongoing, on-the-job activity (White & Kratochwill, 2005).

Communities

Communities—defined as cities, counties, or multicounty regions—have opportunities to help or hinder the application of the practices described here. They are almost always comprised of multiple agencies, which adds to the richness and challenge of implementing the model.

In early intervention, the local programs mentioned above, plus others, band together through formal or informal agreements to meet the needs of early intervention families. An early intervention agency attempting to follow this routines-based approach probably needs to be explicit in its interagency agreements about what it does and does not do.

Many communities have local interagency coordinating committees (LICCs). In Nashville, Tennessee, the FINESSE (described later) was used by the services committee of the LICC to assess typical practices in the district and then to prioritize what to change. LICCs can be characterized as being at different developmental stages (Harbin, Ringwalt,

& Batista, 1998). The FINESSE can be used to propel the LICC to a more mature stage, at least in terms of implementing routines-based interventions across agencies.

In many communities, the single point of entry (SPOE) is the hub of early intervention. This is where referrals to early intervention are made and where eligibility is determined, followed by IFSP development. The SPOE therefore has the opportunity to state how they do business, such as following the IFSP development guidelines presented here. Providers who then implement the IFSP come to learn why families are the primary decision makers, outcomes/goals are participation and context based, and services are not based on diagnosis but on need.

States

Federal law leaves many implementation details to states. Special considerations at the state level are the type of payment system for early intervention, the role of the State Interagency Coordinating Council, policies, and leadership.

One of the most distressing movements in early intervention since the 1980s has been the proliferation of the fee-for-service system to pay for the program. The reasons for this proliferation are known but beyond the scope of this book. Anyway, it's a bit like asking how sausages are made: It's better not to know. The essence of this approach to paying for early intervention is that the state will pay for some things with their federal funds and have third parties pay for ongoing services. In some states, these ongoing services include service coordination. In others, the state pays for service coordination. In this approach, Medicaid and insurance companies are billed for therapies, sometimes special instruction, and sometimes targeted case management. This 1) lulled people into thinking that funding was not an issue and 2) led to an unpleasant fighting among providers to get the business. A fallout was also that pressure has been applied to service coordinators to send the business the way of certain providers. Some states responded to this with a couple of crazy reactions. First, an unhealthy obsession over the predetermination of services has effectively prevented service providers from being involved in assessing needs, leaving this to service coordinators. When service coordinators are only service coordinators (i.e., they are "dedicated" service coordinators), they often do not have intervention or child development knowledge; they are essentially professional case managers (McWilliam, 2006b). For them therefore to be responsible—without the assistance of early interventionists—for assessing needs, helping families select outcomes/goals, and planning services is expecting a lot. At the same time, it is understandable that, in a fee-for-service world, predetermination of services can be a problem.

The second response by states to the fear of predetermining services has been to let families choose their providers. This has been justified on the basis that it seems to be a family-centered practice. But really it is the state's way of avoiding accusations of unfair allocation of services to predatory professionals pimping their programs. So families look at these long lists of meaningless names and have to choose providers, usually with little information. After all, the service coordinator cannot direct families to particular services.

The solutions to these problems are multifaceted. At a large systemic level, states need to reconsider the whole financing structure for Part C services, including reassessing the number of services provided to families at a high frequency and intensity. If that is too big of a task, allowing the use of the "most likely service provider," as described in Section IV of this book, would prevent the service coordinator from having to develop initial IFSPs without the help of other professionals. Even more effective would be the use of PSPs, so the professional helping the service coordinator with initial IFSPs would be a "most likely *primary* service provider."

In some states, the ICC plays a strong role in Part C policy development and implementation. According to IDEA, these bodies are appointed by governors to assist and advise the Part C lead agency. They are interagency and include families. They can be vehicles for supporting innovative approaches, but not surprisingly, in some states they are toothless, rubber-stamping bodies. It depends on how the lead agencies and governors' offices have established them.

Individual leadership at the state level is demonstrated over and over to be a catalyst for high-quality early intervention. States such as Colorado, Connecticut, Georgia, Kentucky, Massachusetts, Minnesota, Missouri, Nevada, New Mexico, Tennessee, and Texas have benefited at one time or another from strong, innovative leaders. Unfortunately, it appears the effects of good, strong leadership are not maintained past the tenure of the leader in question, unless an equally strong leader is the replacement. This list of states is probably not the entire list of states to have benefited from strong leadership, but they are states that have had exemplary policies and management.

Professional Associations

The professional associations representing the major disciplines in early intervention, early childhood special education, occupational therapy, physical therapy, and speech-language pathology can help or hinder the use of innovative approaches.

The DEC of the CEC represents all professions working in early intervention and early childhood special education, but, because the therapists also have their discipline-specific associations, it can be considered the major association for the providers of special instruction, as it is known in Part C. Unlike the allied-health professions, DEC is not involved in licensure or accreditation of training programs. It has, however, established recommended practices in the field (McLean, Snyder, Smith, & Sandall, 2002; Rapport, McWilliam, & Smith, 2004; Smith et al., 2002) and publishes the scholarly journal with the largest circulation in the field, the *Journal of Early Intervention*.

The American Occupational Therapy Association, the American Physical Therapy Association, and the American Speech-Hearing-Language Association provide guidance to their respective professionals, and all have adopted guidelines for working with young children and their families. Although they do promote best practices, I believe that they also exist to protect the interests of their members, which means they have objected to approaches interpreted as decreasing the business of their members. This routines-based approach has been criticized for compromising the livelihood of therapists. Nevertheless, it has not actually prevented implementation of the model, to my knowledge, because in reality there is more demand for therapy services, even with this model, than can be met with the existing workforce. There have been gluts of some therapists in some parts of the country for some age groups of children, but, in general, the demand exceeds the supply.

In collaboration with the national associations are sometimes state associations. When these professional associations apply their considerable professional knowledge to the mission of providing good early intervention, they are powerful allies. Some key players in the national associations have been instrumental in shaping this model.

Service Coordination

IDEA ensures that states offer service coordination to every family eligible for early intervention. A service coordinator is charged with 1) shepherding the family through the process of IFSP development, 2) ensuring families have access to resources including services (although sometimes they forget to look beyond formal services), and 3) helping to coordinate services the family is receiving. Reference has already been made to the dedicated service coordinator. This role has also been called the *individual model* (Bruder & Dunst, 2006). If the service coordinator is in the same agency as providers, it is known as a *within-agency model.* If the service coordinator is also a provider for the same families for which he or she is a service coordinator, it is known as the *combined model.*

The most integrated of all methods is a combined model where the service coordinator/provider is the primary service provider, using a transdisciplinary approach. In this situation, the family is truly dealing with one main professional, and all the other team members are working in concert with that professional and the family. The disadvantage of this method is that the family might not have access to as much information as they should, if this main professional isn't aware of what further information should be provided to the family.

Personnel Preparation

The personnel preparation of early intervention professionals plays a significant role in the implementation of good or bad practices in the field. When a different way of thinking about working with families is presented to professionals, they often say the university programs need to be informed of these new-fangled ideas. To do them justice, however, university faculty will also say they present the students with current thinking about early intervention in natural environments but then students' field experiences or first jobs undo all that instruction. The situation might be different for allied health compared to education and psychology, and then doctoral training has its own issues.

Allied Health

In the training of OTs, PTs, and SLPs, home-based service delivery is barely addressed. In fact, in many early childhood special education training programs, this is true also. A much-needed improvement to the preservice training of early interventionists of all disciplines is effective home-based services, which should look radically different from clinic-based services. As mentioned throughout this book, it is not just a location issue. It is also a scope, role, and orientation issue. A second area of major need is how to work with children in classroom programs, from child care to Early Head Start. Effective consultation with classroom staff requires much skill beyond doing therapy with the child. Finally, university faculty need to shift from traditional definitions of intensity, which treated consultation as an infrequent model considerably less effective than direct services. All "direct" services in early intervention should be consultative, in the sense of exchanging skills and knowledge with adults. Furthermore, monitoring traditionally was also considered an infrequent, watered-down level of service. The highly skilled therapist who makes joint home visits every 3 months (on what some would call a monitoring schedule) can be a highly effective therapist, giving parents and a primary service provider the information needed for the parents to teach their child every day. The current terminology related to intensity is misleading.

Education and Psychology

Personnel preparation in the fields of education and psychology could help with the implementation of this type of approach by focusing on how young children learn, on consultation skills, and again on training in home-based services. A challenge in the last of these foci is supervision during training. Whereas it is relatively simple to have supervision from the cooperating teacher and from a university person when a student is doing a practicum or student teaching in a classroom, the logistics of supervision on home visits are often too challenging for universities to organize.

Doctoral Training

The leaders of the field of early intervention are trained in doctoral programs, so those programs can do much to enhance the implementation of a routines-based approach. First, doctoral students can be given a stronger foundation on research on learning opportunities in early childhood. This kind of research is fraught with challenges, which will either attract or repel doctoral-training faculty. Second, research on consultation needs to be done; students should be nudged into studying this key practice. Consultation is woven throughout early intervention, yet the research on how best to do this, for different kinds of outcomes, with different kinds of consultees has not been determined. Third, the importance of leadership in effecting change has already been made in this chapter. Doctoral programs are leadership programs, but sometimes the behaviors and strategies of leadership as a discipline are suppressed in favor of research and college teaching. We need people trained to be leaders.

Evaluation

Data help make and keep innovations. In our work on routines-based early intervention, we have developed a number of measures that can be used to determine the success of the approach and the quality of implementation. Many of these have been developed for program-planning or individual-improvement purposes and have not yet been determined to produce scores with acceptable reliability or validity. Readers using them should contact me to let me know how the measures perform. Checklists have been included in the appendixes of many chapters, and they should be used for training and for monitoring the fidelity of implementation of practices. When referring to any of these measures, please provide appropriate reference citations.

Program Measures

Five measures that might be particularly helpful for determining the quality of the program and therefore for identifying needs for training and supervision are the Families In

Natural Environments Scale of Service Evaluation (FINESSE); Goal Functionality Scale III; Examination of the Implementation of Embedded Intervention, through Observation (EIEIO); Vanderbilt Ecological Congruence of Teaching Opportunities in Routines (VECTOR), Classroom Version; and Practices for Instruction, Play, and Engagement Rating Scale (PIPERS).

The FINESSE (McWilliam, 2000a) is a 34-item, 7-point rating scale addressing 17 practices in early intervention. Two scaled items pertain to each practice. The first is a score of typical practice, and the second is a score of ideal practice. Each practice is defined with a score of 1 being a description of a practice not at all consistent with recommended practices in early intervention. A score of 7 is a practice highly consistent with such practices. Scores of 1, 3, and 5 are also defined, along this continuum of consistency with recommended practices. The instrument has been used in international studies of early intervention. In a Finnish study of 52 professionals, large differences were found between typical and ideal practices in all 17 items (Rantala, Uotinen, & McWilliam, 2009). A factor analysis conducted on the typical-practice scores with another data set revealed four underlying factors: first encounters, intervention planning, functionality, and service delivery (McWilliam, Rasmussen, & Snyder, 2007). Finally, the FINESSE was found to be sensitive enough to detect differences in scores from six countries (McWilliam & Er, 2003). A copy of the instrument is found in the appendix at the end of the book.

The Goal Functionality Scale III (McWilliam, 2009b) is designed to rate (*1* = not at all, *4* = very much) seven dimensions on each outcome/goal on a child's IFSP: participation, specificity, necessity, acquisition criterion, generalization criterion, meaningfulness, and time frame criterion. A copy is found in the appendix at the end of the book.

The EIEIO (McWilliam & Scott, 2001a) is used to look at how much embedding can be done with each child goal, how much embedding was done, and how appropriate the embedding was. Children are observed in 15-minute observations in each of eight classroom activities, thereby taking at least 2 hours to complete. As the directions state,

> Data can be used to (a) identify which goals should be targeted in particular routines, (b) determine the frequency with which goals are addressed, (c) determine which goals are most functional (those that are easily addressed within daily routines) and which goals need to be revised, and (d) plan for embedding instruction more effectively in future routines.

A copy is found in the appendix at the end of the book.

The VECTOR (Casey, Freund, & McWilliam, 2004) is completed by observing the child for at least 10 minutes during each activity. The frequency with which each routine provides opportunities for the environment and adults to promote engagement, independence, and peer interaction is rated from *rarely* to *most of the time*. Also, the extent to which the child takes advantage of these opportunities is similarly rated from *rarely* to *most of the time*. This instrument, found in the appendix at the end of the book, allows raters to determine which routines work well for the child and whether intervention should begin with teaching the child or modifying the environment.

The PIPERS (McWilliam, 2008) is 48-item discrepancy tool, like the FINESSE. Each of 24 practices is rated by a teacher on a typical-practice and an ideal-practice scale. The content is developmentally appropriate practice and practices from the Engagement Classroom model (McWilliam & Casey, 2008). It can be used to evaluate the quality of a classroom program including young children with disabilities and to plan staff development. A copy is found in the appendix at the end of the book.

Child Measures

Three child measures have been developed for use with this model. The first provides a profile of the child's functioning in routines, the second is used to rate engagement in classroom routines, and the third is a measure to rate child progress on IFSP outcomes/goals.

The Measure of Engagement, Independence, and Social Relationships (MEISR; McWilliam & Hornstein, 2007) has more than 200 items describing functional skills. It is organized by ordinary home routines. The purpose is to develop a profile of functioning in those routines by a child younger than the age of 6. It is completed by a caregiver who has observed the child in the home, such as a parent. Our intention in creating the MEISR was 1) to help families, as members of intervention teams, assess the child's competence in everyday situations, which might help families decide on intervention priorities; 2) to help professionals ask families relevant questions about child functioning in home routines; and 3) to monitor a child's progress. In fact, Naomi Younggren, the brilliant professional development coordinator for the U.S. Army's early intervention program, has reorganized the MEISR items by the three required federal child outcome domains, to help use the tool in completing the Child Outcomes Summary Form (SRI International, 2005). A companion tool, the Classroom Measure of Engagement, Independence, and Social Relationships (ClaMEISR; O'Kelley-Wingate & McWilliam, 2009) lists common skills in group-care routines. Because the MEISR is still being field tested, it is not reproduced here. Readers can obtain it by sending a message to research@siskin.org.

The Scale for Teachers' Assessment of Routines Engagement (STARE; McWilliam, 2000b) is a rating scale for measuring child engagement levels and interactions within the context of classroom routines. The focal child's behavior in terms of engagement is rated along two dimensions: frequency of being engaged with peers and adults, and materials and complexity. For each dimension, there is a scale from 1 to 5, with 1 being *Almost none of the time* or *Nonengaged* and 5 being *Almost all of the time* and *Sophisticated*. Descriptions for the level of complexity of child engagement are provided for each number scale. The focal child is observed for 10 minutes during a classroom routine. The information gained from the STARE is useful for intervention planning and monitoring. Specifically, it provides valuable information for deciding which routines the child seems to handle well and which ones are more problematic. This information is useful for preparing teachers to discuss classroom routines during the routines-based assessment. Teachers have been able to be trained to an acceptable level of interobserver agreement (Casey & McWilliam, 2007). A copy of the STARE is found in the appendix at the end of the book.

The Therapy Goals Information Form (TGIF; McWilliam, 1996; Special Services Research Project, 1993) was developed for describing how a particular child is progressing toward his or her outcomes. The outcomes for the child are listed, and there is a separate column for indicating the priority order of the outcomes. For each outcome, the rater checks the box on a scale from 1 to 5, rating the frequency with which the focal child performs the outcome and rating the level of independence when performing the outcome. The scale also lists an option of indicating *Doesn't apply* or *Don't know.* The TGIF can be completed by a child's teacher, his or her parent, or a specialist. Having ways for keeping track of children's progress toward IFSP or IEP goals is very important, and the TGIF is a quick and efficient way of recording progress relative to goal attainment in terms of frequency and independence. The TGIF can be completed at regular intervals, for instance, on a weekly or quarterly basis. It was used to study the effects of different models of providing therapy services (McWilliam, 1996). A copy is provided in the appendix at the end of the book.

Family Measures

Two family measures support this model: one is used to rate families' satisfaction with their home routines, and the other is used to rate their family quality of life.

The Satisfaction with Home Routines Evaluation (SHoRE) (McWilliam, 2005b) was developed to match the rating done during the RBI, in which the family is asked to rate their satisfaction with home routines on a scale of 1 to 5. The SHoRE is a summated rating scale that can be completed by families in the absence of an RBI. It provides an opportunity to rate 12 common home routines. A copy of this instrument is found in the appendix at the end of the book.

The Family Quality of Life–Autism Spectrum Disorder (FaQoL-ASD) (McWilliam & Hornstein, 2006) is the second in a series of family quality-of-life measures, with each version modified for a specific disability. The autism one is likely to have generality for many families, so it is included here. The instrument is divided into two sections: one consists of family-level concerns (e.g., the information our family has about resources, including services), and the other consists of child competence (e.g., our child's getting along with adults). It is both an expansion (in terms of the weight given to child competence) and a simplification (in terms of the reduced number of factors) of other family quality-of-life measures in early childhood (e.g., Turnbull, Poston, Minnes, & Summers, 2007). A copy is provided in the appendix at the end of the book.

Conclusion

This book describes an approach to early intervention that capitalizes on children's learning opportunities afforded them in their daily routines (Dunst, Bruder, Trivette, Raab, & McLean, 2001). It attempts to take the field back to the original intention of establishing a program for families, including the child, not a program for children with families as an offshoot (Workgroup on Principles and Practices in Natural Environments, 2007). Even before *natural environments* became the term for not segregating children and not making them endure an "abnormal" environment to receive services, the field wrestled with attention to the child's environment versus the family environment, when children were in group care. If children were in group care, such as a child care program, where should early interventionists go? The child care program? The home? And what was their role? To provide enhancements to what the regular caregivers were providing the child? In other words, to work directly with the child? Or was their role to enhance the capabilities of the caregivers?

These questions were only of interest to those who perceived that early intervention was about leaving the office and going to where children are. Other early interventionists were accustomed to children coming to them. The question of relevance to this book is whether they saw the children being transported in by parents, so children could receive instruction and therapy, or whether families were coming with their children, so families could receive support and information. Although I know of no data to substantiate this, it seems that by far the notion was that children were coming in to get "treatment." An issue that has persisted is the dosage issue as it intersects with the model of service delivery (Bailey, Aytch, Odom, Symons, & Wolery, 1999; McWilliam, 1999; Reed, Osborne, & Corness, 2007).

If the median amount of *service* planned is less than 2 hours a week, is this a travesty? The findings from the National Early Intervention Longitudinal Study (Hebbeler et al., 2007) also include the fact that, for 44% of the families, services focused only on the child. If the amount of contact time between a professional and a member of the family, child, or parent is small, the intervention would need to be "highly effective and 'potent' to bring about changes in outcomes for the child" (p. 3). This potency can be achieved by providing a family-level intervention during that time—an intervention that focuses on parenting. Professionals would need to provide emotional, material, and especially informational support to families (McWilliam & Scott, 2001b). If professionals have many hours of contact with the child every week, such as might be found in a full-time group-care program, they have the opportunity to be primary intervention agents for the child. They become caregivers—a label some preschool teachers abhor but should embrace. Care is not a bad thing.

A number of people come with a child: parents, siblings, grandparents, other extended family, the parents' friends, and neighbors. These are the informal supports that can be critical to the well-being of the family, including the child (Bronfenbrenner, 1977; Seligman, Rashid, & Parks, 2006). Add in formal supports, such as services, and intermediate supports, such as work and religious organizations, and a whole family ecology can be seen (Bronfenbrenner, 1986; Weisner, Matheson, Coots, & Bernheimer, 2005). In this approach to early intervention, the child is always viewed in the context of his or her family ecology. This perspective helps professionals see the existing resources families have, so the system does not needlessly and mindlessly pile on formal supports (McKnight, 1996). Developing *ecomaps* with families is the practice in this model that allows the professionals to understand families' ecologies.

Whether children are just at home or are also in group care, the logical division of a day for their caregivers is routines, defined in this model as chunks of the day or common activities. In this book, I have used routines as the hook on to which to hang what has been called the *five-component model for early intervention in natural environments.* Other scholars have noted the importance of routines as "ecocultural niches" (Bernheimer & Weisner, 2007; Weisner, 2002a, 2002b; Weisner et al., 2005) that can be assessed to determine child and family needs (Kristine Ovland & Marya, 2002) and can be the context for working on interventions with the family (Dunlap, Ester, Langhans, & Fox, 2006; Kashinath, Woods, & Goldstein, 2006; Lucyshyn et al., 2007; Woods & Wetherby, 2003). The practice that receives much attention is the RBI. Internet searches show the RBI appearing, in addition to my own, on sites for

- The Family-Guided Routines-Based Intervention (FGRBI) Model at Florida State University (Juliann Woods's project)

- The Birth-to-3 Wisline Training at the Wisconsin Department of Health Services

- First Steps at the Missouri Department of Elementary and Secondary Education

- The Virginia Department of Education and the Training and Technical Assistance Centers of Virginia

- The Kentucky Cabinet for Health and Family Services

- The Minnesota Area Special Education Cooperative

- The Special Education Department of the Minneapolis Public Schools

- Early Intervention Colorado

- Special Education at the State of Washington Office of the Superintendent of Public Instruction

- The Preschool Options Project at the Wisconsin Department of Public Instruction

- Functional Participation-Based IFSP/IEP Meetings at the Nebraska Department of Education

By focusing on routines as the context for much intervention, it allows the team to view the whole day, with all its many learning opportunities, as the "allocated learning time" (Berliner, 1990; Fisher et al., 1979). A major goal of early intervention is then to maximize engaged time, which is essentially the time within the allocated learning time that the child is interacting with the environment (adults, peers, materials) (McWilliam & Casey, 2008). Some specific components of engagement that are foundational to the model are independence and social relationships.

The RBI is designed to produce 6–12 early intervention goals. Some are child-level, some child-related family goals, and some family-level goals. To ensure the IFSP or IEP accurately reflects the need uncovered during the RBI yet also fits criteria for best practice in behavioral goals, I have developed steps for building participation-based child-level goals with multiple measurement criteria. Importantly, however, the other two types of goals, child-related family goals, and family-level goals are also an important part of the sizeable list of goals derived from the RBI. The list is a far cry from the ubiquitous 2–3 outcomes/goals found on most IFSPs. Because this long list is hard to address all at once, the family's priority order is critical.

Once outcomes/goals are selected, what services are needed? Despite the ubiquitous use of the term "needing services," the truth is that this is a judgment often made on the basis of the child's disability or on the basis of political forces—someone persuading the service coordinator that certain services are needed. The pile-on of services is doing families a disservice and bankrupting early intervention, as explained in the chapter on organizing services. The routines-based model described in this book emphasizes the use of a primary service provider as a method of using a transdisciplinary approach. This service delivery approach is probably the hardest practice in the model to put into place in programs and communities where the multidisciplinary approach is commonly used, but it has the potential to make a dramatic impact on families and the field. First, a family can have a true partner (or coach, or professional friend—whatever term seems most appropriate) as they make their way through the myriad events involved in early intervention: teaching the child, organizing routines to meet family needs, adjusting expectations, getting information, and ensuring all family needs are met. Second, the PSP becomes a well-rounded helpgiver, using his or her expertise and continually adding to it, rather than a narrow specialist who can do only a few things. Third, by taking a transdisciplinary approach, the system of early intervention uses the valuable resources—professionals—efficiently.

Just as early intervention professionals in this model need to be highly qualified, flexible, hard working, smart, and convivial, home visits (the most common setting for the delivery of early intervention; Hebbeler et al., 2007) need to be rich, varied, and purposeful. The three big elements of the home-visiting approach in this model are 1) attention to the long list of outcomes/goals that emerge from a routines-based assessment, 2) the use of behavioral consultation on child-level goals to ensure the family has the knowledge and skills to be week-long interventionists, and 3) a support approach so families get the emotional, material, and informational support to press forward with their family lives.

For many children receiving early intervention, child care is one of their natural environments, and the caregivers in those settings need to be supported because of the opportunity they have to teach the children. Support does not mean working one-on-one with the child in such a manner that the teaching staff have no idea what is going on and that the early interventionist is working on skills that might be irrelevant to the child care setting. This model incorporates the findings from our earlier research on *integrated therapy and special instruction*, putting specialists in the classroom, working with the teaching staff, demonstrating for them, trying out interventions with the child, and observing the teachers (McWilliam, 1996; McWilliam & Bailey, 1994; McWilliam & Young, 1996).

In this book, I have mapped out a set of practices that I have been refining since the 1980s, with the significant help of colleagues, mentors, staff, students, and consumer families. There are other ways to conduct early intervention. These five practices—constructing ecomaps, conducting RBIs and writing participation-based outcomes/goals, using primary service providers, using support-based home visits with behavioral consultation, and using collaborative consultation in child care—go together well. They are linked by a strong family-centered philosophy, a fixation on empirical roots, and complete commitment to families' and children's successful functioning at home, school, and in the community.

The routines-based approach to early intervention has the potential to act as a catalyst for change in systems, service coordination, and personnel preparation. A number of instruments have been developed to help measure the quality and impact of services. With change and measurement, children and families can thrive in routines-based early intervention.

References

American Psychiatric Association. (1994). *Diagnostic and Statistical Manual of Mental Disorders* (4th ed.). Washington, DC: Author.

Axtmann, A., & Dettwiler, A. (2005). *The Visit: Observation, reflection, synthesis for training and relationship building.* Baltimore: Paul H. Brookes Publishing Co.

Bailey, D.B. (1987). Collaborative goal setting with families: Resolving differences in values and priorities for services. *Topics in Early Childhood Special Education, 7,* 59–71.

Bailey, D.B., Jr. (2002). Are critical periods critical for early childhood education? The role of timing in early childhood pedagogy. *Early Childhood Research Quarterly, 17,* 281–294.

Bailey, D.B., Jr., Aytch, L.S., Odom, S.L., Symons, F., & Wolery, M. (1999). Early intervention as we know it. *Mental Retardation and Developmental Disabilities Research Reviews, 5,* 11–20.

Bailey, D.B., Jr., Bruder, M.-B., Hebbeler, K., Carta, J., Defosset, M., Greenwood, C., et al. (2006). Recommended outcomes for families of young children with disabilities. *Journal of Early Intervention, 28,* 227–251.

Bailey, D.B., Hebbeler, K., Scarborough, A., Spiker, D., & Mallik, S. (2004). First experience with early intervention: A national perspective. *Pediatrics, 113.*

Bailey, D.B., Jr., McWilliam, R.A., Buysse, V., & Wesley, P.-W. (1998). Inclusion in the context of competing values in early childhood education. *Early Childhood Research Quarterly, 13,* 27–47.

Bailey, D.B., McWilliam, R.A., Darkes, L.A., Hebbeler, K., Simeonsson, R.J., Spiker, D., et al. (1998). Family outcomes in early intervention: A framework for program evaluation and efficacy research. *Exceptional Children, 64,* 313–328.

Bailey, D.B., & Simeonsson, R.J. (1988). Assessing needs of families with handicapped infants. *The Journal of Special Education, 22,* 117–127.

Bairrão, J., & de Almeida, I.C. (2003). Questãões actuais em intervenção precoce. *Psicologia: Revista da Associação Portuguesa Psicologia, 17,* 15–29.

Barnett, D., Clements, M., Kaplan-Estrin, M., & Fialka, J. (2003). Building new dreams: Supporting parents' adaptation to their child with special needs. *Infants and Young Children, 16,* 184.

Bayley, N. (1993). *Bayley scales of infant development: Manual.* San Antonio, TX: Psychological Corporation.

Bennett, F.C. (2004). *Untitled.* Keynote address presented at the Tennessee Association for the Education of Young Children Conference, Nashville.

Berkeley, T.R., & Ludlow, B.L. (1992). Developmental domains: The mother of all interventions; or, the subterranean early development blues. *Topics in Early Childhood Special Education, 11,* 13–21.

Berliner, D.C. (1990). What's all the fuss about instructional time? In M. Ben-Peretz & R. Bromme (Eds.), *The nature of time in schools: Theoretical concepts, practitioner perceptions.* New York: Teachers College Press.

Bernheimer, L.P., & Weisner, T.S. (2007). "Let me just tell you what I do all day...": The family story at the center of intervention research and practice. *Infants and Young Children, 20,* 192–201.

Bess, F., Dodd-Murphy, J., & Parker, R.A. (1998). Children with minimal sensorineural hearing loss: Prevalence, educational performance, and functional status. *Ear & Hearing, 19,* 339–354.

Björck-Akesson, E., & Granlund, M. (1995). Family involvement in assessment and intervention: Perceptions of professionals and parents in Sweden. *Exceptional Children, 61,* 520–535.

Bronfenbrenner, U. (1977). Toward an experimental ecology of human development. *American Psychologist, 32,* 513–531.

Bronfenbrenner, U. (1979). Contexts of child rearing: Problems and prospects. *American Psychologist, 34,* 844–850.

Bronfenbrenner, U. (1986). Ecology of the family as a context for human development: Research perspectives. *Developmental Psychology, 22,* 723–742.

Brookfield, S.D. (1986). *Understanding and facilitating adult learning.* San Francisco: Jossey-Bass.

Bruder, M.B., & Dunst, C.J. (2006). Early intervention service coordination models and service coordination practices. *Journal of Early Intervention, 28,* 155–166.

Campbell, F.A., Ramey, C.T., Pungello, E., Sparling, J., & Miller-Johnson, S. (2002). Early childhood education: Young adult outcomes from the abecedarian project. *Applied Developmental Science, 6,* 42–57.

Campbell, P.H., & Sawyer, L. (2009). Changing early intervention providers? Home visiting skills through participation in professional development. *Topics in Early Childhood Special Education, 28,* 219–234.

Casey, A.M., Freund, P.J., & McWilliam, R.A. (2004). *Vanderbilt Ecological Congruence of Teaching Opportunities in Routines (VECTOR)—Classroom Version.* Nashville, TN: Vanderbilt Center for Child Development.

Casey, A.M., & McWilliam, R.A. (2005). Where is everybody? Organizing adults to promote child engagement. *Young Exceptional Children, 8,* 2–10.

Casey, A.M., & McWilliam, R.A. (2007). The stare: Data collection without the scare. *Young Exceptional Children, 11,* 2–15.

Childress, D.C. (2004). Special instruction and natural environments: Best practices in early intervention. *Infants & Young Children, 17,* 162–170.

Cole, K.N., Dale, P.S., & Mills, P.E. (1992). Stability of the intelligence quotient-language quotient relation: Is discrepancy modeling based on a myth? *American Journal on Mental Retardation, 97,* 131–143.

Cox, R.P., Keltner, N., & Hogan, B. (2003). Family assessment tools. In R.P. Cox (Ed.), *Health related counseling with families of diverse cultures: Family, health, and cultural competencies* (pp. 145–167). Westport, CT: Greenwood Press.

Davis A., & Hind, S. (1999). The impact of hearing impairment: A global health problem. *International Journal of Pediatric Otorhinolaryngology, 49,* S51–S54.

Doke, L.A., & Risley, T.R. (1972). The organization of day-care environments: Required vs. optional activities. *Journal of Applied Behavior Analysis, 5,* 405–420.

Drucker, P. (n.d.). *Peter Drucker quotes.* Retrieved December 30, 2009, from http://www.brainyquote.com/quotes/quotes/p/peterdruck154445.html

Dunlap, G., Ester, T., Langhans, S., & Fox, L. (2006). Functional communication training with toddlers in home environments. *Journal of Early Intervention, 28,* 81–96.

Dunst, C.J. (1985). Rethinking early intervention. *Analysis and Intervention in Developmental Disabilities, 5,* 165–201.

Dunst, C.J. (2000). Revisiting "Rethinking early intervention." *Topics in Early Childhood Special Education, 20,* 95–104.

Dunst, C.J., Boyd, K., Trivette, C.M., & Hamby, D.W. (2002). Family-oriented program models and professional helpgiving practices. *Family Relations: Interdisciplinary Journal of Applied Family Studies, 51,* 221–229.

Dunst, C.J., & Bruder, M.B. (2002). Valued outcomes of service coordination, early intervention, and natural environments. *Exceptional Children, 68,* 361–375.

Dunst, C.J., & Bruder, M.B. (2005). University faculty preparation of students in using natural environment practices with young children. *Psychological Reports, 96,* 239–242.

Dunst, C.J., & Bruder, M.B. (2006). Early intervention service coordination models and service coordinator practices. *Journal of Early Intervention, 28,* 155–165.

Dunst, C.J., Bruder, M.B., Trivette, C.M., Raab, M., & McLean, M. (2001). Natural learning opportunities for infants, toddlers, and preschoolers. *Young Exceptional Children, 4,* 18–25.

Dunst, C.J., Herter, S., & Shields, H. (2000). Interest-based natural learning opportunities. *Young Exceptional Children Monograph Series, 2,* 37–48.

Dunst, C.J., Trivette, C.M., Boyd, K., & Brookfield, J. (1994). Help-giving practices and the self-efficacy appraisals of parents. In C.J. Dunst, C.M. Trivette & A.G. Deal (Eds.), *Supporting and strengthening families: Methods, strategies, and practices* (Vol. 1, pp. 212–220). Cambridge, MA: Brookline Books.

Dunst, C.J., Trivette, C.M., & Deal, A.G. (1994). *Enabling and empowering families.* Cambridge, MA: Brookline Books.

Dunst, C.J., Trivette, C.M., & Thompson, R. (1990). Supporting and strengthening family functioning: Toward a congruence between principles and practice. *Prevention in Human Services, 9,* 19–43.

Education of the Handicapped Act Amendments of 1986, PL 99-457, 20 U.S.C. §§ 1400 *et seq.*

Edwards, J.K., & Bess, J.M. (1998). Developing effectiveness in the therapeutic use of self. *Clinical Social Work Journal, 26,* 89–105.

Erchul, W.P. (1999). Two steps forward, one step back: Collaboration in school-based consultation. *Journal of School Psychology, 37,* 191–203.

Field, T.M., Widmayer, S.M., Stringer, S., & Ignatoff, E. (1980). Teenage, lower-class, black mothers and their preterm infants: An intervention and developmental follow-up. *Child Development, 51,* 426–436.

Fisher, C.W., Berliner, D.C., Filby, N.N., Marliave, R., Cahen, L.S., Dishaur, M.M., & Moore, J.E. (1979). *Teaching and learning in elementary school: A summary of the beginning teacher evaluation study* (No. VIII-1). San Francisco: Far West Laboratory for Educational Research and Development.

Forgatch, M.S., & Toobert, D.J. (1979). A cost-effective parent training program for use with normal preschool children. *Journal of Pediatric Psychology, 4,* 129–145.

Gladwell, M. (2005). *Blink: The power of thinking without thinking.* New York: Little, Brown and Co.

Graham, D.S. (1998). Consultant effectiveness and treatment acceptability: An examination of consultee requests and consultant responses. *School Psychology Quarterly, 13,* 155–168.

Guralnick, M.J. (1998). Effectiveness of early intervention for vulnerable children: A developmental perspective. *American Journal on Mental Retardation, 102,* 319–345.

Guralnick, M.J. (1999). The nature and meaning of social integration for young children with mild developmental delays in inclusive settings. *Journal of Early Intervention, 22,* 70–86.

Haley, S.M., Ni, P., Coster, W.J., Black-Schaffer, R., Siebens, H., & Tao, W. (2006). Agreement in functional assessment: Graphic approaches to displaying respondent effects. *American Journal of Physical Medicine & Rehabilitation, 85,* 747–755.

Hall, G.E., & Loucks, S.F. (1977). A developmental model for determining whether the treatment is actually implemented. *American Educational Research Journal, 14,* 263–276.

Hanft, B., Rush, D.D., & Shelden, M.L. (2004). *Coaching families and colleagues in early childhood.* Baltimore: Paul H. Brookes Publishing Co.

Harbin, G.L. (2005). Designing an integrated point of access in the early intervention system. In M.J. Guralnick (Ed.), *The developmental systems approach to early intervention* (pp. 99–131). Baltimore: Paul H. Brookes Publishing Co.

Harbin, G.L., McWilliam, R.A., & Gallagher, J.J. (2000). Services for young children with disabilities and their families. In S.J. Meisels & J.P. Shonkoff (Eds.), *Handbook of early childhood intervention* (2nd ed., pp. 387–415). Cambridge, UK: Cambridge University Press.

Harbin, G., Ringwalt, S., & Batista, L. (1998). *Local interagency coordinating councils: Purpose, characteristics, and level of functioning. Early childhood research institute: Service utilization. Findings.* Chapel Hill: University of North Carolina.

Hartman, A. (1995). Diagrammatic assessment of family relationships. *Families in Society, 76,* 111–122.

Hebbeler, K., Spiker, D., Bailey, D.B., Scarborough, A.A., Mallik, S., Simeonsson, R.J., et al. (2007). *Early intervention for infants and toddlers with disabilities and their families: Participants, services, and outcomes.* Menlo Park, CA: SRI International.

Higgins, D.J., Bailey, S.R., & Pearce, J.C. (2005). Factors associated with functioning style and coping strategies of families with a child with an autism spectrum disorder. *Autism, 9,* 125–137.

Hoagwood, K.E. (2005). Family-based services in children's mental health: A research review and synthesis. *Journal of Child Psychology and Psychiatry, 46,* 690–713.

Horne, S.G., & Mathews, S.S. (2004). Collaborative consultation: International applications of a multicultural feminist approach. *Journal of Multicultural Counseling and Development, 32,* 366–378.

Hornstein, S., & McWilliam, R.A. (2007). *Measuring family quality of life in families with children with autism.* Paper presented at the 23rd Annual International Conference on Young Children (Division for Early Childhood of CEC), Niagara Falls, Ontario, Canada.

Individuals with Disabilities Education Improvement Act (IDEA) of 2004, PL 108-446, 20 U.S.C. §§ 1400 *et seq.*

Jackson, C.W., & Turnbull, A. (2004). Impact of deafness on family life: A review of the literature. *Topics in Early Childhood Special Education, 24,* 15–29.

Jiyeon, P., & Ann, P.T. (2003). Service integration in early intervention: Determining interpersonal and structural factors for its success. *Infants and Young Children, 16,* 48.

Jung, L.A., & Baird, S.M. (2003). Effects of service coordinator variables on individualized family service plans. *Journal of Early Intervention, 25,* 206–218.

Jung, L.A., & McWilliam, R.A. (2005). Reliability and validity of scores on the IFSP rating scale. *Journal of Early Intervention, 27,* 125–136.

Kaiser, A.P., & Hancock, T.B. (2003). Teaching parents new skills to support their young children's development. *Infants and Young Children, 16,* 9.

Kashinath, S., Woods, J., & Goldstein, H. (2006). Enhancing generalized teaching strategy use in daily routines by parents of children with autism. *Journal of Speech, Language, and Hearing Research, 49,* 466–485.

Knowles, M.S. (1977). Adult learning processes: Pedagogy and andragogy. *Religious Education, 72,* 202–211.

Knowles, M.S. (1978). *The adult learner: A neglected species* (2nd ed). Oxford, United Kingdom: Gulf Publishing.

Kristine Ovland, P., & Marya, M. (2002). The natural environment II: Uncovering deeper responsibilities within relationship-based services. *Infants and Young Children, 15,* 78.

Lattimore, J., Stephens, T.E., Favell, J.E., & Risley, T.R. (1984). Increasing direct care staff compliance to individualized physical therapy body positioning prescriptions: Prescriptive checklists. *Mental Retardation, 22,* 79–84.

Liaw, F.R., & Brooks-Gunn, J. (1993). Pattern of low birthweight children's cognitive development. *Developmental Psychology, 29,* 1024–1035.

Lord, C., & McGee, J.P. (2001). *Educating children with autism.* Washington, DC: National Academy Press.

Lucyshyn, J.M., Albin, R.W., Horner, R.H., Mann, J.C., Mann, J.A., & Wadsworth, G. (2007). Family implementation of positive behavior support for a child with autism: Longitudinal, single-case, experimental, and descriptive replication and extension. *Journal of Positive Behavior Interventions, 9,* 131–150.

Mahoney, G., Robinson, C., & Powell, A. (1992). Focusing on parent-child interaction: The bridge to developmentally appropriate practices. *Topics in Early Childhood Special Education, 12,* 105–120.

Maslow, A.H. (1948). "Higher" and "lower" needs. *Journal of Psychology: Interdisciplinary and Applied, 25,* 433–436.

Maslow, A.H. (1958). A dynamic theory of human motivation. *Psychological Review, 50,* 370–396.

McGee, G.G., Daly, T., Izeman, S.G., Mann, L.H., & Risley, T.R. (1991). Use of classroom materials to promote preschool engagement. *TEACHING Exceptional Children, 23,* 44–47.

McKnight, J. (1996). *The careless society: Community and its counterfeits.* New York: Basic Books.

McLean, M.E., Snyder, P., Smith, B.J., & Sandall, S.R. (2002). The DEC recommended practices in early intervention/early childhood special education: Social validation. *Journal of Early Intervention, 25,* 120–128.

McWilliam, R.A. (1992). *Family-centered intervention planning: A routines-based approach.* Tucson, AZ: Communication Skill Builders.

McWilliam, R.A. (Ed.). (1996). *Rethinking pull-out services in early intervention: A professional resource.* Baltimore: Paul H. Brookes Publishing Co.

McWilliam, R.A. (1999). Controversial practices: The need for a reacculturation of early intervention fields. *Topics in Early Childhood Special Education, 19,* 177–188.

McWilliam, R.A. (2000a). *Families in Natural Environments Scale of Service Evaluation (FINESSE).* Chapel Hill: University of North Carolina.

McWilliam, R.A. (2000b). *Scale for Teachers' Assessment of Routines Engagement (STARE).* Chapel Hill: University of North Carolina.

McWilliam, R.A. (2003). The primary-service-provider model for home- and community-based services. *Psicologia: Revista da Associação Portuguesa Psicologia, 17,* 115–135.

McWilliam, R.A. (2005a). *Family Quality of Life: Deaf and Hard of Hearing.* Nashville: Vanderbilt University Medical Center.

McWilliam, R.A. (2005b). *Satisfaction with Home Routines Evaluation (SHoRE).* Nashville: Vanderbilt Center for Child Development.

McWilliam, R.A. (2006a). *The three foundations for learning for children birth to 6 years of age.* Paper presented at the Associação Nacional de Interventcão Precoce, V Congreso Nacional de Interventcão Precoce, Aveiro, Portugal.

McWilliam, R.A. (2006b). What happened to service coordination? *Journal of Early Intervention, 28,* 166–168.

McWilliam, R.A. (2008). *Practices for Instruction, Play, and Engagement Rating Scale (PIPERS).* Chattanooga, TN: Siskin Children's Institute.

McWilliam, R.A. (2009a). *Protocol for the Routines-Based Interview.* Chattanooga, TN: Siskin Children's Institute.

McWilliam, R.A. (2009b). *Goal Functionality Scale III.* Chattanooga, TN: Siskin Children's Institute.

McWilliam, R.A. (2010a). Support-based home visiting. In R.A. McWilliam (Ed.), *Working with families of young children with special needs* (pp. 27–59). New York: Guilford Press.

McWilliam, R.A. (Ed.). (2010b). *Working with families of young children with special needs.* New York: Guilford Press.

McWilliam, R.A., & Bailey, Jr., D.B. (1994). Predictors of service-delivery models in center-based early intervention. *Exceptional Children, 61,* 56.

McWilliam, R.A., & Casey, A.M. (2008). *Engagement of every child in the preschool classroom.* Baltimore: Paul H. Brookes Publishing Co.

McWilliam, R.A., Casey, A.M., & Sims, J.L. (2009). The Routines-Based Interview: A method for assessing needs and developing IFSPs. *Infants & Young Children, 22,* 224–233.

McWilliam, R.A., & Er, M. (2003). *A model for using natural environments: International applications?* Paper presented at the International Society for Early Intervention, Rome, Italy.

McWilliam, R.A., Ferguson, A., Harbin, G.L., Porter, P., Munn, D., & Vandiviere, P. (1998). The family-centeredness of individualized family service plans. *Topics in Early Childhood Special Education, 18,* 69–82.

McWilliam, R.A., & Hornstein, S. (2006). *Family Quality of Life–Autism Spectrum Disorder (FaQol-ASD).* Nashville: Vanderbilt University.

McWilliam, R.A., & Hornstein, S. (2007). *Measure of Engagement, Independence, and Social Relationships (MEISR).* Nashville: Vanderbilt University.

McWilliam, R.A., McMillen, B.J., Sloper, K.M., & McMillen, J.S. (1997). Early education and child care program philosophy about families. In C.J. Dunst & M. Wolery (Eds.), *Family policy and practice in early child care* (Vol. 9, pp. 61–104). Greenwich, CT: JAI Press.

McWilliam, R.A., Rasmussen, J.L., & Snyder, P. (2007). *Principal components of a tool for measuring typical and ideal practices in early intervention.* Nashville, TN: Vanderbilt University.

McWilliam, R.A., & Scott, S. (2001a). A support approach to early intervention: A three-part framework. *Infants & Young Children, 13,* 55–66.

McWilliam, R.A., & Scott, S. (2001b). *Examination of the Implementation of Embedded Intervention, through Observation (EIEIO).* Chapel Hill: Frank Porter Graham Child Development Center, University of North Carolina.

McWilliam, R.A., Tocci, L., & Harbin, G.L. (1998). Family-centered services: Service providers' discourse and behavior. *Topics in Early Childhood Special Education, 18,* 206–221.

McWilliam, R.A., & Ware, W.B. (1994). The reliability of observations of young children's engagement: An application of generalizability theory. *Journal of Early Intervention, 18,* 34–47.

McWilliam, R.A., Young, H.J., & Harville, K. (1996). Therapy services in early intervention: Current status, barriers, and recommendations. *Topics in Early Childhood Special Education, 16,* 348–374.

Merriam, S.B., Caffarella, R.S., & Baumgartner, L.M. (2007). *Learning in adulthood: A comprehensive guide* (3rd ed.). San Francisco: Jossey-Bass.

Nebraska Department of Education—Department of Health and Human Resources. (n.d.). *Nebraska individualized family service plan.* Retrieved October 28, 2009, from http://www.nde.state.ne.us/edn/ifspform/ifsptable97.doc

Newborg, J. (2005). *Battelle Developmental Inventory, Second Edition.* Itasca, IL: Riverside.

NICHD Early Child Care Research Network. (2002). Parenting and family influences when children are in child care: Results from the NICHD study of early child care. In J. Borkowski, S. Ramey, & M. Bristol-Powers (Eds.), *Parenting and the child's world: Influences on intellectual, academic, and social-emotional development.* (pp. 99–123). Mahwah, NJ: Erlbaum.

Odom, S.L., Hanson, M.J., Lieber, J., Marquart, J., Sandall, S., Wolery, R., et al. (2001). The costs of preschool inclusion. *Topics in Early Childhood Special Education, 21,* 46.

Odom, S.L., Horn, E.M., Marquart, J.M., Hanson, M.J., Wolfberg, P., Beckman, P. et al. (1999). On the forms of inclusion: Organizational context and individualized service models. *Journal of Early Intervention, 22,* 185–199.

Odom, S.L., Vitztum, J., Wolery, R., Lieber, J., Sandall, S., Hanson, M.J., et al. (2004). Preschool inclusion in the United States: A review of research from an ecological systems perspective. *Journal of Research in Special Educational Needs, 4,* 17–49.

O'Kelley-Wingate, K., & McWilliam, R.A. (2009). *Classroom Measure of Engagement, Independence, and Social Relationships (ClaMEISR).* Chattanooga: University of Tennessee at Chattanooga and Siskin Children's Institute.

Palmer, F.B., Shapiro, B.K., Wachtel, R.C., Allen, M.C., Hiller, J.E., Harryman, S.E., et al. (1988). The effects of physical therapy on cerebral palsy. A controlled trial in infants with spastic diplegia. *New England Journal of Medicine, 318,* 803–808.

Parks, S., Furono, S., O'Reilly, K., Inatsuka, T., & Hosaka, C.M. (1997). *Hawaii Early Learning Profile.* Palo Alto, CA: VORT Corporation.

Peck, C.A. (1993). Ecological perspectives on implementation of integrated early childhood programs. In C. Peck, S. Odom, & D. Bricker (Eds.), *Integrating young children with disabilities into community programs: From research to implementation* (pp. 3–16). Baltimore: Paul H. Brookes Publishing Co.

Peterson, C.A., Luze, G.J., Eshbaugh, E.M., Jeon, H., & Kantz, K.R. (2007). Enhancing parent-child interactions through home visiting: Promising practice or unfulfilled promise? *Journal of Early Intervention, 29,* 119–140.

Pohlman, C., & McWilliam, R.A. (1999). Paper lion in a preschool classroom: Promoting social competence. *Early Childhood Education Journal, 27,* 87–94.

Porterfield, J.K., Herbert-Jackson, E., & Risley, T.R. (1976). Contingent observation: An effective and acceptable procedure for reducing disruptive behavior of young children in a group setting. *Journal of Applied Behavior Analysis, 9,* 55–64.

Poston, D.J., & Turnbull, A.P. (2004). Role of spirituality and religion in family quality of life for families of children with disabilities. *Education and Training in Developmental Disabilities, 39,* 95–108.

Powell, D., Fixsen, D., Dunlap, G., Smith, B., & Fox, L. (2007). A synthesis of knowledge relevant to pathways of service delivery for young children with or at risk of challenging behavior. *Journal of Early Intervention, 29,* 81–106.

Pretti-Frontczak, K., & Bricker, D. (2004). *An activity-based approach to early intervention* (3rd ed.). Baltimore: Paul H. Brookes Publishing Co.

Pryzwansky, W.B., & White, G.W. (1983). The influence of consultee characteristics on preferences for consultation approaches. *Professional Psychology: Research and Practice, 14,* 457–461.

Psychopathology Committee of the Group for the Advancement of Psychiatry. (2001). Reexamination of therapist self-disclosure. *Psychiatric Services, 52,* 1489–1493.

Purcell, T., & Rosemary, C.A. (2007). Differentiating instruction in the preschool classroom: Bridging emergent literacy instruction and developmentally appropriate practice. In L. Justice & C. Vukelich (Eds.), *Achieving excellence in preschool literacy instruction* (pp. 221–241). New York: Guilford Press.

Quilitch, H.R., & Risley, T.R. (1973). The effects of play materials on social play. *Journal of Applied Behavior Analysis, 6,* 573–578.

Raab, M., & Dunst, C.J. (2004). Early intervention practitioner approaches to natural environment interventions. *Journal of Early Intervention, 27*, 15–26.

Ramey, C.T., & Campbell, F.A. (1984). Preventive education for high-risk children: Cognitive consequences of the Carolina abecedarian project. *American Journal of Mental Deficiency, 88*, 515–523.

Rantala, A., Uotinen, S., & McWilliam, R.A. (2009). Providing early intervention within natural environments: A cross-cultural comparison. *Infants & Young Children, 22*, 119–131.

Rappaport, J. (1981). In praise of paradox: A social policy of empowerment over prevention. *American Journal of Community Psychology, 9*, 1–25.

Rapport, M.J.K., McWilliam, R.A., & Smith, B.J. (2004). Practices across disciplines in early intervention. *Infants & Young Children, 17*, 32–44.

Ray, R.A., & Street, A.F. (2005). Ecomapping: An innovative research tool for nurses. *Journal of Advanced Nursing, 50*, 545–552.

Realon, R.E., Lewallen, J.D., & Wheeler, A.J. (1983). Verbal feedback vs. verbal feedback plus praise: The effects on direct care staff's training behaviors. *Mental Retardation, 21*, 209–212.

Reed, P., Osborne, L.A., & Corness, M. (2007). Brief report: Relative effectiveness of different home-based behavioral approaches to early teaching intervention. *Journal of Autism and Developmental Disorders, 37*, 1815–1821.

Reinking, R.H., Livesay, G., & Kohl, M. (1978). The effects of consultation style on consultee productivity. *American Journal of Community Psychology, 6*, 283–290.

Ridgley, R., McWilliam, R.A., Snyder, P., & Davis, J. (2009, October). *Improving the quality of IFSPs by integrating supports within state Part C data systems.* Paper presented at the 25th Annual International Conference on Young Children with Special Needs and Their Families (Division for Early Childhood of CEC), Albuquerque, NM.

Roberts, R.N., Wasik, B.H., Casto, G., & Ramey, C.T. (1991). Family support in the home: Programs, policy, and social change. *American Psychologist, 46*, 131–137.

Rush, D.D., Shelden, M.L.L., & Hanft, B. (2003). Coaching families and colleagues: A process for collaboration in natural settings. *Infants & Young Children, 16*, 33–47.

Seligman, M.E.P., Rashid, T., & Parks, A.C. (2006). Positive psychotherapy. *American Psychologist, 61*, 774–788.

Sexton, D., Snyder, P., Lobman, M., & Daly, T. (2002). Comparing the developmentally appropriate practice (dap) beliefs of practitioners in general and special early childhood service settings. *Teacher Education and Special Education, 25*, 247–261.

Sexton, D., Snyder, P., Wolfe, B., & Lobman, M. (1996). Early intervention inservice training strategies: Perceptions and suggestions from the field. *Exceptional Children, 62*, 485–495.

Smith, B.J., Strain, P.S., Snyder, P., Sandall, S.R., McLean, M.E., Broudy-Ramsey, A., et al. (2002). DEC recommended practices: A review of 9 years of EI/ECSE research literature. *Journal of Early Intervention, 25*, 108–119.

Special Services Research Project. (1993). *Therapy goals information form.* Chapel Hill: Frank Porter Graham Child Development Center, University of North Carolina.

Squires, J., & Bricker, D. (2009). *Ages & Stages Questionnaires®, Third Edition (ASQ-3™): A parent-completed child-monitoring system.* Baltimore: Paul H. Brookes Publishing Co.

Squires, J., Bricker, D., & Potter, L. (1997). Revision of a parent-completed developmental screening tool: Ages and stages questionnaires. *Journal of Pediatric Psychology, 22*, 313–328.

Squires, J., Bricker, D., & Twombly, E. (2003). *Ages & Stages Questionnaires®: Social-Emotional (ASQ:SE): A parent-completed, child-monitoring system for social-emotional behaviors.* Baltimore: Paul H. Brookes Publishing Co.

Squires, J., Bricker, D., & Twombly, E. (2004). Parent-completed screening for social emotional problems in young children: The effects of risk/disability status and gender on performance. *Infant Mental Health Journal, 25*, 62–73.

SRI International. (2005). *Child outcomes summary form.* Retrieved June 25, 2009, from http://www.fpg.unc.edu/~eco/pages/outcomes.cfm.

Swick, K.J., Da Ros, D.A., & Kovach, B.A. (2001). Empowering parents and families through a caring inquiry approach. *Early Childhood Education Journal, 29*, 65–71.

Tanner Jones, L.A. (1997). Teacher preference for consultation model: A study of presenting problems and cognitive style. *Dissertation Abstracts International Section A: Humanities and Social Sciences, 58*, 20–90.

Tudor, K.P. (1977). An exploratory study of teacher attitude and behavior toward parent education and involvement. *Educational Research Quarterly, 2*, 22–28.

Turnbull, A.P., Poston, D.J., Minnes, P., & Summers, J.A. (2007). Focus on families: Providing supports and services that enhance a family's quality of life. In I. Brown & M. Percy (Eds.), *A comprehensive guide to intellectual and developmental disabilities* (pp. 561–571). Baltimore: Paul H. Brookes Publishing Co.

Turnbull, A.P., Summers, J., Turnbull, R., Brotherson, M.J., Winton, P., Roberts, R., et al. (2007). Family supports and services in early intervention: A bold vision. *Journal of Early Intervention, 29*, 187–206.

Twardosz, S., Cataldo, M.F., & Risley, T.R. (1974). Open environment design for infant and toddler day care. *Journal of Applied Behavior Analysis, 7*, 529–546.

Valentine, D.P. (1993). Children with special needs: Sources of support and stress for families. *Journal of Social Work and Human Sexuality, 8,* 107–121.

Wasik, B.H., & Bryant, D.M. (2001). *Home visiting: Procedures for helping families.* Thousand Oaks, CA: Sage Publications.

Weisner, T.S. (1996). Contextual approaches (not mere contextualizing) in human development. [Review of L. Winegar & J. Valsiner (Eds.), *Children's development within social context* (Vols. 1 & 2). Mahwah, NJ: Erlbaum.] *Contemporary Psychology, 41,* 1009–1010.

Weisner, T.S. (2002a). Ecocultural pathways, family values, and parenting. *Parenting: Science and Practice, 2,* 325–334.

Weisner, T.S. (2002b). Ecocultural understanding of children's developmental pathways. *Human Development, 45,* 275–281.

Weisner, T.S., Matheson, C., Coots, J., & Bernheimer, L.P. (2005). Sustainability of daily routines as a family outcome. In M.I. Martini & A.E. Maynard (Eds.), *Learning in cultural context: Family, peers, and school* (pp. 41–73). New York: Kluwer Academic.

White, J.L., & Kratochwill, T.R. (2005). Practice guidelines in school psychology: Issues and directions for evidence-based interventions in practice and training. *Journal of School Psychology, 43,* 99–115.

Widerstrom, A.H. (2005). *Achieving learning goals through play: Teaching young children with special needs* (2nd ed.). Baltimore: Paul H. Brookes Publishing Co.

Wilcox, M.J., & Shannon, M.S. (1996). Integrated early intervention practices in speech-language pathology. In R.A. McWilliam (Ed.), *Rethinking pull-out services in early intervention* (pp. 49–69). Baltimore: Paul H. Brookes Publishing Co.

Wilson, L.L., Mott, D.W., & Batman, D. (2004). The asset-based context matrix: A tool for assessing children's learning opportunities and participation in natural environments. *Topics in Early Childhood Special Education, 24,* 110–120.

Wolery, M. (1997). *Individualizing inclusion of young children with disabilities in child care: A model demonstration project.* Chapel Hill: University of North Carolina at Chapel Hill.

Wolery, M., Anthony, L., Caldwell, N.K., Snyder, E.D., & Morgante, J.D. (2002). Embedding and distributing constant time delay in circle time and transitions. *Topics in Early Childhood Special Education, 22,* 14–25.

Wolery, M., Welts, M.G., & Holcombe, A. (1994). Current practices with young children who have disabilities: Issues of placement, assessment, and instruction. *Focus Exceptional Children, 26,* 1–12.

Woodruff, G., & Shelton, T.L. (2006). The transdisciplinary approach to early intervention. In G.M. Foley & J.D. Hochman (Eds.), *Mental health in early intervention: Achieving unity in principles and practice* (pp. 81–110). Baltimore: Paul H. Brookes Publishing Co.

Woods, J., & Goldstein, H. (2003). When the toddler takes over: Changing challenging routines into conduits for communication. *Focus on Autism and Other Developmental Disabilities, 18,* 176–181.

Woods, J.J., & Lindeman, D.P. (2008). Gathering and giving information with families. *Infants & Young Children, 21,* 272–284.

Woods, J.J., & Wetherby, A.M. (2003). Early identification of and intervention for infants and toddlers who are at risk for autism spectrum disorder. *Language, Speech, and Hearing Services in Schools, 34,* 180–193.

Workgroup on Principles and Practices in Natural Environments. (2007). *Agreed-upon practices for providing early intervention services in natural environments.* Retrieved July 6, 2008, from http://www.nectac.org/~pdfs/topics/families/AgreedUponPractices_FinalDraft2_01_08.pdf.

World Health Organization. (2007). *International classification of functioning, disability and health: Children and youth version.* Geneva: Author.

Glossary

ask-to-suggest Asking the family questions about what they have tried, leading to a suggestion.

behavioral consultation A consultation with the parents based upon the question, "How are things going?" A systematic series of coaching behaviors depending on the family's answers—child is not progressing in this target behavior, child is making gradual progress, or child has met this outcome/goal.

collaborative consultation Joint decision making between the consultant and consultee on the problem, the solution, and the evaluation of the solution.

ecomap An illustrative "picture" of the nuclear family surrounded by members of the family's informal, formal, and intermediate supports. The links to those supports depict the level of support the drawer perceives.

engagement The amount of time children spend interacting with their environment (adults, peers, or materials) in a developmentally and contextually appropriate manner.

family concerns The concerns the family mentions during the Routines-Based Interview (RBI) about the child's or family's functioning,

the desire for the child or family to be doing something different, a potential intervention area the interviewer notices while the family member is talking, or any other problem the family mentions. Stars are placed next to family concerns on the interviewer's notes or on the RBI protocol. Family concerns are not listed anywhere and they are not outcomes.

family-level outcomes Individualized family service plan outcomes/goals aimed at something not directly related to the child's development that the parent will do.

formal support Government and private agencies and organizations paid to assist the family, including developmental, medical, and financial services.

functional outcomes/goals Goals that 1) reflect the priorities of the family, 2) are useful and meaningful, 3) reflect real-life situations, 4) are free of jargon, and 5) are measurable.

group activity The consultant interacts with the whole class or a group of the children for the benefit of the child he or she came to see. What the consultant does might have been planned with the teacher or might be spontaneous, but it is consistent with what is going on in the classroom at that time.

individualized family service plan (IFSP) criteria   The measures determining when the child or family has reached the goal.

individualized within routines   The consultant's joining the child in whatever the child is engaged in and weaving intervention into the child's activity. This does not interrupt the activity, and the teaching staff can see what the consultant is doing.

informal support   Generally, families, friends, and neighbors who are not paid to provide support.

intermediate support   Support for families that is neither informal nor formal, such as religious activities, recreation, and work.

intervention   Help the child receives, usually from regular caregivers (parents, teachers), to address an area of need.

joint home visit (JHVs)   A home visit made by the primary service provider (PSP) and a team member for the purpose of providing the team member's service through assessment, demonstration, and parent education.

natural environments   Settings in which children without disabilities participate, including the home and community settings (see Part C of the Individuals with Disabilities Education Improvement Act [IDEA] of 2004, 34 CFR §303.12(b)); "settings that are natural or normal for the child's age peers who have no disabilities" (Part C of IDEA 2004, 34 CFR §303.18).

participation-based outcome   An outcome/goal written with the child's participation in one or more routines first, followed by the specific behavior(s), and then the measurable criteria for acquisition, generalization, and maintenance.

primary service provider (PSP)   The main person having contact with the family on a transdisciplinary team, including supporting services provided through joint home visits as needed by other professionals.

routines   Naturally occurring activities happening with some regularity, including caregiving events and simply hanging-out times.

Routines-Based Interview (RBI)   A semistructured interview for gathering information about a child and family's daily activities and individualized family service plan or individualized education program priorities.

Routines-Based Interview (RBI) outcomes   Specific target behaviors or goals the family chooses at completion of the RBI, after the interviewer has reviewed ("recapped") the family concerns.

service   Help the family or other caregivers receive, usually from professionals (e.g., early interventionists, occupational therapists, physical therapists, speech-language pathologists), to address an area of need the child or family has.

social relationships   Children's communication and positive interactions (getting along) with others.

support-based home visits   Home visits providing emotional, material, and informational support, not direct hands-on instruction or therapy with the child for any reason other than demonstration to the family.

Vanderbilt Home Visit Script (VHVS)   An alternative to the toy bag, involving a guide for talking to the family about new events in the family's life, functional goals/outcomes, other family members, appointments with other professionals, and amount of suggestions.

Appendix
Blank Forms

Families In Natural Environments Scale of Service Evaluation (FINESSE)

Goal Functionality Scale III

Examination of the Implementation of Embedded Intervention, through Observation (EIEIO)

Vanderbilt Ecological Congruence of Teaching Opportunities in Routines (VECTOR), Classroom Version

Practices for Instruction, Play, and Engagement Rating Scale (PIPERS)

Scale for Teachers' Assessment of Routines Engagement (STARE)

Therapy Goals Information Form (TGIF)

Satisfaction with Home Routines Evaluation (SHoRE)

Family Quality of Life–Autism Spectrum Disorder (FaQoL-ASD)

Families In Natural Environments Scale of Service Evaluation (FINESSE)

Name _____   Date _____

Directions

This scale focuses on your program's typical and ideal practices in providing quality, family-centered services to children with special needs birth to 5 years old. The scale consists of 17 items that address various program components. Each item can be scored from 1 to 7. In rating each item, first read all of the descriptors. On the scale above the descriptors, circle the number that best represents your program's typical response. Then, on the scale below the descriptors, circle the number that represents where you would like your program to be (ideal) on this dimension. Use the even numbers if your program falls between the descriptors specified under the odd-numbered headings.

1. Written Program Descriptions (e.g., brochures, flyers)

Typical Practice

1	2	3	4	5	6	7
Written materials exclusively **describe** services for the child only, such as therapy and instruction.		Written materials **emphasize** services for the child only, such as therapy and instruction.		Written materials **mention** emotional, informational, and material support for families.		Written materials **emphasize** emotional, informational, and material support for families.

Ideal Practice

1	2	3	4	5	6	7

2. Initial Referral Call

Typical Practice

1	2	3	4	5	6	7
Person handling the initial referral call describes the program **solely** in terms of therapy and instruction for children.		Person handling the initial referral call describes the program **primarily** in terms of intervention for children.		Person handling the initial referral call describes the program primarily in terms of intervention for the child and **mentions** support to families.		Person handling the initial referral call describes the program **primarily** in terms of support to families.

Ideal Practice

1	2	3	4	5	6	7

(continued)

Routines-Based Early Intervention: Supporting Young Children and Their Families by R.A. McWilliam

3. Intake

Typical Practice

1	2	3	4	5	6	7
Intake consists **entirely** of a description of services, especially therapy and instruction for the child.		Intake consists **primarily** of a description of services, especially therapy and instruction for the child.		Intake consists primarily of a description of child intervention and includes **some** questions to find out what questions the family wants answered.		Intake consists **primarily** of questions to the family about what questions they would like answered and of questions to get to know the family.

Ideal Practice

1	2	3	4	5	6	7

4. Assessment for Intervention Planning

Typical Practice

1	2	3	4	5	6	7
Only **standardized instruments** that focus on traditional developmental domains are used for intervention planning.		**Curriculum-based instruments** that focus on traditional developmental domains are used for intervention planning.		Curriculum-based instruments and Routines-Based Interviews that focus on **both** traditional developmental domains and family functioning, child engagement, social relationships, and independence are used for intervention planning.		**Routines-Based Interviews** that focus on family functioning, child engagement, social relationships, and independence are used for intervention planning.

Ideal Practice

1	2	3	4	5	6	7

(continued)

5. Identifying Family Needs

Typical Practice

1	2	3	4	5	6	7
Professionals do **not** ask parents about their concerns and priorities.		Professionals **ask** parents about their concerns and priorities during IFSP meetings.		Professionals **occasionally** (e.g., twice yearly) have conversations with families about families' aspirations.		Professionals **regularly** (e.g., monthly) have conversations with families about families' aspirations.

Ideal Practice

1	2	3	4	5	6	7

6. Intervention Planning Meetings

Typical Practice

1	2	3	4	5	6	7
During IFSP/IEP meetings, professionals **primarily** discuss test scores and services offered by the program; parents listen.		During IFSP/IEP meetings, professionals **occasionally** discuss test scores; meeting focuses on child deficits and services; parents mostly listen.		During IFSP/IEP meetings, professionals **discuss child/family needs and functional intervention strategies;** parents are actively involved in discussion (not routines based).		During IFSP/IEP meetings, parents discuss routines, priorities, and concerns; professionals **ask questions and listen.**

Ideal Practice

1	2	3	4	5	6	7

(continued)

7. Outcome/Goal Selection

Typical Practice

1	2	3	4	5	6	7
Outcomes/goals are selected from **tests, curricula, and checklists**.		Outcomes/goals are selected from **professional recommendations**.		Outcomes/goals are selected from **family concerns** (not a Routines-Based Interview).		Outcomes/goals are selected from a **Routines-Based Interview**.

Ideal Practice

1	2	3	4	5	6	7

8. Family Outcomes/Goals

Typical Practice

1	2	3	4	5	6	7
Only **child** outcomes/goals are included in the IFSP/IEP.	Only **child-related family** outcomes/goals are included in the IFSP/IEP (along with child goals).		Family **involvement** outcomes/goals and child-related family goals are included in the IFSP/IEP (along with child goals).		Family goals **unrelated** to the child are included in the IFSP/IEP (along with child goals).

Ideal Practice

1	2	3	4	5	6	7

(continued)

9. Outcome/Goal Purpose

Typical Practice

1	2	3	4	5	6	7
Purpose for each outcome/goal is **not clear**.		Purpose for each outcome/goal is simply **overall improvement** in a general developmental or skill area (e.g., talking).		Purpose for each outcome/goal is stated **implicitly** (i.e., we can guess why we're working on it).		Purpose for each outcome/goal is stated **explicitly** (i.e., we know exactly why we're working on it).

Ideal Practice

1	2	3	4	5	6	7

10. Intervention Embeddedness

Typical Practice

1	2	3	4	5	6	7
Activities require **specific places or specialized equipment**.		Activities require the family to set aside **specific times** (not routines based).		Activities involve **significant** modification of existing routines.		Activities involve **minor** modifications of existing routines.

Ideal Practice

1	2	3	4	5	6	7

(continued)

11. Equipment

Typical Practice

1	2	3	4	5	6	7
Much specialized equipment, even when it s not necessary or effective for successful functioning in everyday routines, is usec.		**Some** specialized equipment, even when it is not necessary or effective for successful functioning in everyday routines, is used.		Some specialized equipment that is designed to **facilitate** future development and/or prevent future problems is used.		Only specialized equipment **necessary** for successful functioning in everyday routines is used.

Ideal Practice

1	2	3	4	5	6	7

12. Necessity of Target Behaviors

Typical Practice

1	2	3	4	5	6	7
Target behaviors only **indirectly related** to functioning in current routines are recommended.		Target behaviors with **some developmental benefit** are recommended.		Target behaviors **useful** for functioning in current routines are recommended; without the behaviors, the child can just manage but not very well.		Target behaviors **necessary** for functioning in current routines are recommended; until the behavior is accomplished, the child cannot function well in the routine(s).

Ideal Practice

1	2	3	4	5	6	7

(continued)

13. Intervention Philosophy

Typical Practice

1	2	3	4	5	6	7
Intervention philosophy is **providing** education and therapy to children.		Intervention philosophy is **training parents** to teach their child.		Intervention philosophy is training parents to teach their child **and to be advocates.**		Intervention philosophy is **supporting the family.**

Ideal Practice

1	2	3	4	5	6	7

14. Focus of Intervention

Typical Practice

1	2	3	4	5	6	7
Interventions and outcomes/goals are **discipline specific.**		Interventions and outcomes/goals are **domain specific.**		Interventions and outcomes/goals are context specific but are **not** routines based.		Interventions and outcomes/goals are **routines based.**

Ideal Practice

1	2	3	4	5	6	7

(continued)

15. Group Care Consultation

Typical Practice

1	2	3	4	5	6	7
When consulting in classrooms, we use individual or small-group **pull-out**.		When consulting in classrooms, we use **1:1 in classroom**.		When consulting in classrooms, we use **group activities**.		When consulting in classrooms, we use **individualized activities within routines**.

Ideal Practice

1	2	3	4	5	6	7

16. Home-Based Service Delivery Model

Typical Practice

1	2	3	4	5	6	7
Multidisciplinary by two or more professionals: Professionals provide regular home visits and do not communicate with each other.		**Interdisciplinary** home visits by multiple professionals: Professionals provide regular home visits and exchange information occasionally.		**Modified** transdisciplinary: A teacher or other "generalist" provides regular home visits and receives consultation from specialists.		**Pure** transdisciplinary: Any professional team member provides regular home visits and receives consultation from other professionals.

Ideal Practice

1	2	3	4	5	6	7

(continued)

17.   Home Visitor's Primary Role

Typical Practice

1	2	3	4	5	6	7
To provide direct, hands-on instruction to the child while the parent **might be doing other things**.				To **listen** to parent concerns and **model** for and **instruct** the parent.		To provide material, informational, and emotional **support** by talking with families.

Ideal Practice

1	2	3	4	5	6	7

Now look back over your responses. If there is generally a difference between your typical practices and what you consider to be ideal practices, what factors contribute to the discrepancy?

Goal Functionality Scale III

Child _____ IFSP date _____

District _____ Rater _____

Outcome 1

To what extent does the goal/outcome	Not at all	Somewhat	Much	Very much
1. Emphasize the child's *participation* in a routine (i.e., activity)? (*Child will participate in outside play time* not *child will participate in running*)	1	2	3	4
2. State specifically (i.e., in an observable and measurable manner) what the child will do?	1	2	3	4
3. Address a skill that is either *necessary or useful* for participation in home, "school," or community routines?	1	2	3	4
4. State an acquisition criterion (i.e., an indicator of when the child can do the skill)?	1	2	3	4
5. Have a **meaningful** acquisition criterion (i.e., one that shows improvement in *functional* behavior)? (*We will know he can do this when he holds a spoon for 2 minutes,* not *...when he holds a spoon on 5 out of 7 trials*)	1	2	3	4
6. Have a generalization criterion (i.e., using the skill across routines, people, places, materials, etc.)? (*...when he holds a spoon for 2 minutes at lunch and dinner*)	1	2	3	4
7. Have a criterion for the time frame? (*...when he holds a spoon for 2 minutes at lunch and dinner on three consecutive days* or *...at lunch and dinner on 3 days in 1 week*)	1	2	3	4

(continued)

Outcome 2

To what extent does the goal/outcome	Not at all	Somewhat	Much	Very much
1. Emphasize the child's *participation* in a routine (i.e., activity)? (*Child will participate in outside play time* not *child will participate in running*)	1	2	3	4
2. State specifically (i.e., in an observable and measurable manner) what the child will do?	1	2	3	4
3. Address a skill that is either *necessary or useful* for participation in home, "school," or community routines?	1	2	3	4
4. State an acquisition criterion (i.e., an indicator of when the child can do the skill)?	1	2	3	4
5. Have a **meaningful** acquisition criterion (i.e., one that shows improvement in *functional* behavior)? (*We will know he can do this when he holds a spoon for 2 minutes* not *...when he holds a spoon on 5 out of 7 trials*)	1	2	3	4
6. Have a generalization criterion (i.e., using the skill across routines, people, places, materials, etc.)? (*...when he holds a spoon for 2 minutes at lunch and dinner*)	1	2	3	4
7. Have a criterion for the time frame? (*...when he holds a spoon for 2 minutes at lunch and dinner on three consecutive days* or *...at lunch and dinner on 3 days in 1 week*)	1	2	3	4

(continued)

Outcome 3

To what extent does the goal/outcome	Not at all	Somewhat	Much	Very much
1. Emphasize the child's *participation* in a routine (i.e., activity)? (*Child will participate in outside play time* not *child will participate in running*)	1	2	3	4
2. State specifically (i.e., in an observable and measurable manner) what the child will do?	1	2	3	4
3. Address a skill that is either *necessary or useful* for participation in home, "school," or community routines?	1	2	3	4
4. State an acquisition criterion (i.e., an indicator of when the child can do the skill)?	1	2	3	4
5. Have a **meaningful** acquisition criterion (i.e., one that shows improvement in *functional* behavior)? (*We will know he can do this when he holds a spoon for 2 minutes* not *...when he holds a spoon on 5 out of 7 trials*)	1	2	3	4
6. Have a generalization criterion (i.e., using the skill across routines, people, places, materials, etc.)? (*...when he holds a spoon for 2 minutes at lunch and dinner*)	1	2	3	4
7. Have a criterion for the time frame? (*...when he holds a spoon for 2 minutes at lunch and dinner on three consecutive days* or *...at lunch and dinner on 3 days in 1 week*)	1	2	3	4

(continued)

Outcome 4				
To what extent does the goal/outcome	Not at all	Somewhat	Much	Very much
1. Emphasize the child's *participation* in a routine (i.e., activity)? (*Child will participate in outside play time* not *child will participate in running*)	1	2	3	4
2. State specifically (i.e., in an observable and measurable manner) what the child will do?	1	2	3	4
3. Address a skill that is either *necessary or useful* for participation in home, "school," or community routines?	1	2	3	4
4. State an acquisition criterion (i.e., an indicator of when the child can do the skill)?	1	2	3	4
5. Have a **meaningful** acquisition criterion (i.e., one that shows improvement in *functional* behavior)? (*We will know he can do this when he holds a spoon for 2 minutes* not *...when he holds a spoon on 5 out of 7 trials*)	1	2	3	4
6. Have a generalization criterion (i.e., using the skill across routines, people, places, materials, etc.)? (*...when he holds a spoon for 2 minutes at lunch and dinner*)	1	2	3	4
7. Have a criterion for the time frame? (*...when he holds a spoon for 2 minutes at lunch and dinner on three consecutive days* or *...at lunch and dinner on 3 days in 1 week*)	1	2	3	4

(continued)

Outcome 5				
To what extent does the goal/outcome	Not at all	Somewhat	Much	Very much
1. Emphasize the child's *participation* in a routine (i.e., activity)? (*Child will participate in outside play time* not *child will participate in running*)	1	2	3	4
2. State specifically (i.e., in an observable and measurable manner) what the child will do?	1	2	3	4
3. Address a skill that is either *necessary or useful* for participation in home, "school," or community routines?	1	2	3	4
4. State an acquisition criterion (i.e., an indicator of when the child can do the skill)?	1	2	3	4
5. Have a **meaningful** acquisition criterion (i.e., one that shows improvement in *functional* behavior)? (*We will know he can do this when he holds a spoon for 2 minutes* not *...when he holds a spoon on 5 out of 7 trials*)	1	2	3	4
6. Have a generalization criterion (i.e., using the skill across routines, people, places, materials, etc.)? (*...when he holds a spoon for 2 minutes at lunch and dinner*)	1	2	3	4
7. Have a criterion for the time frame? (*...when he holds a spoon for 2 minutes at lunch and dinner on three consecutive days* or *...at lunch and dinner on 3 days in 1 week*)	1	2	3	4

(continued)

Outcome 6

To what extent does the goal/outcome	Not at all	Somewhat	Much	Very much
1. Emphasize the child's *participation* in a routine (i.e., activity)? (*Child will participate in outside play time* not *child will participate in running*)	1	2	3	4
2. State specifically (i.e., in an observable and measurable manner) what the child will do?	1	2	3	4
3. Address a skill that is either *necessary or useful* for participation in home, "school," or community routines?	1	2	3	4
4. State an acquisition criterion (i.e., an indicator of when the child can do the skill)?	1	2	3	4
5. Have a **meaningful** acquisition criterion (i.e., one that shows improvement in *functional* behavior)? (*We will know he can do this when he holds a spoon for 2 minutes* not *...when he holds a spoon on 5 out of 7 trials*)	1	2	3	4
6. Have a generalization criterion (i.e., using the skill across routines, people, places, materials, etc.)? (*...when he holds a spoon for 2 minutes at lunch and dinner*)	1	2	3	4
7. Have a criterion for the time frame? (*...when he holds a spoon for 2 minutes at lunch and dinner on three consecutive days* or *...at lunch and dinner on 3 days in 1 week*)	1	2	3	4

(continued)

Outcome 7

To what extent does the goal/outcome	Not at all	Somewhat	Much	Very much
1. Emphasize the child's *participation* in a routine (i.e., activity)? (*Child will participate in outside play time* not *child will participate in running*)	1	2	3	4
2. State specifically (i.e., in an observable and measurable manner) what the child will do?	1	2	3	4
3. Address a skill that is either *necessary or useful* for participation in home, "school," or community routines?	1	2	3	4
4. State an acquisition criterion (i.e., an indicator of when the child can do the skill)?	1	2	3	4
5. Have a **meaningful** acquisition criterion (i.e., one that shows improvement in *functional* behavior)? (*We will know he can do this when he holds a spoon for 2 minutes* not *...when he holds a spoon on 5 out of 7 trials*)	1	2	3	4
6. Have a generalization criterion (i.e., using the skill across routines, people, places, materials, etc.)? (*...when he holds a spoon for 2 minutes at lunch and dinner*)	1	2	3	4
7. Have a criterion for the time frame? (*...when he holds a spoon for 2 minutes at lunch and dinner on three consecutive days* or *...at lunch and dinner on 3 days in 1 week*)	1	2	3	4

(continued)

Outcome 8

To what extent does the goal/outcome	Not at all	Somewhat	Much	Very much
1. Emphasize the child's *participation* in a routine (i.e., activity)? (*Child will participate in outside play time* not *child will participate in running*)	1	2	3	4
2. State specifically (i.e., in an observable and measurable manner) what the child will do?	1	2	3	4
3. Address a skill that is either *necessary or useful* for participation in home, "school," or community routines?	1	2	3	4
4. State an acquisition criterion (i.e., an indicator of when the child can do the skill)?	1	2	3	4
5. Have a **meaningful** acquisition criterion (i.e., one that shows improvement in *functional* behavior)? (*We will know he can do this when he holds a spoon for 2 minutes* not *...when he holds a spoon on 5 out of 7 trials*)	1	2	3	4
6. Have a generalization criterion (i.e., using the skill across routines, people, places, materials, etc.)? (*...when he holds a spoon for 2 minutes at lunch and dinner*)	1	2	3	4
7. Have a criterion for the time frame? (*...when he holds a spoon for 2 minutes at lunch and dinner on three consecutive days* or *...at lunch and dinner on 3 days in 1 week*)	1	2	3	4

(continued)

Outcome 9				
To what extent does the goal/outcome	Not at all	Somewhat	Much	Very much
1. Emphasize the child's *participation* in a routine (i.e., activity)? (*Child will participate in outside play time* not *child will participate in running*)	1	2	3	4
2. State specifically (i.e., in an observable and measurable manner) what the child will do?	1	2	3	4
3. Address a skill that is either *necessary or useful* for participation in home, "school," or community routines?	1	2	3	4
4. State an acquisition criterion (i.e., an indicator of when the child can do the skill)?	1	2	3	4
5. Have a **meaningful** acquisition criterion (i.e., one that shows improvement in *functional* behavior)? (*We will know he can do this when he holds a spoon for 2 minutes* not *...when he holds a spoon on 5 out of 7 trials*)	1	2	3	4
6. Have a generalization criterion (i.e., using the skill across routines, people, places, materials, etc.)? (*...when he holds a spoon for 2 minutes at lunch and dinner*)	1	2	3	4
7. Have a criterion for the time frame? (*...when he holds a spoon for 2 minutes at lunch and dinner on three consecutive days* or *...at lunch and dinner on 3 days in 1 week*)	1	2	3	4

(continued)

Outcome 10

To what extent does the goal/outcome	Not at all	Somewhat	Much	Very much
1. Emphasize the child's *participation* in a routine (i.e., activity)? (*Child will participate in outside play time* not *child will participate in running*)	1	2	3	4
2. State specifically (i.e., in an observable and measurable manner) what the child will do?	1	2	3	4
3. Address a skill that is either *necessary or useful* for participation in home, "school," or community routines?	1	2	3	4
4. State an acquisition criterion (i.e., an indicator of when the child can do the skill)?	1	2	3	4
5. Have a **meaningful** acquisition criterion (i.e., one that shows improvement in *functional* behavior)? (*We will know he can do this when he holds a spoon for 2 minutes* not *...when he holds a spoon on 5 out of 7 trials*)	1	2	3	4
6. Have a generalization criterion (i.e., using the skill across routines, people, places, materials, etc.)? (*...when he holds a spoon for 2 minutes at lunch and dinner*)	1	2	3	4
7. Have a criterion for the time frame? (*...when he holds a spoon for 2 minutes at lunch and dinner on three consecutive days* or *...at lunch and dinner on 3 days in 1 week*)	1	2	3	4

(continued)

Outcome 11

To what extent does the goal/outcome	Not at all	Somewhat	Much	Very much
1. Emphasize the child's *participation* in a routine (i.e., activity)? (*Child will participate in outside play time* not *child will participate in running*)	1	2	3	4
2. State specifically (i.e., in an observable and measurable manner) what the child will do?	1	2	3	4
3. Address a skill that is either *necessary or useful* for participation in home, "school," or community routines?	1	2	3	4
4. State an acquisition criterion (i.e., an indicator of when the child can do the skill)?	1	2	3	4
5. Have a ***meaningful*** acquisition criterion (i.e., one that shows improvement in *functional* behavior)? (*We will know he can do this when he holds a spoon for 2 minutes* not *...when he holds a spoon on 5 out of 7 trials*)	1	2	3	4
6. Have a generalization criterion (i.e., using the skill across routines, people, places, materials, etc.)? (*...when he holds a spoon for 2 minutes at lunch and dinner*)	1	2	3	4
7. Have a criterion for the time frame? (*...when he holds a spoon for 2 minutes at lunch and dinner on three consecutive days* or *...at lunch and dinner on 3 days in 1 week*)	1	2	3	4

(continued)

Outcome 12

To what extent does the goal/outcome	Not at all	Somewhat	Much	Very much
1. Emphasize the child's *participation* in a routine (i.e., activity)? (*Child will participate in outside play time* not *child will participate in running*)	1	2	3	4
2. State specifically (i.e., in an observable and measurable manner) what the child will do?	1	2	3	4
3. Address a skill that is either *necessary or useful* for participation in home, "school," or community routines?	1	2	3	4
4. State an acquisition criterion (i.e., an indicator of when the child can do the skill)?	1	2	3	4
5. Have a **meaningful** acquisition criterion (i.e., one that shows improvement in *functional* behavior)? (*We will know he can do this when he holds a spoon for 2 minutes* not *...when he holds a spoon on 5 out of 7 trials*)	1	2	3	4
6. Have a generalization criterion (i.e., using the skill across routines, people, places, materials, etc.)? (*...when he holds a spoon for 2 minutes at lunch and dinner*)	1	2	3	4
7. Have a criterion for the time frame? (*...when he holds a spoon for 2 minutes at lunch and dinner on three consecutive days* or *...at lunch and dinner on 3 days in 1 week*)	1	2	3	4

Examination of the Implementation of Embedded Intervention, through Observation (EIEIO)

The EIEIO addresses individualized goals identified for children with disabilities who attend inclusive child care centers. Data are gathered by observing a child and recording the frequency with which intervention is embedded within classroom activities.

Directions

Identify seven target goals from the child's individualized family service plan (IFSP) or individualized education program (IEP). Number the goals 1 through 7 in the leftmost column of the form. The columns to the right of the target goals represent 15-minute intervals of observation. At the top of each of the eight columns, identify the routine in which the child participated for the majority of the interval. The seven goals in the leftmost column of the form and eight activities in the top row of the form create a grid; each block within the grid represents a specific goal and a specific activity within the observation.

Each block within the grid contains three spaces, labeled *C*, *W*, and *A*. Mark a *Y* ("yes") or *N* ("no") in each space.

- In the **C** space, indicate whether or not the goal **could have been** addressed. Did the structure of the activity make it possible for the goal to be addressed?

- In the **W** space, indicate whether or not the goal **was** addressed in the activity.

- In the **A** space, indicate whether or not the goal was addressed **appropriately** (place a mark in this space only if the goal was addressed). When determining if a goal was addressed appropriately, consider the developmental, individual, and contextual appropriateness of the goal. In other words, ask yourself the following: (a) Is the child developmentally ready for the skill? (b) Is he or she capable of demonstrating the skill? (c) Was the least intrusive intervention strategy used? (d) Was the goal addressed during a routine in which it was needed? and (e) Was the goal relevant to what the other children were doing?

There are eight 15-minute intervals in the 2-hour observation. It is best to include a variety of routines within the observation. If only one or two different routines (i.e., free play and lunch) are observed, the data will not be representative of how often goals are being addressed throughout the day. Observations may be completed in eight consecutive intervals or at various times of the day (in order to witness a wider variety of routines).

Data can be used to (a) identify which goals should be targeted in particular routines, (b) determine the frequency with which goals are addressed, (c) determine which goals are most functional (those that are easily addressed within daily routines) and which goals need to be revised, and (d) plan for embedding instruction more effectively in future routines.

(continued)

McWilliam, R.A., & Scott, S. (2001). *Examination of the Implementation of Embedded Intervention, through Observation (EIEIO).* Chapel Hill: The University of North Carolina, FPG Child Development Institute.

From McWilliam, R.A., & Casey, A.M. (2008). *Engagement of every child in the preschool classroom* (pp. 161–162). Baltimore: Paul H. Brookes Publishing Co.; reprinted by permission. Copyright © 2008 Paul H. Brookes Publishing Co., Inc. All rights reserved.

(Also reproduced in *Routines-Based Early Intervention: Supporting Young Children and Their Families* by R.A. McWilliam; 2010, Paul H. Brookes Publishing Co., Inc.)

Examination of the Implementation of Embedded Intervention, through Observation (EIEIO)

Center _____ Class _____ Teacher _____

Child _____ Date _____ Observer _____

15-Minute Blocks of Observation

(Write the name of the routine in which the child with disabilities is participating for each 15-minute block of observation)

Questions	C	W	A	Notes	C	W	A	Notes	C	W	A	Notes	C	W	A	Notes
List high priority goals (check all that are addressed in each 15-minute block of observation)																

(continued)

McWilliam, R.A., & Scott, S. (2001). Examination of the Implementation of Embedded Intervention, through Observation (EIEIO). Chapel Hill: The University of North Carolina, FPG Child Development Institute.

From McWilliam, R.A., & Casey, A.M. (2008). Engagement of every child in the preschool classroom (pp. 161–162). Baltimore: Paul H. Brookes Publishing Co.; reprinted by permission. Copyright © 2008 Paul H. Brookes Publishing Co., Inc. All rights reserved.

(Also reproduced in Routines-Based Early Intervention: Supporting Young Children and Their Families by R.A. McWilliam; 2010, Paul H. Brookes Publishing Co., Inc.)

15-Minute Blocks of Observation

(Write the name of the routine in which the child with disabilities is participating for each 15-minute block of observation)

Feedback Given?

List any Feedback given	C	W	A	Notes	C	W	A	Notes	C	W	A	Notes	C	W	A	Notes

C = *Could* the goal be addressed? W = *Was* the goal addressed? A = Was the goal addressed *appropriately?*

Appropriately: Developmentally appropriate, individually appropriate, normalization principles, relevant to what others are doing, doable by teaching staff, contextually appropriate

Vanderbilt Ecological Congruence of Teaching Opportunities in Routines (VECTOR), Classroom Version

Rationale

Ecological congruence is a measure of the fit between the provision of particular types of supports and the need for those supports. We propose that, when assessing the fit between a child and his or her environment, the *opportunities* available in the environment must be considered, as well as the frequency with which the child takes *advantage* of the opportunities. Opportunities may be provided in the physical environment or by the adults present in the environment. Incongruence is found when the opportunities being provided do not fit with the child's use of supports; too few opportunities are provided by adults or the physical environment or the child is not taking advantage of the opportunities provided. Incongruence between a child and his or her environment can be resolved by making changes in the environment, changing the expectations for the child or activity, or intervening with the child to teach a particular skill. The VECTOR is designed to focus assessment of ecological congruence on three developmental domains: engagement, independence, and peer interactions.

Population and Setting

The VECTOR, Classroom Version, is designed to be used with children 18 months to school age in a group setting. There is no prescribed schedule for when to use the VECTOR. It could be completed

1. Periodically to monitor fit and determine potential changes needed in the environment and adult interventions
2. To monitor child progress
3. When particular concerns have been identified

Completing the Scale

1. Observe the child for at least 10 minutes during each of the routines applicable to the child's group setting.
2. For each of the 10 routines, rate nine items concerning the environment, adult interventions, and the child's performance.
   a. For environment and adult interventions, rate the frequency with which each routine provides the opportunities referred to with the scale from 1 (*rarely*) to 5 (*most of the time*).
   b. Then rate the child's performance, using the same scale, indicating if the child takes advantage of the opportunities provided.

Scoring

1. Sum the scores for **O**pportunity and divide by 6. Enter scores at the bottom.
2. Sum the scores for **A**dvantage and divide by 3. Enter scores at the bottom.
3. Sum the scores for **O**pportunity (environment and adult interventions) for all routines and divide by 10 or by the number of routines observed if fewer than 10. Enter score in far right hand column.
4. Sum the scores for **A**dvantage for all routines and divide by 10 or by the number of routines observed if fewer than 10. Enter score in far right hand column.
5. Analyze scores based on information provided below.
6. Implement changes and monitor success.

(continued)

Casey, A.M., Freund, P.J., & McWilliam, R.A. (2004). *Vanderbilt Ecological Congruence of Teaching Opportunities in Routines (VECTOR)— Classroom Version*. Nashville: Vanderbilt University Medical Center, Center for Child Development.

From McWilliam, R.A., & Casey, A.M. (2008). *Engagement of every child in the preschool classroom* (pp. 163–165). Baltimore: Paul H. Brookes Publishing Co. Copyright © 2008 Paul H. Brookes Publishing Co., Inc. All rights reserved.

(Adapted with permission and included in *Routines-Based Early Intervention: Supporting Young Children and Their Families* by R.A. McWilliam; 2010, Paul H. Brookes Publishing Co., Inc.)

Analyses

1. *Determine the overall goodness of the fit* between the child and his or her environment across the routines of the day. Compare the **O**pportunity and **A**dvantage scores for each routine at the bottom of the table. If the scores are consistently high and scores for **O**pportunity and **A**dvantage are similar, the fit is most likely good. If the **O**pportunity and **A**dvantage scores are all low or dissimilar the fit may not be good and further analysis is needed (see below).

2. *Determine the fit between the environment and the child specific routines.* Compare **O**pportunity and **A**dvantage scores for each routine at the bottom of the table. If the **O**pportunity score and **A**dvantage score for a routine are both low, look within the data for the routine to determine where environmental change may be needed (in the physical environment, in adult interventions, or in both the physical environment and adult interventions). Examine the scores for the three areas of functioning (engagement, independence, and peer interactions) to determine where specific change may be needed.

3. *Determine whether or not the child is taking advantage of the opportunities provided by the physical environment and adults.* Compare **O**pportunity and **A**dvantage scores for each routine at the bottom of the table. If **A**dvantage scores are low and **O**pportunity scores are notably higher, it might suggest that the child is not taking full advantage of the opportunities provided. This discrepancy may be the result of skill deficits or challenging behaviors. Examining child scores within routines should help you identify specific areas of concern related to the child's engagement, independence, and peer interactions.

4. *Determine and monitor the child's engagement, independence, and peer interactions across routines of the day.* Examine the total child scores (column at right, second page) for engagement, independence, and peer interactions. If scores are lower than desired, examine individual scores across routines to determine strengths, needs, and trends.

Note: In some instances you might find that child **A**dvantage scores are higher than environmental scores. In this case, making specific changes to the environment might not be necessary for the child, although enriching the environment might further enhance the child's learning experiences.

(continued)

Casey, A.M., Freund, P.J., & McWilliam, R.A. (2004). *Vanderbilt Ecological Congruence of Teaching Opportunities in Routines (VECTOR)— Classroom Version.* Nashville: Vanderbilt University Medical Center, Center for Child Development.

From McWilliam, R.A., & Casey, A.M. (2008). *Engagement of every child in the preschool classroom* (pp. 163–165). Baltimore: Paul H. Brookes Publishing Co. Copyright © 2008 Paul H. Brookes Publishing Co., Inc. All rights reserved.

(Adapted with permission and included in *Routines-Based Early Intervention: Supporting Young Children and Their Families* by R.A. McWilliam; 2010, Paul H. Brookes Publishing Co., Inc.)

Child's Name _____ Date _____

Teacher _____ Observer _____

Observer's role _____ Typical day for child Yes ☐ No ☐

If not typical, why? _____

Directions:
1. Rate 9 items across 10 routines
2. Sum scores for Opportunity and divide by 6. Enter score at bottom
3. Sum scores for Advantage and divide by 3. Enter score at bottom
4. Sum all Opportunity scores for all routines, divide by 10, enter last column
5. Sum all Advantage scores for all routines, divide by 10, enter last column

Rating Scale

1	2	3	4	5
Rarely		Some of the time		Most of the time

		Arrival		Free Play		Meals/Snacks		Circle		Structured Activities	
		O	A	O	A	O	A	O	A	O	A
Engagement	**Environment** 1. Physical environment and available materials promote engagement.										
	Adults 2. Adults are responsive to the child and consistently promote higher levels of engagement.										
	Child 3. Child is consistently engaged at his/her most sophisticated level.										
Independence	**Environment** 4. Routine allows independence.										
	Adults 5. Adults provide the least prompts necessary for independence.										
	Child 6. Child completes routine independently.										
Peer Interaction	**Environment** 7. The routine provides multiple opportunities for peer interaction.										
	Adults 8. Adults promote and reinforce peer interactions.										
	Child 9. Child interacts frequently and appropriately with peers.										
	Totals										

O = **Opportunities** provided within the routine

A = Child takes **advantage** of the opportunities and instruction

Casey, A.M., Freund, P.J., & McWilliam, R.A. (2004). *Vanderbilt Ecological Congruence of Teaching Opportunities in Routines (VECTOR)—Classroom Version*. Nashville: Vanderbilt University Medical Center, Center for Child Development.

From McWilliam, R.A., & Casey, A.M. (2008). *Engagement of every child in the preschool classroom* (pp. 163–165). Baltimore: Paul H. Brookes Publishing Co. Copyright © 2008 Paul H. Brookes Publishing Co., Inc. All rights reserved.

(Adapted with permission and included in *Routines-Based Early Intervention: Supporting Young Children and Their Families* by R.A. McWilliam; 2010, Paul H. Brookes Publishing Co., Inc.)

(continued)

Rating Scale

1	2	3	4	5
Rarely		Some of the time		Most of the time

Directions:
1. Rate 9 items across 10 routines
2. Sum scores for Opportunity and divide by 6. Enter score at bottom
3. Sum scores for Advantage and divide by 3. Enter score at bottom
4. Sum all Opportunity scores for all routines, divide by 10, enter last column
5. Sum all Advantage scores for all routines, divide by 10, enter last column

		Outdoor Activity		Centers		Personal Hygiene		Story time		Movement and Music		Totals
		O	A	O	A	O	A	O	A	O	A	
Engagement	**Environment** 1. Physical environment and available materials promote engagement.												E
	Adults 2. Adults are responsive to the child and consistently promote higher levels of engagement												
	Child 3. Child is consistently engaged at his/her most sophisticated level.												
Independence	**Environment** 4. Routine allows independence.												I
	Adults 5. Adults provide the least prompts necessary for independence.												
	Child 6. Child completes routine independently.												
Peer Interaction	**Environment** 7. The routine provides multiple opportunities for peer interaction.												PI
	Adults 8. Adults promote and reinforce peer interactions.												
	Child 9. Child interacts frequently and appropriately with peers.												
	Totals												

O = **Opportunities** provided within the routine

A = Child takes **advantage** of the opportunities and instruction

Casey, A.M., Freund, P.J., & McWilliam, R.A. (2004). *Vanderbilt Ecological Congruence of Teaching Opportunities in Routines (VECTOR)—Classroom Version.* Nashville: Vanderbilt University Medical Center, Center for Child Development.

From McWilliam, R.A., & Casey, A.M. (2008). *Engagement of every child in the preschool classroom* (pp. 163–165). Baltimore: Paul H. Brookes Publishing Co. Copyright © 2008 Paul H. Brookes Publishing Co., Inc. All rights reserved.

(Adapted with permission and included in *Routines-Based Early Intervention: Supporting Young Children and Their Families* by R.A. McWilliam; 2010, Paul H. Brookes Publishing Co., Inc.)

Practices for Instruction, Play, and Engagement Rating Scale (PIPERS)

Directions

Each item on the PIPERS has two scales, one for typical practice and one for ideal practice. Both scales should be completed for all items. Circle the number nearest the description that best matches your typical or ideal practice. The PIPERS can be completed by an individual or by a group of people. If it is completed by a group, they should come to consensus about each rating. It is about classroom practices for children 1–5 years of age.

Name of person or group _____

1. Needs Assessment

Typical practice (Circle the number that most closely matches what typically happens in your classroom or program)

1	2	3	4	5	6	7
Goals are determined by specialists based on professionals' assessment.		Goals are suggested by professionals.		Goals are determined by parents alone or parents and professionals together, but without a Routines-Based Interview.		Goals are determined by parents as the result of a Routines-Based Interview.

Ideal practice (Circle the number that most closely matches what would be ideal for your classroom or program)

1	2	3	4	5	6	7

2. Organization of Adults

Typical practice (Circle the number that most closely matches what typically happens in your classroom or program)

1	2	3	4	5	6	7
All adults follow the classroom schedule.		Adults generally follow the classroom schedule but go where needed.		Adults know where they are supposed to be at each time of the day, but individual schedules are not written.		Each adult has a list of responsibilities scheduled throughout the day.

Ideal practice (Circle the number that most closely matches what would be ideal for your classroom or program)

1	2	3	4	5	6	7

(continued)

3. Room Arrangement

Typical practice (Circle the number that most closely matches what typically happens in your classroom or program)

1	2	3	4	5	6	7
The room is open with similar objects stored together.		The room has centers around a central open space.		The room is organized in clearly demarcated zones, named in professional-centered ways (e.g., fine motor, symbolic play, sensory).		The room is organized in clearly demarcated zones, named in child-centered ways (e.g., small toys, dress-up, sand and water).

Ideal practice (Circle the number that most closely matches what would be ideal for your classroom or program)

1	2	3	4	5	6	7

4. Responsiveness

Typical practice (Circle the number that most closely matches what typically happens in your classroom or program)

1	2	3	4	5	6	7
Almost all actual teaching occurs with a teacher asking a child to perform a task unrelated to the child's current interest (i.e., what the child is attending to at the teaching moment)—a task the teacher had planned to have the child do.		Much teaching occurs with a teacher asking a child to perform a task unrelated to the child's current interest, but some occurs in response to children's interests and abilities.		Much teaching occurs in response to children's interests and abilities, but some occurs with a teacher asking a child to perform a task unrelated to the child's current interest.		Almost all teaching occurs in response to children's interests and abilities, even when those interests have nothing to do with planned activities.

Ideal practice (Circle the number that most closely matches what would be ideal for your classroom or program)

1	2	3	4	5	6	7

(continued)

5. Elaboration

Typical practice (Circle the number that most closely matches what typically happens in your classroom or program)

1	2	3	4	5	6	7
Almost all teaching involves praise but children are not prompted to do more.		**Occasionally,** children are prompted to do more than they are currently doing.		**Quite often,** teaching involves eliciting more sophisticated behavior related to the child's interest.		**Almost all** teaching involves the provision of prompts or models to elicit more sophisticated behavior related to the child's current interest (i.e., what the child is attending to at the teaching moment).

Ideal practice (Circle the number that most closely matches what would be ideal for your classroom or program)

1	2	3	4	5	6	7

6. Context of Teaching

Typical practice (Circle the number that most closely matches typically happens in your classroom or program)

1	2	3	4	5	6	7
Almost all teaching occurs in teacher-directed interactions, which can be in large groups, small groups, or one on one.		**Much** teaching occurs in teacher-directed interactions, but some occurs while children are playing.		**Much** teaching occurs while children are playing, but some occurs in teacher-directed large groups, small groups, or one on one.		**Almost all** teaching occurs while children are playing.

Ideal practice (Circle the number that most closely matches what would be ideal for your classroom or program)

1	2	3	4	5	6	7

(continued)

7. Integration with Ongoing Routines

Typical practice (Circle the number that most closely matches what typically happens in your classroom or program)
If you have multiple therapists, circle a number for each discipline with the following initials beside each circle: PT (physical therapist or PT assistant), OT (occupational therapist or certified OT assistant), or SLP (speech-language pathologist)

1	2	3	4	5	6	7
Therapists pull the child out of the classroom for intervention.		Therapists work with the child in the classroom, doing their own interventions, regardless of the ongoing classroom activity.		Therapists join the child in whatever the child is engaged in and weave their intervention into the ongoing activity.		Therapists coach the teaching staff, with modeling and feedback as appropriate, to intervene with the child in the ongoing activity.

1	2	3	4	5	6	7

Ideal practice (Circle the number that most closely matches what would be ideal for your classroom or program)

8. Role Release and Acceptance

Typical practice (Circle the number that most closely matches what typically happens in your classroom or program)
If you have multiple therapists, circle a number for each discipline with the following initials beside each circle: PT (physical therapist or PT assistant), OT (occupational therapist or certified OT assistant), or SLP (speech-language pathologist)

1	2	3	4	5	6	7
Therapists convey an attitude that their strategies cannot be used by classroom staff, and classroom staff do not want to use the strategies.		Therapists convey an attitude that their strategies cannot be used by classroom staff, but classroom staff want strategies to use.		Therapists convey an attitude that their strategies are for use by classroom staff, but classroom staff do not willingly accept the strategies.		Therapists convey an attitude that their strategies are for use by classroom staff, and classroom staff willingly accept the strategies.

1	2	3	4	5	6	7

Ideal practice (Circle the number that most closely matches what would be ideal for your classroom or program)

(continued)

9. Least Prompts/Devices Necessary

Typical practice (Circle the number that most closely matches what typically happens in your classroom or program)
If you have multiple therapists, circle a number for each discipline with the following initials beside each circle: PT (physical therapist or PT assistant), OT (occupational therapist or certified OT assistant), or SLP (speech-language pathologist)

1	2	3	4	5	6	7
Therapists recommend a) devices that do not have direct relevance to the ongoing routine (e.g., weighted vests, chewy tubes, facial vibrators) and b) noncontingent stimulation (adult actions on the child that require no response from the child other than cooperation, such as stretching, massage, oral-motor stimulation, and brushing). They do not *teach* the child.		Therapists recommend noncontingent stimulation but the minimal necessary devices.		Therapists recommend *teaching* the child to function but they use devices that do not have direct relevance to the ongoing routine, such as weighted vests, chewy tubes, and facial vibrators.		Therapists recommend *teaching* the child to function in routines with the minimal necessary devices such as augmentative communication systems, supportive seating, and splints.

Ideal practice (Circle the number that most closely matches what would be ideal for your classroom or program)

1	2	3	4	5	6	7

(continued)

10. Big-Picture Goals for Children

Typical practice (Circle the number that most closely matches what typically happens in your classroom or program)

1	2	3	4	5	6	7
The overall goals for children are to maximize their potential.		The overall goals for children are to maximize their cognitive, communication, motor, social, and adaptive development.		The overall goals for children are to maximize their positive social-emotional skills (including social relationships), acquisition and use of knowledge and skills (including early language/communication and early literacy), and use of appropriate behaviors to meet their needs.		The overall goals for children are to maximize their engagement, independence, and social relationships.

Ideal practice (Circle the number that most closely matches what would be ideal for your classroom or program)

1	2	3	4	5	6	7

11. Play

Typical practice (Circle the number that most closely matches what typically happens in your classroom or program)

1	2	3	4	5	6	7
Children spend almost all their time in adult-directed activities such as circle, prepared small-group lessons, and one-on-one work.		Children spend about three quarters of their time in adult-directed activities and about one quarter of their time in play.		Children spend about half their time in adult-directed activities and about half their time in play.		Children spend most of their time in play that consists of free, uninterrupted time; access to interesting materials; adults following children's lead in play; opportunities for messy behavior, rough-and-tumble behavior, and nonsense behavior.

Ideal practice (Circle the number that most closely matches what would be ideal for your classroom or program)

1	2	3	4	5	6	7

(continued)

12. Complete Learning Interactions

Typical practice (Circle the number that most closely matches what typically happens in your classroom or program)

1	2	3	4	5	6	7
Adults pay little attention to setting events, antecedents, and prompts and little attention to consequences of children's behavior.		Adults set the stage for children to produce a desired behavior but pay little attention to consequences of children's behavior.		Adults pay little attention to setting events, antecedents, and prompts but they do ensure child behaviors are followed by natural or adult-delivered consequences.		Adults set the stage for children to produce a desired behavior and, when the child responds, a natural or adult-delivered consequence ensues.

1	2	3	4	5	6	7

Ideal practice (Circle the number that most closely matches what would be ideal for your classroom or program)

13. Attention to IFSP/IEP Child-Level Goals

Typical practice (Circle the number that most closely matches what typically happens in your classroom or program)

1	2	3	4	5	6	7
Goals are addressed in sessions with specialists (e.g., therapists) but not during ongoing classroom routines.		Goals are addressed in some ongoing classroom routines but are also addressed in lessons or sessions with teachers or specialists.		Goals are addressed in sessions with specialists during ongoing classroom routines but not throughout the rest of the day.		Goals are addressed throughout the day by whomever is interacting with the child.

1	2	3	4	5	6	7

Ideal practice (Circle the number that most closely matches what would be ideal for your classroom or program)

(continued)

14. Room Furnishings

Typical practice (Circle the number that most closely matches what typically happens in your classroom or program)

1	2	3	4	5	6	7
Rooms are utilitarian, with few decorations; insufficient materials that children can handle; no soft area; and no area where children are allowed to be messy.		Rooms have interesting materials and an area where children can be messy but are utilitarian and have no soft area.		Rooms are attractive and have a soft area but insufficient materials and no area where children are allowed to be messy.		Rooms are attractive to children and adults with objects of beauty; interesting materials that children can handle; a soft, tucked-away area; and an area where children can be messy.

Ideal practice (Circle the number that most closely matches what would be ideal for your classroom or program)

1	2	3	4	5	6	7

15. Type of Engagement

Typical practice (Circle the number that most closely matches what typically happens in your classroom or program)

1	2	3	4	5	6	7
Children are encouraged to be engaged with adults most of the day, watching or listening to adults in adult-directed activities, or in one-on-one interactions with adults.		Children are encouraged to be engaged with adults most of the day, but specific activities are planned for peer interactions or engagement with materials.		Children are encouraged to be engaged with peers and materials for about half the day and with adults for about half the day.		Children are encouraged to be engaged with peers and materials for most of the day, with adults supporting such engagement.

Ideal practice (Circle the number that most closely matches what would be ideal for your classroom or program)

1	2	3	4	5	6	7

(continued)

16. Peer Interactions

Typical practice (Circle the number that most closely matches what typically happens in your classroom or program)

1	2	3	4	5	6	7
Teachers often discourage peer interactions, instead encouraging children to be on task in independent activities with materials.		Teachers sometimes discourage peer interactions and sometimes encourage peer interactions.		Teachers often encourage peer interactions.		Teachers almost always encourage peer interactions.

Ideal practice (Circle the number that most closely matches what would be ideal for your classroom or program)

1	2	3	4	5	6	7

17. Self-Direction versus Compliance

Typical practice (Circle the number that most closely matches what typically happens in your classroom or program)

1	2	3	4	5	6	7
Children are expected to comply with rules and directions so they learn appropriate behavior, good manners, and rules.		Children are taught to comply with rules and directions but some latitude is given.		Children are encouraged to be independent but they are taught to do things the "right" way (e.g., rules for walking down the hall, sitting at the table).		Children are encouraged to be independent even if they don't do things the "right" way.

Ideal practice (Circle the number that most closely matches what would be ideal for your classroom or program)

1	2	3	4	5	6	7

(continued)

18. Language Promoting Developmentally Appropriate Practice (DAP)

Typical practice (Circle the number that most closely matches what typically happens in your classroom or program)

1	2	3	4	5	6	7
Children are consistently referred to as "students."		Children are usually referred to as "students" but sometimes as "children."		Children are usually referred to as "children" but sometimes as "students."		Children are consistently referred to as "children" or "kids."

Ideal practice (Circle the number that most closely matches what would be ideal for your classroom or program)

1	2	3	4	5	6	7

19. Language Promoting Membership ("Children")

Typical practice (Circle the number that most closely matches what typically happens in your classroom or program)

1	2	3	4	5	6	7
All children are frequently called "program child(ren)" or "peer(s)."		All children are frequently called "child(ren) with disabilities," "child(ren) without disabilities," or "typically developing child(ren)."		All children are called "child(ren)" or "kid(s)," only designating whether they have disabilities or not when necessary; when necessary, the terms "program child(ren)" and "peer(s)" are used.		All children are called "child(ren)" or "kid(s)," only designating whether they have disabilities or not when necessary; when necessary, the terms "with disabilities" and "without disabilities" or "typically developing" are used; "peers" refers to same-age or classroom children, whether or not they have disabilities.

Ideal practice (Circle the number that most closely matches what would be ideal for your classroom or program)

1	2	3	4	5	6	7

(continued)

20. Individualization for All

Typical practice (Circle the number that most closely matches what typically happens in your classroom or program)

1	2	3	4	5	6	7
All children learn the core curriculum with little attention to any individual goals.		Children with disabilities have individual goals with little attention to overall curricular goals; typically developing children have overall curricular goals.		Children with disabilities have individual goals in addition to their overall curricular goals; typically developing children have overall curricular goals.		All children in the classroom have individual goals (outcomes) in addition to their overall curricular goals.

Ideal practice (Circle the number that most closely matches what would be ideal for your classroom or program)

1	2	3	4	5	6	7

21. Partnership with Families

Typical practice (Circle the number that most closely matches what typically happens in your classroom or program)

1	2	3	4	5	6	7
In their interactions with families, professionals are professional, with clear boundaries to ensure there is no confusion about who is the professional and who is the consumer.		In their interactions with families, professionals are usually positive and friendly, but they expect to be in charge of education, with parents in charge of *parenting*.		In their interactions with families, professionals are consistently positive, responsive, friendly, and sensitive, but make many of the decisions about interventions.		In their interactions with families, professionals are consistently positive, responsive, friendly, and sensitive, including supporting families in making decisions about interventions.

Ideal practice (Circle the number that most closely matches what would be ideal for your classroom or program)

1	2	3	4	5	6	7

(continued)

22. Attention to Family-Level Needs

Typical practice (Circle the number that most closely matches what typically happens in your classroom or program)

1	2	3	4	5	6	7
Professionals assess child performance and restrict themselves to addressing child-level needs related to the "school" day.		Professionals assess child performance but make suggestions to families as they hear, by chance, about child-level needs in the home.		Professionals assess child needs but make suggestions to families as they hear, by chance, about family-level needs.		Professionals conduct an in-depth needs assessment, capturing both child- and family-level needs, and they ensure families receive support to address any family-level needs, including making suggestions about parenting at home and in the community.

Ideal practice (Circle the number that most closely matches what would be ideal for your classroom or program)

1	2	3	4	5	6	7

23. Behavior Management

Typical practice (Circle the number that most closely matches what typically happens in your classroom or program)

1	2	3	4	5	6	7
Adults react inconsistently to children's inappropriate behavior with voice control (i.e., "shouting"), physical handling (e.g., moving a child), and timed time-out (e.g., one minute for every year of the child's age).		Adults follow a consistent "behavior management" plan that involves applying timed time-out when children violate certain classroom rules.		Adults generally follow reinforcement principles, attending to desired behaviors and ignoring inappropriate behaviors when possible (i.e., no talk, no explanations at the time of the infraction).		Adults teach children to behave appropriately through systematic application, when necessary, of reinforcement principles, including the tactical withholding of reinforcement, shaping, and manipulating prompts.

Ideal practice (Circle the number that most closely matches what would be ideal for your classroom or program)

1	2	3	4	5	6	7

(continued)

24. Participation

Typical practice (Circle the number that most closely matches what typically happens in your classroom or program)

1	2	3	4	5	6	7
During most activities, children with any disabilities are not present because they are not enrolled, are in the classroom but not involved in the main activity, or are present in the activity but not meaningfully participating.		During some activities, children with disabilities *other than* significant motor or cognitive impairments are present but not meaningfully participating; children with significant motor or cognitive disabilities are not present in activities.		During most activities, children with disabilities *other than* significant motor or cognitive impairments have some meaningful way to participate actively.		During most activities, all children, including those with significant motor or cognitive impairments, have some meaningful way to participate actively—not just watching.

Ideal practice (Circle the number that most closely matches what would be ideal for your classroom or program)

1	2	3	4	5	6	7

Scale for Teachers' Assessment of Routines Engagement (STARE)

Child _____ Date _____

Observer _____

Directions

Observe the child for 10 minutes in each of the following routines. First, rate the amount of time the child is engaged with adults, peers, and materials. Second, rate the complexity of the child's engagement: *Nonengaged* = inappropriate behavior, zoning out; *Unsophisticated* = repetitive play, casually looking around; *Average* = following routines, participating; *Advanced* = talking, creating; *Sophisticated* = symbolic talk, pretending, and persisting. There is space to add additional or alternate routines at the end of the scale.

Arrival	Almost none of the time	Little of the time	Half of the time	Much of the time	Almost all of the time
With adults	1	2	3	4	5
With peers	1	2	3	4	5
With materials	1	2	3	4	5
Complexity	Nonengaged 1	Unsophisticated 2	Average 3	Advanced 4	Sophisticated 5

Circle Time	Almost none of the time	Little of the time	Half of the time	Much of the time	Almost all of the time
With adults	1	2	3	4	5
With peers	1	2	3	4	5
With materials	1	2	3	4	5
Complexity	Nonengaged 1	Unsophisticated 2	Average 3	Advanced 4	Sophisticated 5

Centers/Free Play	Almost none of the time	Little of the time	Half of the time	Much of the time	Almost all of the time
With adults	1	2	3	4	5
With peers	1	2	3	4	5
With materials	1	2	3	4	5
Complexity	Nonengaged 1	Unsophisticated 2	Average 3	Advanced 4	Sophisticated 5

(continued)

McWilliam, R.A. (2000b). *Scale for Teachers' Assessment of Routines Engagement (STARE).* Chapel Hill: University of North Carolina.

From McWilliam, R.A., & Casey, A.M. (2008). *Engagement of every child in the preschool classroom* (pp. 168–170). Baltimore: Paul H. Brookes Publishing Co.; reprinted by permission. Copyright © 2008 Paul H. Brookes Publishing Co., Inc. All rights reserved.

(Also reproduced in *Routines-Based Early Intervention: Supporting Young Children and Their Families* by R.A. McWilliam; 2010, Paul H. Brookes Publishing Co., Inc.)

Teacher-Directed Activity	Almost none of the time	Little of the time	Half of the time	Much of the time	Almost all of the time
With adults	1	2	3	4	5
With peers	1	2	3	4	5
With materials	1	2	3	4	5
Complexity	Nonengaged 1	Unsophisticated 2	Average 3	Advanced 4	Sophisticated 5

Snack/Lunch (circle one)	Almost none of the time	Little of the time	Half of the time	Much of the time	Almost all of the time
With adults	1	2	3	4	5
With peers	1	2	3	4	5
With materials	1	2	3	4	5
Complexity	Nonengaged 1	Unsophisticated 2	Average 3	Advanced 4	Sophisticated 5

Outside	Almost none of the time	Little of the time	Half of the time	Much of the time	Almost all of the time
With adults	1	2	3	4	5
With peers	1	2	3	4	5
With materials	1	2	3	4	5
Complexity	Nonengaged 1	Unsophisticated 2	Average 3	Advanced 4	Sophisticated 5

	Almost none of the time	Little of the time	Half of the time	Much of the time	Almost all of the time
With adults	1	2	3	4	5
With peers	1	2	3	4	5
With materials	1	2	3	4	5
Complexity	Nonengaged 1	Unsophisticated 2	Average 3	Advanced 4	Sophisticated 5

(continued)

McWilliam, R.A. (2000b). Scale for Teachers' Assessment of Routines Engagement (STARE). Chapel Hill: University of North Carolina.

From McWilliam, R.A., & Casey, A.M. (2008). Engagement of every child in the preschool classroom (pp. 168–170). Baltimore: Paul H. Brookes Publishing Co.; reprinted by permission. Copyright © 2008 Paul H. Brookes Publishing Co., Inc. All rights reserved.

(Also reproduced in Routines-Based Early Intervention: Supporting Young Children and Their Families by R.A. McWilliam; 2010, Paul H. Brookes Publishing Co., Inc.)

	Almost none of the time	Little of the time	Half of the time	Much of the time	Almost all of the time
With adults	1	2	3	4	5
With peers	1	2	3	4	5
With materials	1	2	3	4	5
Complexity	Nonengaged 1	Unsophisticated 2	Average 3	Advanced 4	Sophisticated 5

	Almost none of the time	Little of the time	Half of the time	Much of the time	Almost all of the time
With adults	1	2	3	4	5
With peers	1	2	3	4	5
With materials	1	2	3	4	5
Complexity	Nonengaged 1	Unsophisticated 2	Average 3	Advanced 4	Sophisticated 5

Therapy Goals Information Form (TGIF)

Directions

Complete the top portion of the form by filling in your name and the date you completed the form. Please indicate the approximate time span that the ratings cover (i.e., last 4 weeks) in the space after *For period ending*. Please list the outcomes that have been assigned the highest priority for the child and assign them a number to indicate their priority order. Beside each outcome are two rows of boxes. The top row is used to indicate how often the outcome behavior is performed (ranging from *Never* to *All of the time*). The bottom row is used to indicate the independence with which the outcome behavior is performed (ranging from *Needs total assistance* to *With no help*). In each row there is also an option for indicating that frequency and independence considerations do not apply for a particular outcome goal. For each outcome goal listed, please check one box for *Frequency* and one box for *Independence*.

Child's name _____   Date _____

Teacher's name _____   For period ending _____

How well does the child do each of the following? (Check one box for frequency and one box for independence for each outcome.)

Outcome #	Outcome	1	2	3	4	5	
		Never	Almost never	About half the time	Almost all of the time	All of the time	FREQUENCY
		Needs total assistance	With lots of help	With some help	With very little help	With no help	INDEPENDENCE
		Never	Almost never	About half the time	Almost all of the time	All of the time	FREQUENCY
		Needs total assistance	With lots of help	With some help	With very little help	With no help	INDEPENDENCE
		Never	Almost never	About half the time	Almost all of the time	All of the time	FREQUENCY
		Needs total assistance	With lots of help	With some help	With very little help	With no help	INDEPENDENCE

(continued)

From McWilliam, R.A. (1996). *Rethinking pull-out services in early intervention: A professional resource* (p. 165). Baltimore: Paul H. Brookes Publishing Co. Copyright © 1996 by Paul H. Brookes Publishing Co., Inc. All rights reserved.

(Adapted with permission and included in *Routines-Based Early Intervention: Supporting Young Children and Their Families* by R.A. McWilliam (2010, Paul H. Brookes Publishing Co., Inc.)

Outcome #	Outcome	1	2	3	4	5		
		Never	Almost never	About half the time	Almost all of the time	All of the time	Doesn't apply (Don't know)	FREQUENCY
		Needs total assistance	With lots of help	With some help	With very little help	With no help	Doesn't apply (Don't know)	INDEPENDENCE
		Never	Almost never	About half the time	Almost all of the time	All of the time	Doesn't apply (Don't know)	FREQUENCY
		Needs total assistance	With lots of help	With some help	With very little help	With no help	Doesn't apply (Don't know)	INDEPENDENCE
		Never	Almost never	About half the time	Almost all of the time	All of the time	Doesn't apply (Don't know)	FREQUENCY
		Needs total assistance	With lots of help	With some help	With very little help	With no help	Doesn't apply (Don't know)	INDEPENDENCE
		Never	Almost never	About half the time	Almost all of the time	All of the time	Doesn't apply (Don't know)	FREQUENCY
		Needs total assistance	With lots of help	With some help	With very little help	With no help	Doesn't apply (Don't know)	INDEPENDENCE
		Never	Almost never	About half the time	Almost all of the time	All of the time	Doesn't apply (Don't know)	FREQUENCY
		Needs total assistance	With lots of help	With some help	With very little help	With no help	Doesn't apply (Don't know)	INDEPENDENCE
		Never	Almost never	About half the time	Almost all of the time	All of the time	Doesn't apply (Don't know)	FREQUENCY
		Needs total assistance	With lots of help	With some help	With very little help	With no help	Doesn't apply (Don't know)	INDEPENDENCE

Satisfaction with Home Routines Evaluation (SHoRE)

Name _____ Date _____

Directions

1. Rate how satisfied you are with each routine by circling one number beside each routine. A routine is an event, activity, or time of day, as listed below. The specific time of day is unimportant.

2. Write NA next to routines that do not apply to your family.

Routine	Not at all satisfied		Satisfied		Very satisfied
1. Waking up	1	2	3	4	5
2. Diaper change/toileting	1	2	3	4	5
3. Meals/feeding	1	2	3	4	5
4. Dressing	1	2	3	4	5
5. Playtime	1	2	3	4	5
6. In the car	1	2	3	4	5
7. At the store	1	2	3	4	5
8. Hanging out	1	2	3	4	5
9. Dinner preparation time	1	2	3	4	5
10. Bath	1	2	3	4	5
11. Bedtime	1	2	3	4	5
12. Child care	1	2	3	4	5

Family Quality of Life–Autism Spectrum Disorder (FaQoL-ASD)

Please rate the following aspects of your family's life as *poor, fair, good, very good,* or *excellent.* Answer every question by circling one number. *Family* generally refers to the people living with the child, but you can define it any way that makes sense to you and your family.

	Poor	Fair	Good	Very good	Excellent
1. Our family's ability to solve problems together[a]	1	2	3	4	5
2. The communication within our family [a,b]	1	2	3	4	5
3. Our family's relationships with extended family[a]	1	2	3	4	5
4. The information our family has about our child's condition or disability[a,c]	1	2	3	4	5
5. The information our family has about child development[a,c]	1	2	3	4	5
6. The information our family has about resources, including services[a,c]	1	2	3	4	5
7. The information our family has about what to do with our child[a,c]	1	2	3	4	5
8. The alliances our family has, such as with friends and others[a]	1	2	3	4	5
9. Our family's socializing with others[a]	1	2	3	4	5
10. Our family's connections to ASD organizations	1	2	3	4	5
11. Our family's ability to pay for things[a]	1	2	3	4	5
12. Our family's access to health care[a]	1	2	3	4	5
13. Our family's knowledge about how children who have ASDs learn[a]	1	2	3	4	5
14. Our family's knowledge about parenting[a]	1	2	3	4	5
15. Our family's knowledge of what to do when our child engages in difficult behavior	1	2	3	4	5
16. Our family's time to spend with our child[a]	1	2	3	4	5
17. Our family's access to services for our child[a]	1	2	3	4	5
18. The support available to our family to help our child make friends[a]	1	2	3	4	5
19. Our family's participation in community events and activities, including outings[a,b]	1	2	3	4	5
20. Our family's health[b]	1	2	3	4	5

(continued)

		Poor	Fair	Good	Very good	Excellent
21.	Employment by at least one adult in our family[b]	1	2	3	4	5
22.	Our family's time to spend one on one with each of our children	1	2	3	4	5
23.	The amount of agreement between the adult family members concerning our family's approach to ASDs	1	2	3	4	5
24.	How welcome we feel in our faith-based community	1	2	3	4	5
Please rate the following aspects of your child's functioning as *poor, fair, good, very good,* or *excellent.*						
25.	Our child's understanding what is said to him or her[b,c]	1	2	3	4	5
26.	Our child's expressing him- or herself[b,c]	1	2	3	4	5
27.	Our child's getting along with adults[b,c,d]	1	2	3	4	5
28.	Our child's getting along with other children[b,c,d]	1	2	3	4	5
29.	Our child's ability to get along with his or her sibling(s)	1	2	3	4	5
30.	Our child's participating in home routines[c]	1	2	3	4	5
31.	Our family's ability to take our child on routine errands (e.g., grocery store; mall; haircut, dentist, or doctor appointment)	1	2	3	4	5
32.	Our family's ability to take our child on social outings (e.g., movies, zoo, library)	1	2	3	4	5
33.	Our child's participating in school or group care activities[c]	1	2	3	4	5
34.	Our child's playing with toys and using objects[c]	1	2	3	4	5
35.	Our child's behaving appropriately[b,c,d]	1	2	3	4	5
36.	Our child's ability to fall asleep and stay asleep	1	2	3	4	5
37.	Our child's independence[c]	1	2	3	4	5
38.	Our child's health[b,d]	1	2	3	4	5
39.	Our family's overall life situation now[e]	1	2	3	4	5
40.	Our child's overall life situation now[e]	1	2	3	4	5

Sources: [a]Jackson and Turnbull (2004); [b]Davis and Hind (1999); [c]McWilliam (2005a); [d]Bess, Dodd-Murphy, and Parker (1998); and [e]NEILS (Bailey, Hebbeler, Scarborough, Spiker, & Mallik, 2004).

Index

Page references followed by *b*, *f*, and *t* indicate boxes, figures, and tables, respectively.